TREVOR LYNCH:

PART FOUR OF THE TRILOGY

by

TREVOR LYNCH

EDITED BY GREG JOHNSON

Counter-Currents Publishing Ltd.
San Francisco
2020

Cover design by
Kevin I. Slaughter

Published in the United States by
COUNTER-CURRENTS PUBLISHING LTD.
P.O. Box 22638
San Francisco, CA 94122
USA
http://www.counter-currents.com/

Hardcover ISBN: 978-1-64264-151-6
Paperback ISBN: 978-1-64264-152-3
E-book ISBN: 978-1-64264-153-0

CONTENTS

PREFACE

This is my fourth volume of essays and reviews on film and television. It took me eighteen years to write the first three, a little more than a year to write this one. What's going on?

It's nothing mysterious. I have been writing a lot more on film and television since 2019, when I started doing two pieces a month for *The Unz Review*, where everything in this volume was first published. I want to thank Ron Unz for exposing my work to a wider audience and making this book possible. Thus it is fitting that I dedicate it to him.

I also wish to thank Kevin Slaughter for his work on the cover; Scott Weisswald, James O'Meara, and Alex Graham for help with the proofs and index; the commentators at *The Unz Review*; and, of course, the whole *Counter-Currents* community.

I can hardly wait for volume five!

November 1, 2020

AD ASTRA

Ad Astra (2019), starring Brad Pitt and directed by James Gray, is the best science fiction movie since Christopher Nolan's *Interstellar* (2014). Like *Interstellar*, *Ad Astra* is visually striking and emotionally powerful, stimulating to both thought and imagination, and unfolds at a leisurely pace—all traits inviting comparisons to Kubrick and Tarkovsky, although I hasten to add that I found both *Ad Astra* and *Interstellar* so absorbing that my attention never wavered.

Ad Astra is set sometime later in this century. The US has permanent bases on the Moon and Mars, but the farthest any manned missions have gone is Neptune, where the Lima Project was sent to scan the universe for signs of intelligent life outside the interference of the sun's magnetic field. However, when the Lima Project went silent—sixteen years into its mission and thirteen years before the time of the film—the US ended deep space missions.

Brad Pitt plays astronaut Roy Mcbride, a Major in the US Space Command. Roy is the son of astronaut Clifford Mcbride, the Commander of the Lima Project (brilliantly played by Tommy Lee Jones). The film begins with Roy McBride working on a communication tower that extends from Earth into space. It is a modern tower of Babel. The tower is struck by a mysterious power surge, and Roy literally falls to Earth. Luckily, he is equipped with a parachute that allows him to land more-or-less safely. The whole sequence is as thrilling as it is bizarre.

It turns out that the power surge has affected the whole planet, leading to thousands of deaths. After recuperating in the hospital for a few days, Roy is called in to be debriefed and meets some top brass in Space Command (a white, a Latino, and a black woman—from intelligence, no less—for in diversity casting this film is as depressingly predictable as NASA).

It turns out that the surge was caused by an anti-matter discharge near Neptune. The Lima Project was powered by anti-matter. Space Command believes that Clifford McBride is alive and may be responsible for the surge, which if unstopped might destroy the Earth. They ask Roy to broadcast a message to his father from Space Command's last secure communication hub on Mars. They hope he will respond, which will give Space Command a fix on his location, at which point they can dispatch someone to stop the surge by any means necessary.

The rest of the movie follows Roy from Earth to the Moon, from the Moon to Mars, and from Mars to Neptune—where he finds his father—then back home. This much is not a spoiler, since it can be gathered from the trailer—which is actually quite different than the final film. For one thing, Liv Tyler as Roy's wife Eve was almost eliminated from the final cut. I don't wish to give away any more of the plot, because I want you to see this film. But I do want to discuss some of the themes, which will require mentioning some details.

Ad Astra is interesting because it meditates on the personality traits necessary to explore and settle the cosmos. Clifford McBride left his ailing wife and thirteen-year-old son on a one-way mission to find intelligent life in the cosmos. What kind of people are capable of leaving their homes and saying goodbye to their family, friends, and neighbors—*forever*? Obviously, such people need to have weak ties to the people and places of their birth, or they would never be able to leave them.

Beyond that, they need to have some sort of *mission* to sustain them, a counter-weight to the things they leave behind. In *Ad Astra*, Clifford McBride is portrayed as an intensely religious man. His faith is twofold: in God, the creator of the cosmos, and in the existence of intelligent extraterrestrial life, which is for many people a kind of religion as well. The four astronauts who take Roy McBride from the Moon to Mars are also intensely religious Christians. There is no sign that Roy McBride shares any of their beliefs. He seems like more of a secular Stoic.

Of course, weak roots and powerful senses of mission are the same traits possessed by past generations of explorers and settlers. Not even a century ago, when people departed on ships for new lands, they could be reasonably certain they would never be coming back. They knew how to say goodbye *forever*.

Ad Astra also confronts us with just how hard space exploration is on people. Clifford McBride chose to widow his wife and orphan his son to explore the cosmos. Roy chose to follow his father's career, but he chose not to have children of his own, and his sense of mission destroyed his own marriage. (In a news-flash, Eve informs him that she is "her own person.")

Many people, however, can't really leave the Earth behind, so they replicate the best and worst of it wherever they go. Or they simply go a bit mad out in the void, sometimes to the point of mutiny. In one suspenseful and shocking sequence, we see that even the animals we bring into space can go mad and mutiny.

Ad Astra can be taken as an anti-religious film in two ways. First, Roy's absent father out in space is very much analogous to the Biblical God. Roy can't help loving the man who abandoned him, but in the end, he finds the strength to let him go. Second, Roy's father is sustained by his faith in the existence of extra-terrestrial life, a faith to which he sacrificed first his family then his crew. But the Lima Project found no evidence of extraterres-trial life. Clifford begs his son to help him continue his quest. "You can't let me fail." But Roy responds, "But dad, you haven't failed. Now we know, we're all we've got." It is an extremely touching scene, because as the movie shows, men like Roy McBride can do great things without faith in higher powers.

Since the same causes give rise to the same effects, it seems inevitable that the causes that gave rise of intelligent life on Earth will give rise to intelligent life elsewhere in the cosmos. Furthermore, given how big the universe is, it is likely that other intelligent life exists *right now*. Frankly, though, I find that a chilling thought, since if intelligent extraterrestrials arrived on Earth, the human race will be in the same position as primitive peoples around the globe when white explorers first arrived. *We wouldn't have a chance.* I would much prefer to know that "We're all we've got," that—free of gods and aliens—our kind is free to expand unopposed into the universe.

Both Clifford and Roy McBride are magnificent portraits of Faustian European man. As Clifford tells his son, "Sometimes, the human will must overcome the impossible." Roy does just that. He is a study in what I consider the real meaning of "cool." He is the intelligent man of action, the taciturn, unflappable Nordic explorer. He has nerves of steel. He is "focused on the essential, to the exclusion of all else." He has a slow pulse, which helps him stay cool in tight spots. (When a spaceship is in trouble and the captain is paralyzed, Roy coolly steps in and saves the day. Roy's pulse only gets elevated when he hears that his father is really alive.)

If Roy is a Faustian hero, Clifford is a Faustian anti-hero, like Captain Ahab, whose indomitable will is twisted by an obsession, ultimately destroying him and everyone around him.

The most poignant thing Clifford says is, "We're a dying breed, Roy." No kidding. Roy McBride is the childless white Atlas on whose shoulders the whole world rides. He dutifully takes orders from affirmative action blacks and browns, wimpy man-buns and pushy dykes. He obediently shares his feelings with machines. They use him to get what they want, then shove him aside. When he sticks up for himself, Space Comm sends a black, an Oriental, and a gutless white to "neutralize" him, and they can't even kill him without his help. Disavowed by his "superiors," he saves the world on his own. When men like Roy McBride finally take the red pill, they will finish this system in short order. But don't expect Jewish director James Gray to direct *that* epic.

Ad Astra isn't a perfect movie. The script is highly intelligent, and I enjoyed the deliberate pace, but early on, I had the feeling that Gray was throwing arbitrary action sequences at us, just to keep people with short attention spans occupied. But even these sequences illustrated the larger themes of the film, such as the madness induced by losing one's roots. I also found the music by Max Richter and Lorne Balfe to be undistinguished, although there is one beautiful theme that brings to mind Jerry Goldsmith's *Alien* score. But by the time this movie gets to Mars, it is absolutely riveting, largely thanks to the magnetic performances of Brad Pitt and Tommy Lee Jones. Although *Ad Astra* doesn't dazzle the eye with special effects and quick cuts, it is often simply beautiful to look at. But above all, *Ad Astra* is a feast for the mind. You'll be *thinking* about this movie long after the final frames.

The Unz Review, January 21, 2020

AGE OF CRINGE:
ALT-RIGHT: AGE OF RAGE

Based on a few clips, I was certain that *Alt-Right: Age of Rage* (2018) would lead to permanent physical damage from sheer cringiness. But I was delighted to have been proven wrong. This is a remarkably fair-minded documentary. On balance, though, I think it will be good for white identity politics. *Age of Rage* was directed by Adam Bhala Lough, an American of partial South Asian descent.

The film starts quite tendentiously, with footage of a German American Bund meeting in New York City in the 1930s. A line of young women walking into the meeting is accompanied by a stock sound effect of marching feet. The speaker, Fritz Kuhn, has a German accent that sounds comical and sinister. He speaks of taking America back from Jewish power. At one point, a certain Isadore Greenbaum rushes the stage and is tackled by Storm Troopers. New York's finest then hustle in to break up the fight.

Then we read the words:

We learn from history
that we do not learn from history.
— Friedrich Hegel.

At this point, I knew that Lough would cut either to Hailgate or Unite the Right in Charlottesville. It was the latter.

From that point on, however, the tone became generally more balanced, and the tide began to turn in the direction of the Alt Right. Basically, Lough made a practice of balancing pro-white speakers with anti-white speakers. The main pro-white voices are Richard Spencer of the National Policy Institute and Jared Taylor of American Renaissance. The main anti-white voices are Daryl Lamont Jenkins of One People's Project and Mark Potok formerly of the Southern Poverty Law Center.

We also hear from Gavin McInnes of the Alt Lite, an Alt-Right video blogger known as TV KWA, Sikh activist Simran Jeet Singh, and Lacy MacAuley and John Carico of Antifa. There are also brief clips of Milo Yiannopoulos and David Duke.

In Lough's hands, all of his interviewees come off as articulate and sincere. Since it is child's play to make even experienced speakers look exactly the opposite, we have the filmmaker's integrity and honesty to thank for that.

There are some embarrassing moments.

For instance, we are treated to a debauched-looking Richard Spencer obviously posing with a cigarette and Gavin McInnes preening before a mirror, then loudly blowing his nose (clearly for show), before beginning his interview. But these were not candid moments included to be embarrassing. Both men were obviously posturing before the camera. No doubt they thought they were being "alpha" and "badass." So the inclusion of these gaffes is on them, not Lough. (Also, in spite of his bizarre introduction, McInnes gives a compelling performance.)

And, of course, there is Hailgate.

But the worst moments came in the last 45 minutes of the film, where we are treated to extensive footage of the 2017 American Renaissance conference and Unite the Right in Charlottesville a couple weeks later.

The Amren footage decidedly favors the pro-white side. The Antifa are mostly fat, unattractive, self-righteous, and shrill misfits, with really lame chants, whereas the conference-goers are well-dressed and well-behaved, with conspicuously more fit people. At 63 minutes there is a welcome cameo of the *Counter-Currents* table.

The Charlottesville footage has cringe on both sides.

The torchlight march to the statue of Thomas Jefferson the night before the rally was, in terms of optics and messaging, extremely impressive.

But on the day of the rally, there are numerous shots of goofy and gross-looking people—from both Unite the Right and Antifa—wearing home-made uniforms, including armor, and carrying improvised weapons. When the two sides started fighting, it was sometimes hard to tell which side people were on. So the net effect on the normie viewer should be a wash.

There is also ample footage of the police doing nothing while the Antifa attack Unite the Right. Reporters and bystanders repeatedly ask them why they are doing nothing. Then, after countless fights and injuries, we hear the state's declaration of an unlawful assembly. Riot cops move in (again to a cue of marching feet), and in the ensuing chaos and violence, Unite the Right attendee James Fields crashes into a crowd (to a stock cue of a race car engine), killing Heather Heyer and injuring a many more.

The worst moments on the pro-white side included Richard Spencer donning his bullet-proof vest, his security detail scrambling through a drill, and his big entrance saying "hail victory." According to Jason Kessler, who is suing the city of Charlottesville over Unite the Right, Spencer had declined a police escort to the park so he and his guys could "look strong" in their entrance. If this is true, it undermines the narrative that the authorities are completely responsible for the obvious decision not to protect the rally from the Antifa mob. We can only hope that a fuller picture of events emerges as Kessler's suit continues.

As for the interview footage of Taylor and Spencer, I thought both men did admirable jobs. They made telling points with eloquence and sincerity. I was particularly impressed at the end, when both Spencer and Taylor answer the question of whether or not white demographic decline depresses them and makes them want to give up. Spencer offers an excellent rebuttal that I use as well: White demographic decline is precisely what is driving the rise of white identity politics. Taylor responds by arguing that he does not act based on calculations of outcomes but out of duty to his ancestors and his descendants. Still, he believes he can win.

The final question of the film is posed to Spencer and Jenkins: Is America now too divided to come together? Spencer's response is excellent in both content and delivery. This gist of his answer is: Maybe America can't come back together. Maybe race and religion and ethnicity really do matter. Maybe this country has become too diverse to survive. I think a lot of sensible white people who are growing weary of increasing political polarization—driven mostly by Left-wing anti-Trump hysteria—will find Spencer's remarks quite credible.

Jenkins' response, moreover, is wholly unconvincing. He simply denies that America is divided. We are merely "frustrated" and in need of answers. It is patent nonsense in light of everything we have seen before it, but Jenkins is so adamant that unthinking people might actually find him convincing.

Although I disagree with them profoundly, I have to admit that Jenkins and MacAuley acquitted themselves well. Both have killer shill instincts, immediately trying to frame events in their favor even as they unfold before them. But both of them state their core views in a creditable way.

Jenkins is a black man with a large chocolate chip on his shoulder. He speaks ebonic English ("dat," "dere," "gone" as a verb) with great dignity and conviction but little by way of argument. Still, his judgment on Unite the Right while the rally was still winding down was prescient, namely, that this was the beginning of the end for the Alt Right.

MacAuley is a strong, independent womyn who has come a long way, baby, and will never be feminine, agreeable, barefoot, pregnant, or make sandwiches for anyone but her fellow protesters.

Potok is the slickest anti-white voice, but the most problematic, since everything he says is a cliché. These clichés are necessary, he says, because the old technique of Jewish organizations—namely to work with the media to quarantine pro-white ideas—no longer works because of the proliferation of alternative media. Thus people have to be inoculated from pro-white ideas with such talking points as the following.

❖ The idea of an ethnostate is a prescription for genocide. This is followed by information about the botched India-Pakistan partition rather than the peaceful Czech-Slovak one. We are told that one to two million people died in the India-Pakistan partition, but given the hatreds between Muslims, Hindus, and Sikhs, it might have saved more lives in the long run.

❖ We can't differentiate between white and black people because of people who are mixed race.

❖ Genetic determinism is a pseudo-science, like phrenology.

❖ Eugenics leads to Nazi genocide.

❖ People become haters because of envy for their betters, guilt that they externalize by blaming others, and out of a desire to give meaning to their otherwise empty lives.

Potok justifies the Taliban-style destruction of Confederate monuments, which he says are explicit expressions of white supremacism. As an example, he gives a monument in Colfax, Louisiana to three white men who died in a battle with black unionists. "That can come right down," he says. Here he tips his hand.

If one really wanted to create a peaceful multiracial society, wouldn't one seek a position *beyond* the racial conflicts of the past? Why not pursue reconciliation between both sides of the conflict? Why not, for instance, create a monument to the blacks who died, rather than remove a monument to the whites? Or better yet, why not let sleeping dogs lie, since most blacks and whites in Louisiana have long forgotten such historical events anyway?

But Potok does not want racial peace and reconciliation. He wants to refight the race wars of the past. And he sides with non-whites against whites. But this time, he wants the whites to lose.

Many people believe that the Southern Poverty Law Center and other such organizations wish to create a world of multiracial harmony. White Nationalists believe that diversity is just a euphemism for white dispossession. Diversity just means fewer white people. Today, it is our monuments that are being erased. Tomorrow it is our racial consciousness that will be erased. But if sub-replacement white fertility, miscegenation, and non-white immigration are not stopped, eventually our race itself will disappear.

A yellow post-it note by Potok's desk is captured by Lough's camera. On it, Potok keeps track of the decline of America's white population decade by decade. But if diversity simply adds richness to America, why specifically keep tabs on white decline? I would love to hear Potok's explanation for this. Perhaps, someday, he can be asked under oath.

Lough asks his interviewees about violence. McInnes whole-heartedly endorses it. Jared Taylor and Mark Potok reject it as counter-productive. Simran Singh says it is only justified in self-defense. Jenkins and MacAuley would cry out as they strike you. Spencer is not included.

Taylor, McInnes, and Yiannopoulos all defend freedom of speech. Potok, Singh, and Jenkins at least acknowledge that it is protected by the First Amendment to the US Constitution. But they prefer to emphasize the terrible consequences of respecting free speech for white people by trotting out Wade Michael Page and Dylann Roof. Again, Spencer is not included, which is just as well, because he doesn't believe in free speech.

Age of Rage ends on an apocalyptic but rather sour note with Matt Christman, some sort of Marxist podcaster, ranting about how neoliberalism will create ecological and economic disasters that will displace millions of people. This will force a choice: to appropriate and redistribute the ill-gotten gains of the First World to guarantee the existence of all—or to embrace genocide. The Alt Right, he says, is paving the way for the latter solution.

This analysis comes out of nowhere, and frankly it seems nutty. Is it meant as an illustration of the views that guide Jenkins, Potok, etc.? Does it represent the filmmaker's own views? The film seems too well-balanced for that to be the case.

Whatever the filmmaker's motive—to say nothing of the foolishness of the Marxist analysis of fascism, or anything else, for that matter—the truth is that, politically speaking, the center will not hold. Instead, it will be increasingly abandoned for white and anti-white identity politics, then what remains will be pulverized when these two blocs clash for dominance.

Although it is certainly not the director's intention, I think *Alt-Right: Age of Rage* will tip the outcome in our direction. Thus I highly recommend it, and I especially urge you to show it to select normies.

The Unz Review, February 20, 2019

AMERICAN PIMP

American Pimp is a 1999 documentary directed by the Hughes Brothers, the half-black, half-Armenian twins who also directed *Menace II Society* and *Dead Presidents*. *American Pimp* has fallen into obscurity and is now hard to find. But it deserves to be better-known, especially among race-realists. *American Pimp* is just under ninety minutes. It consists primarily of interviews with black pimps and their prostitutes.

The film opens with clips of white people sharing their views about pimps, which are universally negative: disgusting, immoral, exploiters of women, parasites, gaudy, tasteless, extravagant, etc. It is hard to know if we are supposed to think these are all negative "stereotypes" for which white people should be ashamed. As the movie unfolds, however, we see that these descriptions are all true — and then some.

American Pimp also intercuts clips from so-called Blaxploitation films such as *The Mack* and *Willie Dynamite*. Again, it is hard to tell if we are supposed to think that these films are sinister parodies and exaggerations of the truth about pimps. But the documentary goes on to demonstrate that the truth about pimps is far more clownish and sinister than the movie portrayals. Beyond that, the very term "Blaxploitation" strikes me as *faux*-victimhood whining, since these films generally glamorize and glorify ghetto black behavior for the entertainment of ghetto black consumers.

Judging from the film, the typical African-American pimp is ugly, dark-black, unspeakably foul-mouthed, utterly cynical and materialistic, and has hideous, gaudy tastes in clothes, cars, and jewelry. Gold teeth are optional.

Only a couple of the pimps interviewed speak anything close to standard English. The rest are mush-mouthed bix-nooders whose every third word is "bitch" or some version of "motherfucker." Usually, they end their sentences with "Ya know whum sayin,'" to which my truthful answer is "no." It seems odd that this spark of self-knowledge doesn't seem to lead to self-improvement in their communication skills. Sadly, there are no subtitles for the ebonically challenged, although the French and Spanish subtitles might come in handy.

If, however, one looks beyond the ghetto *patois* and clown-costumes, the truth is that most of these pimps aren't stupid in the low-IQ sense. It takes some brains to run any kind of business, and some of the things they say are actually witty. Thus they probably have IQs above the African-American average of eighty-five. This is useful, because if low IQ is taken out of the equation, it highlights other racial differences, particularly moral ones.

Pimps aren't necessarily stupid, but all of them are "moral imbeciles." They manifest the Dark Triad of narcissism, sociopathy, and Machiavellianism.

The gaudy and extravagant peacocking of pimps is obviously narcissistic. The constant parade of expensive clown costumes and tasteless pimpmobiles is one of the most entertaining aspects of *American Pimp.*

The exploitation of women is obviously sociopathic. One of the funniest sequences of the film is where pimps explain the cut that whores get from their work. They are unanimous: "zero percent." One of them asks, "How can I give you 100% of my pimpin' unless you give me 100% of yo' money?"

Pimps also take pride in their use of manipulation to control whores. Primarily, they use false promises and emotional manipulation. But they aren't above beating them. One pimp, who is now a Christian minister, claims that if you don't beat a whore, she'll start thinking that you don't care about her. Although I didn't manage to catch it on my recent viewing, I recall one pimp says that he "didn't steal nothin' except bitches' minds." (Clearly my ear for ebonics has gotten rusty.)

American Pimp doesn't offer much insight into the psychology of the sad hookers who allow themselves to be exploited. By the looks of them, they are mostly below-average in the looks and IQ departments, although the vacant faces could be products of drug use. A large percentage of these women are white. Most of them want to have — or think they have — relationships with their pimps, which bespeaks a huge capacity for self-deception. Many hookers end up dead due to drug overdoses. Others are murdered. Still others end up in mental hospitals. One white hooker ended up married to her pimp. Although most of these women lack much potential, a decent society would protect them from such predators.

The most articulate pimp in the movie styles himself Gorgeous Dre. His real name is Andrè [sic] Taylor. He is clearly smarter than the average pimp. He's also better-looking and better-dressed. Dre has a great patter about character, manliness, and integrity. One can almost forget he is a ruthless, bottom-feeding sociopath. Later in the film we revisit him in jail. He has been arrested for pimping and sleeping with a sixteen-year-old.

I was rather hoping Dre would be sentenced to life, and maybe shanked in the joint. But it turns out that he did less than a year. He has put his first-class bullshitting skills to good use. He is now a "life coach" and a "community organizer" in Seattle, working to make it easier for black people to commit crimes.

Near the end of the movie, we meet a white pimp, Dennis Hof, owner of the Moonlight Bunny Ranch and other legal Nevada brothels. Hof is clearly a major pervert, but he seems free of the black pimps' Dark Triad traits. He is a businessman, not a parasite. The women who work for him do so for salaries. They are not manipulated and bullied into giving all their money to him. It is far more humane than the black system, but should a decent society allow even this sort of prostitution?

It is tempting for white people to view black pimps as pathological. But I think black pimps are authentic expressions of blackness. As outlaws, pimps reject white norms entirely. They can do what comes natural to them. Polygamy, the exploitation of women, and peacocking are all quite common in pre- and post-colonial Africa. So it makes sense that they would emerge spontaneously in black diaspora societies among subcultures that reject white norms.

I highly recommend *American Pimp* as an entertaining tour of the heart of darkness in America today. It definitely deserves a Blu-ray edition with improved picture and sound, as well as English subtitles.

THE AVIATOR

My favorite Martin Scorsese film is *Gangs of New York*, but his follow-up film, *The Aviator* (2004), is a close second and rises in my estimation with each viewing. *The Aviator* is an epic depiction of the career of Howard Hughes, spanning the years 1927 to 1947, from the creation of his WWI flying epic *Hell's Angels* to the successful test flight of the Hercules transport plane, dubbed by his enemies the "Spruce Goose."

In its feel, Scorsese's depiction of a heroic industrialist battling philistines, nay-sayers, corrupt politicians, and unethical rivals is the closest thing we will ever get to a decent film adaptation of Ayn Rand's *The Fountainhead* or *Atlas Shrugged*, and in some ways it is far more interesting than Rand's stories because Hughes was real. He was, furthermore, more heroic than any Rand protagonist because he not only overcame the whole world but also a far more formidable adversary: namely, his own mental illness.

Hughes inherited the Hughes Tool Company from his father, which he used to finance his work in two industries that centered around his personal obsessions: film and aviation. (He also invested his film and aviation profits in extensive real estate and hotel holdings.) Hughes directed two films, *Hell's Angels* (1930) and *The Outlaw* (1943), and produced a number of others, first as an independent producer, then by acquiring a controlling interest in RKO. Hughes' taste in film was unabashedly masculine (war and boobs). And although he was a playboy, he was conservative in his politics if not his morals and worked to purge RKO of Communists.

But above all else, Hughes was an aviator. He created Hughes Aircraft while filming *Hell's Angels*. He set a number of aviation records. He was intimately involved in the design, development, and testing of a number of airplanes. He revolutionized commercial aviation. And he survived four airplane crashes (two of which are depicted in the film).

Leonardo Di Caprio is wonderfully believable in his por-

trayal of Hughes as a stubborn visionary who combined technological mastery and shrewd business instincts with a strong
aesthetic sensibility, although in truth his airplanes were more
artful than his movies. Di Caprio is particularly brilliant in capturing Hughes' mood swings from charismatic, boyish enthu-
siasm to obsessive-compulsive paranoia. Cate Blanchett won
an Oscar for her role of Katherine Hepburn. Other solid performances are Kate Beckinsale as Ava Gardner, Alec Baldwin
as Juan Trippe, and Alan Alda as Senator Owen Brewster.

One of my favorite parts of *The Aviator* is Hughes' romance
with Katherine Hepburn, especially their golf match (in gorgeous two-color Technicolor), her compassionate response to
his mounting obsessive-compulsive disorder and paranoia, and
his disastrous dinner with her rich, snobbish, and obnoxiously
Left-wing family.

There's a strong populist feel to *The Aviator*, for Hughes was a
Texan who was constantly at odds with the Hollywood Jewish
and Eastern liberal WASP establishments. Although Hughes inherited wealth like the Hepburns, he did not hold people who
work for a living in contempt. When Hepburn finally left him,
Hughes became increasingly unmoored from reality and consumed by his obsessions.

I also very much enjoyed Scorsese's handling of the aviation
sequences in the making of *Hell's Angels*; the building, test-
flight, and crash of the H1-Racer after setting a speed record;
the building, test-flight, and crash of the XF-11 reconnaissance
plane (Hughes called it his "Buck Rodgers" ship); and finally
the test flight of the Hercules.

Scorsese used models, not computer animation, in these sequences, and the payoff in terms of realism is palpable. The use
of Eugene Ormandy's orchestration of Bach's Toccata and
Fugue in D-Minor for the XF-11 sequence was an inspired
choice. (The soundtrack contains original music by Howard
Shore, which to my surprise made no impression on me, and a
large number of well-chosen pieces of popular music from the
period.)

Another excellent sequence is Hughes' triumph over a Senator Owen Brewster and Juan Trippe of Pan Am, who cooked

up legislation that would give Pan Am a monopoly on international air travel from the United States. Brewster also launched a Congressional investigation of Hughes, digging up embarrassing information and accusing him of defrauding the US government out of $56 million. Then Brewster offered to call off the hearings if Hughes would sell TWA to Pan Am. It was transparent blackmail.

Hughes refused, then retreated into a cocoon, holing up in a screening room for months, communicating only by tape recordings and intercom, peeing in bottles, etc. Hughes finally pulled himself together with the help of Ava Gardner (best lines: "I love what you've done with the place" and "Nothing's clean, Howard. But we do our best anyway"). Yes, Hughes actually did things like this, though the sequence of events may have been altered for dramatic effect.

Hughes goes to Congress and in a fiery speech flays the hypocrisy of the charges against him. For instance, $800 million in aircraft were not delivered during the war because of research and development failures, but only Hughes was being investigated. Then he exposes Brewster's real agenda: to cripple TWA because it threatened Pan Am with competition. It is thrilling drama. Alan Alda is brilliant in his portrayal of oily operator Senator Brewster.

The movie ends with the triumphant flight of the Hercules, the prototype of which was finished by Hughes at great expense, even though the war was over and the military had cancelled the project. It was a matter of personal pride for Hughes, and it was a magnificent engineering achievement.

At the afterparty, an ebullient Hughes declares that jet aircraft are the way of the future. Then his OCD takes over. He can't stop repeating the phrase "the way of the future, the way of the future." His business manager and chief engineer hustle him into isolation so he can regain control. Scorsese wisely ends the film here, with Hughes alone in the throes of his compulsions.

This was indeed "the way of the future" for Hughes. He spent his last twenty-nine years in increasing seclusion, living in luxury hotel suites, moving from triumph to triumph building his business empire and vast fortune. Racked with chronic pain from the XF-11 crash, which nearly killed him, and increasingly consumed by OCD, Hughes apparently became addicted to painkillers. He died at the age of seventy. His six-foot four-inch frame weighed only ninety-six pounds. He had apparently starved himself to death. The pitiful final triumph of an unbridled Faustian will.

The Aviator is a masterpiece, a work of tragic grandeur encompassing everything that made America both great and terrible, a biopic raised to the level of myth.

The Unz Review, May 1, 2019

"Now It's Dark"
Blue Velvet

JEFFREY: I'm seeing something that was always hidden.
I'm involved in a mystery. And it's all secret.
SANDY: You like mysteries that much?
JEFFREY: Yeah. You're a mystery. I like you. Very much.

Blue Velvet (1986) is the quintessential David Lynch film, filled with quirky humor and shocking violence. It features one of the most terrifying villains in all of film: Frank Booth, brilliantly portrayed by Dennis Hopper. *Blue Velvet* is a "mystery" story. But it is more than just a crime drama. Sometimes it is described as neo *noir*. But it is a much darker shade of *noir*.

Blue Velvet is about the great mysteries of life. It is a coming-of-age tale about callow college-boy Jeffrey Beaumont (Kyle MacLaughlin) becoming a man. It is also an initiation tale, with sexual, spiritual, and political dimensions. A good mystery can be engaging but superficial. *Blue Velvet* is powerful and moving because its archetypal, religious, and philosophical themes stir deeper parts of the soul.

Jeffrey's initiation into the mysteries is a descent into the underworld: both a literal, criminal underworld as well as the "deep river" of the unconscious, including obsessive and sadomasochistic sexuality. But Lynch also hints that the unconscious is not merely human, but a portal through which essentially demonic powers enter our world.

Jeffrey conquers and controls these forces, returning to the sunlit world not only as a man but as a guardian of the social and the family order. In his journey, he has encountered the libidinal, criminal, and demonic forces that can tear society apart, and he has learned about the artifices of civilization that keep chaos at bay. Politically speaking, this is a profoundly conservative vision.

After the nocturnal opening titles, with their elegant script, shimmering blue-velvet backdrop, and lush, Italianate theme music by Angelo Badalamenti, the famous opening sequence sets up the whole story. To Bobby Vinton's oldie "Blue Velvet," we see a clear blue sky, then our eyes descend to red roses in front of the archetypal white picket fence. An old-fashioned firetruck drives by, complete with a Dalmatian and a fireman benevolently waving from the running board, a gesture that subtly puts the viewer in the position of a child. Then we see yellow tulips. A crossing guard carefully shepherds little girls across the street.

It is a vision of childlike wholesomeness and safety. Indeed, all the adults are people charged with keeping the public safe. The guardians of public safety are an important theme in *Blue Velvet* and *Twin Peaks*.

Then we see the modest Beaumont house. Mr. Beaumont is watering the yard. Mrs. Beaumont is watching a crime drama on TV—the first hint of darkness—although the gun on the screen usually elicits a laugh, and it is all tidily contained on the tube. Then we hear an amplified gurgling and see Mr. Beaumont's hose snagged and kinked on a branch. As he yanks the hose, he is suddenly stricken and falls to the ground, water geysering everywhere. Then we see him on his back, a baby in diapers watching as a terrier seems to attack the water squirting from the hose. The film slows, giving the dog both maniacal and mechanical qualities. Then we dive into the well-watered lawn, down to the roots, where in the darkness we find a writhing mass of beetles and other insects fighting and devouring one another.

Next we hear a corny radio jingle, which welcomes us to Lumberton, an idyllic North Carolina logging town, the model for the titular town in *Twin Peaks*, Lynch's next project.

Young Jeffrey Beaumont has been called home from college to visit his stricken father and help run the family hardware store. On the way home from the hospital, Jeffrey discovers a severed human ear in a field. It has greenish splotches of decay on it, and it is crawling with bugs. Bugs, again, are associated with evil.

Jeffrey puts the ear in a paper bag and takes it to Detective Williams (George Dickerson) at the Lumberton Police Department. Detective Williams immediately begins an investigation.

He and Jeffrey first take the ear to the morgue, where the medical examiner observes that it had been cut off with scissors. Then they go to the field to search for evidence.

Cut to later that evening. A door opens, and light descends into a darkened stairwell. Jeffrey descends into the darkness as well. His journey into the underworld has begun. He tells his mother (Priscilla Pointer) and fretful aunt Barbara (Frances Bay) that he is going out walking. "You're not going down by Lincoln, are you?" asks aunt Barbara fearfully. Jeffrey says no. It seems a silly prejudice, but later we realize that it was well-founded. Bad things happen down by Lincoln. (Odd that Lynch chose that name, associated with a president unpopular in North Carolina.)

As Jeffrey walks the neighborhood, we cut to a closeup of the ear in the morgue. There is a loud humming as we enter the ear, then everything fades to black. This too is a descent into mystery, into the underworld.

Cut to Jeffrey knocking at the door of the Williams house. Jeffrey wants to know more about the ear, but Detective Williams can't tell him, and asks him not to disclose anything he already knows, until the case is concluded. Detective Williams is stern but warm, a surrogate for Jeffrey's stricken father. He tells Jeffrey that he understands his curiosity. It is what got him into police work in the first place. "It must be great," Jeffrey volunteers. "It's horrible too," he replies. But Jeffrey seems undaunted. He is on a path that may lead him to becoming a guardian of public order, someone who exposes himself to evil, risking his life to serve the common good.

When Jeffrey leaves the Williams house, he hears a voice: "Are you the one that found the ear?" He looks into the darkness. Detective Williams' daughter Sandy (Laura Dern) emerges from the night, a pink-clad blonde vision of loveliness. She is coy and mysterious, teasing Jeffrey with her knowledge of the case.

As they walk together, she tells him that she overheard her father talking. The ear may somehow be connected to the case of Dorothy Vallens (Isabella Rossellini), a singer who lives nearby. Sandy leads Jeffrey to Dorothy's apartment building.

With a slightly comic/ominous music cue, the camera pans up to the sign: Lincoln St.

The next afternoon, Jeffrey picks Sandy up after school. They go to Arlene's, a diner that is the prototype of the RR in *Twin Peaks*, right down to the passing logging truck. Jeffrey then tries to involve Sandy in a scheme. He wants to look around Dorothy Vallens' apartment. He will pretend that he is the pest control man, there to spray for bugs (which are of course already associated with darkness and evil). Sandy will pretend to be Jehovah's witness, with copies of *Awake!* magazine, who will draw Dorothy away, allowing Jeffrey to open one of the windows for a later visit. (There is an interesting Manichean polarity in their covers, mirrored in Jeffrey's near black and Sandy's golden blonde hair.)

How Jeffrey plans to get in a seventh-floor window is not explained, but he hasn't really thought it out. He doesn't even know Dorothy's name or apartment number without Sandy's help. When we arrive, we see that Dorothy lives in the Deep River Apartments, a nomen that may also be an omen of Jeffrey getting in way over his head. (Betty Elms, in Lynch's *Mulholland Drive*, hails from Deep River, Ontario.)

Dorothy's apartment is pure Lynch: retro, slightly dingy, with dusky pink walls and carpets, dark red draperies (shades of *Twin Peaks*), lavender sofas, magenta cushions, and putrid green accents in the form of pots with spiky "mother in law's tongue" plants. The warm colors have a womblike feel, but the overall effect is seedy and sluttish, not maternal. Jeffrey does not manage to find a window, and before Sandy can knock, Dorothy is visited by a glowering man in a bright yellow sport jacket. But he does manage to pocket an extra pair of keys, hoping they will unlock the apartment.

That evening, Jeffrey takes Sandy to dinner at The Slow Club to watch Dorothy Vallens sing. She doesn't have much of a voice, but she still makes a captivating spectacle, with her huge retro microphone and blue-lit band against dark red draperies, more foreshadowing of *Twin Peaks*. Then Jeffrey and Sandy return to Dorothy's apartment. When Sandy says good-bye, she tells him, "I don't know if you're a detective or a pervert." Jeffrey sneaks inside. When Dorothy comes home suddenly, Jeffrey hides in the closet. Peering through the slats, he watches her undress. It turns out he's both a detective and a pervert.

Dorothy hears a rustling in her closet and confronts Jeffrey with a knife, jabbing him in the cheek when he does not answer one of her questions. She thinks he is a voyeur. But instead of calling the police, she orders him to undress. Then she kneels, with a worshipful look on her face, and pulls down his boxer shorts. She kisses and caresses him but also threatens to kill him, demanding that he neither look at nor touch her. Then she asks if he likes that kind of talk. He doesn't. She tells him to lie down on a couch, following him knife held high like a stage actress. Then she gets on top of him, knife poised, and kisses him.

Terrified by a loud pounding on the door, Dorothy hustles Jeffrey into the closet and orders him to stay silent. Jeffrey is the voyeur again, poised to witness one of the weirdest and sickest scenes in all of cinema. Enter Frank Booth, a middle-aged man in a leather jacket and rockabilly shirt, seething with unfocused rage. Frank and Dorothy then role-play a sexual scenario not unlike the one that has just transpired with Jeffrey, although this time Frank is in control.

Frank's scenario is very specific. Dorothy has to wear a blue velvet robe, provide him with a glass of bourbon, dim the lights and light a candle ("Now it's dark," he says), and sit on a particular chair. He demands that Dorothy not look at him and punches her savagely when she does. (She looks at least three times.) Loosening his inhibitions by swigging the bourbon, then huffing some sort of gas from a cylinder under his jacket, he refers to her as "mommy" and himself as "baby" and "daddy."

He begins by viewing her vagina, then pinching her breasts, then, red-faced and maniacal, he hurls her to the floor, threatens her with a pair of scissors, then pantomimes intercourse, yelling "Daddy's coming home, daddy's coming home."

He has a fetishistic attachment to her blue velvet bathrobe. She stuffs it in his mouth, he stuffs it in her mouth, and he even carries around a piece of it that he has cut from the hem, perhaps with the scissors he uses to threaten her. When it is all over, he blows out the candle. "Now it's dark," he repeats.

As Jeffrey later says, "Frank is a very sick and dangerous man." A drug dealer, he has kidnapped Dorothy's husband Don and their small boy, Donny, holding them hostage to force Dorothy into sexual bondage. It is Don's ear that Jeffrey found, cut off as a threat to Dorothy, perhaps with the same scissors with which he menaced her. Frank has removed Dorothy's real baby and daddy so he can have "mommy" all to himself.

But Dorothy's own disturbing behavior makes it hard to view her as simply a victim. When Frank screams "Don't you fucking look at me" and punches Dorothy, her head lolls back with an ecstatic smile on her face. When she looks at him again and again, is she asking for it? She herself has forced Jeffrey to strip at knife point, ordering him not to look at or touch her while she looks at and touches him. One way to make someone into an object is to forbid him to be a subject.

When Frank leaves, Jeffrey creeps out of the closet to comfort Dorothy, who first claims she is all right. Then she asks Jeffrey to hold her, referring to him as her husband Don. Either she is delirious or simply playing a role. The latter seems more likely. For without missing a beat, she begins to seduce Jeffrey, asking him to look at her, then touch her . . . then hit her. Now she's *literally* asking for it.

A feminist would automatically claim that Dorothy has been so traumatized by Frank that she is simply reenacting her trauma with Jeffrey. But another possibility suggests itself. Dorothy is very much in control with Jeffrey. She is not so worried about Frank or her husband and son that she cannot start an affair with a new man.

It is interesting that when Jeffrey tells Dorothy that he knows what has happened to her husband and son, she is impassive. She only reacts when he suggests telling the police, and she uses her reaction to finally goad Jeffrey into hitting her.

This awakens something in both of them, represented by a burst of flames bringing to mind similar effects in Lynch's next movie, *Wild at Heart*, as well as slowing down the film and replacing the sound of their lovemaking by distorted animal shrieks and growls. This is Jeffrey's baptism in the deep river of repressed animal sexuality. Jeffrey is in way over his head, but Dorothy is in firm control.

Did Frank undergo a similar initiation? Was the kidnapping his way of seeking somehow to regain a semblance of control in the throes of an obsession?

Now it's *really* dark.

There are a number of clues that point to Frank's deep sexual abjection. As the "baby" he can pinch Dorothy's breasts. But as "daddy" he merely pantomimes intercourse. Frank may actually be impotent. At least he is with Dorothy.

When Jeffrey returns to The Slow Club, he sees Frank in the audience, fondling his blue velvet fetish, deeply moved by Dorothy's performance, almost at the edge of tears.

The night Dorothy goads Jeffrey into hitting her, he bumps into Frank and his gang as he leaves her apartment. Frank flies into a jealous rage, forcing Jeffrey and Dorothy to go on a "joy ride." At their first stop, Frank says: "This. Is. It." And sure enough, a red neon sign reads: "This Is It."

But it is hard to say what "it" is. It seems like a retirement home for old fat whores. The interior color scheme is very much like Dorothy's apartment. It is littered with beer and prescription bottles and presided over by a flamboyant aging homosexual named Ben, hilariously played by Dean Stockwell, all pursed lips and rolling eyes. Ben is involved with Frank's drug trade and is holding Dorothy's husband and son hostage.

Frank goes on and on about how "suave" Ben is, with his smoking jacket, ruffled shirt, and long cigarette holder. Every other word is "fuck." When Ben proposes a toast to Frank's health, he hilariously rejects it, suggesting "Here's to your fuck" instead. After transacting some drug business, Frank asks Ben to lip-sync to Roy Orbison's "In Dreams," which Frank childishly refers to as "candy-colored clown," a phrase in the first line of the song.

Ben switches on an inspection light, which he uses as a fake microphone, giving his powdered face a ghastly pallor. One gets the feeling that Ben has done this kind of thing before in a thousand drag shows. When we get to the words, "In dreams you're mine, all the time," Frank's face becomes agitated, and Ben fearfully cuts short the mime. Frank shuts off the tape, Ben shuts off the light, and Frank says, "Now it's dark." Then they make to leave, Frank's departing words: "Let's fuck. I'll fuck anything that moves!"

Next stop is a sawmill near Meadow Lane. Frank begins huffing his gas, then tells Jeffrey, "You're like me." Thanks to Dorothy, that's now truer than Jeffrey would like to think. Then Frank begins to pinch Dorothy's breasts, hurting her. Jeffrey tells Frank "Leave her alone," then punches him in the face. He's already slapped Dorothy around that evening. He's getting comfortable with this.

Frank flies into absolute fury. His henchmen drag Jeffrey out of the car and hold him. There's an ominous industrial thrumming and thumping in the background, as in *Eraserhead*. Frank puts on Dorothy's lipstick then kisses Jeffrey all over his face, saying "pretty, pretty," huffing more fumes, and threatening to kill him if he sees Dorothy again.

While "In Dreams" plays in the car and one of Ben's vacant whores dances on the roof, Frank repeats the words "In dreams, I walk with you. In dreams, I talk to you. In dreams you're mine, all the time. We're together in dreams, in dreams," adding the words "forever in dreams." He places a hand to Jeffrey's ear and "lip-syncs" the words like it is a sock puppet. One thing is for sure: Frank is going to haunt Jeffrey's dreams for the rest of his life. Frank is putting his disease in him.

Frank caresses Jeffrey's face with his blue velvet fetish, wiping off the lipstick. Flexing his biceps, he tells Jeffrey to feel them. "You like that? You like that?" Then Frank begins beating Jeffrey senseless while Dorothy screams. Cut to a guttering candle. And now it's dark.

Frank's constant talk of fucking, as well as merely pantomiming the act with Dorothy, suggest he is impotent. The song "In Dreams" is also about unrequited love for someone who can be possessed only in dreams, itself very close to sexual impotence. Frank's repeated compliments to Ben, as well as the lipstick, kisses, and "feel my muscles" routine with Jeffrey, strongly suggest latent homosexuality.

The guy is a mess.

Jeffrey recovers consciousness in the morning. In addition to the pain of the beating, he feels pangs of guilt as well, for he too has tasted the pleasures of sadism. In some way, he really is like Frank.

Jeffrey resolves to go to Detective Williams at the police station but discovers that Williams' partner, Detective Gordon, is the "yellow man," one of Frank's partners in crime. That evening, we see Jeffrey emerge from the dark carrying an envelope, suggesting his return from the underworld. He shares his findings with Detective Williams, who begins plotting to take down Frank and his gang.

A couple days pass. It is Friday. Jeffrey waters the lawn, visits his dad, then picks up Sandy to go to a party. They are now officially dating. After the party, they are followed by a menacing car. They think it is Frank, but when the car pulls alongside, Sandy sees that it is her jealous ex-boyfriend Mike. When they pull up to the Beaumont house, Mike threatens to beat up Jeffrey, but then Dorothy Vallens staggers out of the dark, beaten and bloody. Mike stammers out an apology, and Jeffrey and Sandy take Dorothy to the Williams house to call an ambulance.

Sandy cringes in horror as Dorothy calls Jeffrey her "secret lover" and repeats, "He put his disease in me." In truth, Dorothy is the one who put her sadomasochistic disease in Jeffrey.

After Dorothy is taken to the hospital, Jeffrey goes to her apartment and finds evidence of Frank's fury. Dorothy's husband Don is dead, his brains blown out, Frank's strip of blue velvet stuffed in his mouth. The yellow man is standing in the middle of the room in shock, a huge hole blown in the side of his head, brain matter visible. Over the yellow man's police radio, Jeffrey hears that the raid on Frank's apartment has commenced. As Jeffrey leaves, however, he sees Frank approaching the apartment. He rushes back inside, calls for help on the police radio, grabs the yellow man's gun, and hides in the closet.

Frank, who has heard the call on his police radio, bursts into the apartment. Yanking his swatch of blue velvet from Don's mouth and draping it over the silencer of his pistol, then huffing his mysterious fumes, he searches for Jeffrey in the bedrooms, calling out "Here pretty, pretty" like he is summoning a dog. Returning to the living room, he silences the TV and topples the yellow man with bullets, then realizes Jeffrey is in the closet. Huffing more fumes, he ecstatically closes in for the kill, but Jeffrey sees him coming through the slats and shoots him in the head. The voyeur has become an actor.

The slow-motion headshot is accompanied by a terrifying simian shrieking. The bulbs in the floor lamp then surge with electricity and burn out, as if Frank's life force is fleeing through the wiring. In the visual code established in *Eraserhead*, this signifies the presence of the supernatural, especially the demonic. Frank is somehow both more and less than human.

There is a strong spiritual-religious element to *Blue Velvet*, as with all of Lynch's work. Although Lynch himself is a practitioner of Transcendental Meditation, which makes him a Hindu of sorts, the spiritual imagery of his movies tends to be Western, primarily Christian but also Gnostic. I read *Eraserhead*, for instance, as a Gnostic anti-sex film.[1] Like *Eraserhead*, *Blue Velvet* treats sex as a form of bondage to subhuman powers, both animal and demonic. But *Blue Velvet* is far less nihilistic than *Eraserhead*. The demonic forces are balanced out by angelic ones, represented by robins and light from above, as opposed to electric light, which for Lynch has demonic connotations.

The night after his first terrifying encounter with Frank, Jeffrey tells Sandy what he has seen. Sandy picks him up in her car, an odd role reversal putting her in the driver's seat. She parks near a church with colorful stained-glass windows, brightly lit from inside. Organ music plays in the background.

Jeffrey prefaces the story of Frank and Dorothy with the words, "It's a strange world," which becomes something of a *Leitmotif* in the film. After telling Sandy who Frank is and what

---

[1] See my "*Eraserhead*: A Gnostic Anti-Sex Film," in *Return of the Son of Trevor Lynch's CENSORED Guide to the Movies* (San Francisco: Counter-Currents, 2019).

he has done, Jeffrey asks "Why are there people like Frank? Why is there so much trouble in this world?" His face is anguished and childlike, for he is just discovering the darkness of the adult world. Jeffrey's question is not merely psychological. Given the backdrop of church and organ music, it is also theological. It is *the* problem of evil: If God is perfect in his power and goodness, why are there people like Frank? Why is there so much trouble in this world?

Sandy says she doesn't know the answer. But she does in a way. For she tells Jeffrey of the dream she had the night they met:

> In the dream, there was our world, and the world was dark, because there weren't any robins. And the robins represented love. And for the longest time, there was just this darkness. And all of a sudden, thousands of robins were set free, and they flew down and brought this blinding light of love. And it seemed like that love would be the only thing that would make any difference. And it did. So I guess it means, there is trouble till the robins come.

As Sandy speaks of the blinding light of love, one realizes the organ music is not coming from the church. It is part of the score, underscoring the essentially religious nature of her dream. Love, light from above, and robins are the forces that will beat back hate, darkness, and bugs. Evil is only temporary, until the robins come. Sandy has essentially delivered a religious sermon, sitting in the driver's seat.

After Jeffrey's first encounter with Frank and Dorothy, we see him on the sidewalk. He emerges from darkness. Then he freezes as a light comes from above. Is this the light of judgment? Then we see distorted images of Jeffrey's father in the hospital, then Frank raving, then the guttering candle, then Dorothy saying "Hit me." We then see Frank punch at the camera. Is he hitting Dorothy or Jeffrey at this point? Jeffrey then awakens from a nightmare.

After Jeffrey kills Frank, Sandy, her father, and a legion of police and paramedics arrive on the scene. Even though Jeffrey has rescued himself, we only really breathe again when we see the flashing lights and guardians of order. In the middle of the bustling crime scene, Jeffrey and Sandy embrace and kiss, bathed in white light from above. There is trouble till the robins come.

Cut to an extreme closeup of an ear. Near the beginning of the story, we were drawn into the mystery by entering the dead ear to ominous industrial noise. Now we are at the end of the story, the mystery solved, emerging from a pink and living ear to Julee Cruise's ethereal "Mysteries of Love" (yet another foreshadowing of *Twin Peaks*).

As the camera pulls back, we see that the ear belongs to Jeffrey, sleeping in the sunshine. He opens his eyes and sees a robin perched in a tree. Sandy calls out, "Jeffrey, lunch is ready." Mr. Beaumont is out of the hospital, up on his feet, working on something in the yard with Detective Williams. Jeffrey's mother and Mrs. Williams are chatting together in the living room. The families have come together. It is a sign that Jeffrey and Sandy have a serious relationship. Perhaps marriage is in the future.

Aunt Barbara and Sandy are preparing lunch in the kitchen when the robin appears on the windowsill with a bug squirming in its beak. The forces of good have quelled the forces of evil. "Maybe the robins are here," says Jeffrey.

"I don't see how they could do that. I could never eat a bug" volunteers aunt Barbara, before stuffing something that looks vaguely bug-like in her mouth. Aunt Barbara is a robin without even knowing it. Thus *Blue Velvet* vindicates all guardians of public order, even the silliest and least self-conscious form, namely *prejudice*: "You're not going down by Lincoln, are you?"

"It's a strange world, isn't it?" observes Sandy.

Then we see the yellow tulips, the friendly fireman, and the red roses. But before we return to the blue sky, we see Dorothy Vallens and her little boy in a park. She picks him up and holds him, smiling, although her face then takes on a sad and haunted look.

It is the happiest ending possible after such a hellish journey.

What is the political philosophy of *Blue Velvet*? I read Lynch
as fundamentally conservative. The typical sneering Leftist
take on Lynch's opening is that the idyllic surface of Lumberton is fake and kitschy, whereas the truth about Lumberton is
the bloody struggle of vermin in the dark. But Lynch's own
view is far more nuanced.

Lynch knows that civilization is artificial, a construct, a triumph over nature. But Lynch is not a liberal or a Leftist because he does not think that nature is good. Thus he does not
conclude that the conventions that constrain nature are bad.
Lynch thinks that nature is profoundly dangerous, especially
sex and sadism, which for him have a supernatural, demonic
quality. Lynch does not believe in the "natural goodness" of
man. He believes in the natural—and supernatural—badness of
man. Which means that human nature needs to be constrained
by human conventions.

Frank Booth is Lynch's portrait of what you get when nature
is liberated by the breakdown of social repressions. The French
Revolution ended with the Terror. The Sixties ethic of sex,
drugs, and rock-and-roll didn't lead us back to the Garden of
Eden. It gave us the Tate-LaBianca murders, the Weathermen,
and Frank Booth.

Frank is not just a sex maniac. He is a drug dealer. His partner in crime, Ben, sells both sex and drugs. Frank uses alcohol
and also his mysterious gas to break down his inhibitions and
release his sadism. Moreover, Frank always has his Roy Orbison soundtrack tape handy. Finally, to channel F. Roger Devlin
for a moment, Dorothy Vallens can also be seen as an example
of the havoc created by female narcissism, masochism, and hypergamy when social conventions break down.[2]

Sade knew human nature better than Rousseau.

Many viewers note that the robin at the end is clearly fake,
some sort of puppet. It might simply have been the best effect
that Lynch could create with the available budget. But it could

---

[2] See F. Roger Devlin's *Sexual Utopia in Power* (San Francisco:
Counter-Currents, 2015).

very well have been intentional. The bugs represent hate and evil whereas the robins represent love and goodness. The bugs are darkness; the robins are light. If the bugs represent nature, then the robins have to represent something other than nature. In Sandy's dream, they clearly have a supernatural aspect.

But another opposite of nature is convention, in which case it makes sense to have an obviously artificial robin. The robin represents the conventions that hold the savagery of nature in check, including the guardians of public order: the police, firemen, paramedics, even the crossing guards. These conventions also include moral principles, manners, and even Aunt Barbara's prejudices.

Although *Blue Velvet* was Lynch's fourth feature film, it was really the first where he had both creative control and an adequate budget. (Well, maybe not for the robin.) *The Elephant Man* (1980) and *Dune* (1984) gave Lynch adequate funding but no creative control. *Eraserhead* (1977) was entirely Lynch's baby, but he created it over a period of years on a shoestring budget. It is a measure of Lynch's genius that the very first time he had the financial and creative freedom to fully realize his vision, he created what is arguably his greatest film. Certainly it is his most Lynchian.

The Unz Review, July 26, 2019

BLUE VELVET:
THE LOST FOOTAGE

The Criterion Collection's 2019 Blu-ray of *Blue Velvet* contains 53 minutes of lost footage. Does this footage in any way alter my reading of the film's psychological and political meaning? The short answer is no, but read on.

Blue Velvet was released as a two-hour film, but originally the film was about two hours and fifty minutes long. The material Lynch removed is not raw footage that was never part of the film. Instead, it was edited into the film, scored by Angelo Badalamenti, and then removed by Lynch. For years, this footage was lost, but we knew the basic content from the shooting script and still photos of the scenes. But, to quote Lynch, through some "amazing grace," what once was lost has now been found, and thanks to the Criterion Collection, now we all can see.

Lynch does not present the lost footage in the order in which it appeared in the film, but my commentary on it will mostly follow the story.

In the theatrical release of *Blue Velvet*, we first glimpse Jeffrey Beaumont walking across a field to a hospital to visit his father. In the lost footage, our first view of him is at college, in the basement of a dorm, hidden in the dark, watching a couple kissing on a mattress. As the woman's demands to "stop" become more strident, Jeffrey shouts, "Hey, leave her alone!" — the very words he later says to Frank Booth when he is pinching Dorothy Vallens' breasts.

This opening strongly establishes two themes that are prominent throughout *Blue Velvet*: Jeffrey's peeping Tom behavior and the connection between sex and violence. This scene also foreshadows the questions the movie raises about the blurry lines between rape and role-playing, victim and perpetrator, for the couple do not react as if Jeffrey has just stopped a crime. In fact, the woman looks at her partner with an expression that seems to say: "Are you gonna take that? Are you gonna let this guy stop you?"

Jeffrey receives a phone call from his mother, telling him that his father has been stricken with a mysterious ailment and is in the hospital. She tells Jeffrey that he will have to withdraw from college and come home for good because of the expense of his father's illness and the need for him to help run the family hardware store. This scene is vintage Lynch, with excellent music by Badalamenti and quirky touches like the mother's bedside table cluttered with prescription bottles and the dirty, cracked mint green walls the camera lingers on.

It also reveals dimensions of the mother's character entirely absent from the finished film. She is sinister and manipulative, giving the strong vibe that she is less concerned with having Jeffrey take on adult responsibilities than with reeling him back into the nest before he can fully escape.

The other scenes with Jeffrey at college—including a surreal sock hop and Jeffrey's farewells with his friends and his insincere, airheaded girlfriend Louise—are completely dispensable. Like practically everything that Lynch cut, they feel like TV.

Night time. A small airplane lands. Jeffrey's mother picks him up at the airport. At first we wonder why Jeffrey is riding in the back seat like a child. Then we see that his aunt Barbara is in the front passenger seat. We see the car pull into the driveway, the family enter the living room, Jeffrey ascend the stairs. He surveys his childhood room. Returning feels like defeat. Then he goes to the blinds and peeks into the night, more peeping Tom behavior foreshadowing him spying on Dorothy Vallens through the slats of her closet door. The whole sequence really adds nothing. It is TV-like padding for people who can't imagine characters traveling from point A to B without actually seeing it.

The following morning at breakfast, Jeffrey's mother asks him not to mention to his father than he has withdrawn from college, adding to her manipulative quality. Then, finally, we arrive at the point where Jeffrey first appears in the final release, on his way to the hospital to see his father.

There are several more scenes with Jeffrey's mother and aunt Barbara: the women singing "Clementine" as they wash the dishes, the mother receiving a shot from a Dr. Gunn for some unknown ailment, the mother waiting up for Jeffrey in the dark and startling him when he comes come. (He has just seen Frank Booth for the first time and doesn't need any more surprises.) And finally an amusing sequence where aunt Barbara hunts for termites and leaves her quarry with a note to Jeffrey on a table next to an overflowing ashtray.

There are a couple of entirely dispensable scenes at the house of Detective Williams. In the first, Jeffrey has coffee and cake with Mrs. Williams while waiting for her husband to return. In the final version, we cut directly to the conversation with Detective Williams, although without establishing that he has just come home, it seems odd for him to be wearing his shoulder holster in his house.

The other sequence involves a dinner with Jeffrey, the Williams, their daughter Sandy, and Sandy's boyfriend Mike, which establishes nothing except that Mike is jealous of Jeffrey and that Mike is a vitamin-popping prude whereas Jeffrey (like Lynch) loves sweets and coffee. There is also a brief scene where Jeffrey and Detective Williams look at crime scene photos and Jeffrey focuses in on a swatch of (dunn-dunn-dunn) blue velvet. It all feels like TV and is well lost.

The sequence in which Jeffrey and Sandy go to the Slow Club to see Dorothy Vallens sing is much longer. Their car's approach is dragged out, but the music is gorgeous. The club itself is quite droll, with its Maitre D' and uniformed waiters clashing with the background twitter of electronic games. The opening acts are pure Lynch. First, we see a dog eating from a green bowl, a neon rabbit above his head, and a winds arrangement of the "Battle Hymn of the Republic" being looped in the background. Then we are treated to an excruciating comic, accompanied by "Beautiful Dreamer" and an exotic dancer. Both acts go on much, much too long.

There are three additional scenes with Frank Booth. In the first, Jeffrey tails Frank to a field on a windy night, watching him moving frantically through the dark to Dorothy Vallens' apartment, then emerging sometime later. Frank is shot at such a distance that it is hard to see who he is, much less understand what he is doing.

In another scene, Jeffrey calls Dorothy's apartment, and Frank answers. There are a few seconds of seething tension followed by Frank's terrifying "Speak, fucker!"

The longest sequence takes place after Frank and his gang arrive at This Is It. In the theatrical version, they simply enter Ben's apartment. Originally, the sequence was much more complex. A grotesque old black man sings about a dog chasing a rabbit, accompanied on guitar by a white man, while a vacant, topless whore stares off-screen. It goes on much, much too long.

This is apparently the back room of a bar/whorehouse. Frank and his crew burst in the front, then head straight to the back where Frank threatens the life of one of the male customers.

None of these scenes add anything to the story, but the brief phone call is genuinely terrifying.

There are two scenes involving Dorothy Vallens. One is an alternative take of Jeffrey's second visit to her apartment. In this version, the yellow man (Detective Gordon) shows up briefly to hassle Dorothy while Jeffrey hides in the closet and eavesdrops. But from his point of view, we can barely make out the dialogue. It adds nothing.

In the second scene, Dorothy and Jeffrey go to the roof of her building. Dorothy tries to throw herself over the parapet, but Jeffrey drags her back. Then they make love on the rooftop. The whole scene is murky, both visually and psychologically. The only loss is Angelo Badalamenti's truly wonderful music.

There are a few other bits that I will not discuss: just hellos, goodbyes, phone calls, and other filler, none of it a loss.

Every fan of Lynch and *Blue Velvet* will love this footage. But *Blue Velvet* is a better movie without it. Some of the lost scenes underscore themes found in the final cut, particularly Jeffrey's scopophilia, the association of sex and violence, and the association of bugs and evil. We also get a bit more of eccentric aunt Barbara and Jeffrey's playful relationship with her. But really the only surprise is the sinister side of Jeffrey's mother. Cinematically, the only distinctively Lynchian scenes are Jeffrey's phone conversations with his mother and Frank, the events at the Slow Club and This Is It, and aunt Barbara's bug hunt.

Will there ever be a "director's cut" of *Blue Velvet*? Lynch had complete creative control over *Blue Velvet,* so the theatrical version *is* the director's cut. It is nice to have the lost footage, but it should not be part of the film.

What does the lost footage reveal about Lynch as an artist? Some of the lost scenes are fluff and filler. Some are self-indulgent and boring. Some are interesting and well done. But none of them were essential to the story. This is why their removal does not fundamentally alter *Blue Velvet*'s meaning but instead brings it into greater focus.

The Unz Review, August 9, 2019

BREAKFAST AT TIFFANY'S

Blake Edwards' 1961 film *Breakfast at Tiffany's*—loosely based on Truman Capote's 1958 novel of the same name—stars Audrey Hepburn in her iconic role of Holly Golightly, a charming, flighty, feminine, haunted young woman trying to create a life—and an identity—in a gorgeous Technicolor New York City at what is arguably the peak of American civilization, just before the plunge.

I have seen *Breakfast at Tiffany's* six times, twice on the big screen, and although I loved it every time, for the first four viewings, the movie played a strange trick on my memory. If you had asked me what *Breakfast at Tiffany's* is about, I would have said it is a wholesome romantic comedy. But that's not really true. Yes, it has plenty of comic elements, but overall, *Breakfast at Tiffany's* is a very sad and serious film. As Sally Tomato says, the story of Holly Golightly's life would be a book that "would break the heart." That's certainly true of Truman Capote's novel, which is indeed so heartbreaking that Blake Edwards rewrote the ending for the movie to give us a little hope to cling to.

And, as for wholesomeness, it has that too in the end. But somehow I repeatedly forgot that *Breakfast at Tiffany's* is the tale of the romantic misadventures of two gold-diggers, Holly Golightly and her upstairs neighbor, Paul Varjak, both of whom are skating through their 20s by having sex with and taking money from older and richer people. Of course, they both maintain their self-respect by keeping a discreet distance between the sex-giving and money-taking, so that the *quid pro quo* is not too brazenly obvious. Capote said that Holly stopped short of simple prostitution, describing her as an "American geisha."

Both Holly and Paul rationalize their choices by reference to a mission. Holly wants to buy land and horses and care for her sweet but slow brother Fred, who is currently in the Army. (The novel is set in 1943, so being in the army is a rather dangerous undertaking.) Paul is a writer who needs a patron to give him time to work on his great novel. But it is not working. He's got writer's block. As Holly notes, he doesn't even have a ribbon in his typewriter.

Paul is the prouder and more serious of the two. Holly is top banana in the flake department. Which, of course, means that Paul suffers greatly at Holly's hands when he falls in love with her.

Maybe the false memories are due to Henry Mancini's music, which won two Oscars, for best score and best song for the haunting cornball classic "Moon River," with lyrics by Johnny Mercer, which casts a silvery shimmer of nostalgia over the whole heartbreaking tale. Whatever the cause, I am grateful to this amnesia, for it has allowed *Breakfast at Tiffany's* to surprise me again and again with each new viewing.

The basic plot of *Breakfast at Tiffany's* is quite simple. Paul Varjak—played by George Peppard at the peak of his Nordic, preppy good looks—moves into an apartment on Manhattan's upper east side and meets his ditzy downstairs neighbor, Holly Golightly. Holly has lived there for a year but looks like she is still moving in. That's because she's rootless, a drifter, a flake. She has an orange cat, but she hasn't given him a name, because she doesn't want the commitment. Her favorite place in the world is Tiffany's, the jewelers on Fifth Avenue. She declares to Paul that if she ever finds a place that makes her feel like Tiffany's, she'll put down roots and give the cat a name. Of course it is hard to imagine a home that would feel like Tiffany's. Buckingham Palace, perhaps? Holly, in short, is not too practical. Her conditions for settling down are a fanciful way of saying "never."

Paul's apartment isn't exactly "him" either. It looks like an expensive European hotel room. It was decorated before his arrival by his patron, Mrs. Failenson, nicknamed "2E," played by a radiant Patricia Neal (who once played opposite a certain Ellsworth Toohey in King Vidor's film of Ayn Rand's *The Fountainhead*). The movie creates the character of Paul from the novel's unnamed narrator. 2E and her relationship with Paul are inventions of the screenwriter, which considerably deepens the character and his relationship with Holly, creating dramatic conflict through "irreconcilable similarities."

Holly finds Paul to be a sympathetic, useful, and highly pre-
sentable neighbor. As fellow gold-diggers, they also have a certain understanding. But in her eyes, their shared mode of life
also precludes a relationship, for Paul has no gold, and Holly
has set her sights on older, uglier men with more money. For
Paul, gold-digging is a short-term strategy, to get his start in life,
at which time he will settle down with a nice girl and take care
of her. For Holly, however, gold-digging is a long-term strategy
to find a husband, who will take care of her forever.

One of the most captivating sequences in *Breakfast at Tiffany's*
is when a mysterious stalker shows up outside Paul and Holly's
building. 2E thinks her husband is having her followed. Paul,
who is a red-blooded male under his gorgeous wardrobe, is
game for a confrontation. After some cat and mouse in the east
side and Central Park, the stalker approaches Paul and says,
"Son, I need a friend."

It turns out that the stalker, played by Buddy Ebsen, is Doc
Golightly, a veterinarian from Texas and Holly's . . . no, not her
father, her *husband*, whom she married at the age of fourteen.
Holly's real name is Lula Mae Barnes. Lula Mae and Fred were
runaways who showed up on Doc's farm. Doc was a widower
with children who needed a helpmeet. Hence the marriage. Doc
has tracked Lula Mae down to persuade her to return home to
"her husband and her chirren."

Holly will have none of it. The marriage was annulled long
ago, and she's just not Lula Mae anymore. She has constructed a
whole new identity for herself. She got rid of her Okie accent
with French lessons, courtesy of a Hollywood producer, O. J.
Berman (Martin Balsam), and she has a fabulous circle of rich
male friends—whom she rates as "rats" and "super-rats"—
competing for her attention.

When she sees a heartbroken Doc off at the Greyhound bus
station, she tells him that she's a "wild thing" and that one
should never fall in love with wild things, because they will just
break your heart. In truth, Holly is just a flake who doesn't know
who she is or what she wants and is afraid of real relationships
and real commitments. Berman thinks Holly is a phony, but he
debates whether she is a real phony or not—a real phony being

someone who believes his own nonsense.

The whole sequence moves from creepy, to comical, to corny, to deeply moving. That's the magic of this film.

Once Doc has been sent on his way, Holly gets roaring drunk. It is a catharsis, a crisis, a crossroads. Paul now knows her story but loves her all the more. He hopes that she will get a little more serious about life, and maybe about him. Paul enjoys taking care of Holly. It makes him feel strong and manly. Being taken care of by 2E is convenient but emasculating. Unsurprisingly, Holly proves to be the better muse than 2E. Awakening Paul's manliness also awakens his creativity.

Thus Paul is appalled when Holly declares that she is no longer going to play the field. She is going to set her sights on marrying Rusty Trawler, the ninth-richest man in America under fifty, despite the fact that he is a tittering pig-faced manlet. (In the novel, Trawler is a known Nazi sympathizer who once proposed marriage to Unity Mitford.)

When Trawler falls into the clutches of another gold-digger, Holly coolly turns to pursuing José da Silva Pereira (played by Spanish aristocrat José Luis de Vilallonga), a dashing but strait-laced Brazilian from a prominent family. It is not clear to Paul, though, if he means to marry her or merely keep her as a mistress. Holly is oblivious, however.

Whatever José's intentions, however, he calls it off when Holly is arrested. Holly has received $100 per week to visit Sally Tomato, an elderly mobster incarcerated at Sing Sing, and deliver his "weather report" — obviously coded messages about the narcotics trade — to his people outside.

Berman gets Holly bailed out. Paul packs her belongings and the cat and picks her up at a police station to take her to a hotel where she can hide out from the press. In the cab, he breaks the bad news about José. While adjusting her lipstick, Holly coolly decides to jump bail, use her ticket to Brazil, and marry some other rich South American. In an act of consummate bitchcraft, she tells the cab to pull over and abandons the cat in an alleyway in a downpour. In the novel, she follows through with her plan and disappears: a realistic but terrible outcome that puts Holly Golightly into the lower circle of flaky heartless bitches like *Cabaret*'s Sally Bowles.

In the film, Paul gives Holly a powerful talking to. He tells her that people really do belong to one another and that it is the only real chance we have of happiness. In today's rabidly individualistic society, these are unfashionable sentiments, but deeply romantic and stirring ones. Paul actually reaches Holly. He actually changes her heart. She runs into the rain, searching for the cat, whom she finds, then Paul and Holly embrace, the prototype of a human family that may come to be. (Holly definitely wants children.) The end—a happy one, we hope.

Unsurprisingly, modern arbiters of virtue don't like *Breakfast at Tiffany's* very much. It is obviously heteronormative, anti-feminist, and otherwise "problematic." But their ire is focused mostly on Mickey Rooney's portrayal of Holly's upstairs neighbor, Mr. I. Y. Yunioshi, as a buck-toothed Jap buffoon, straight out of World War II propaganda cartoons. Frankly, even I am offended by Mr. Yunioshi.

Capote's novel makes much more of race, but it is hard to say if it is "problematic" or "woke." For instance, Holly notes that José has a touch of black blood. But she doesn't mind the prospect of having slightly "coony" babies as long as the father is rich and respected. (Eventually, they'll come for Capote as well.)

I highly recommend *Breakfast at Tiffany's*. But what is most enchanting about this film can't be captured in prose. It simply must be *seen*—for the beautiful people, the iconic fashions (one of the little black dresses Audrey Hepburn wore in this film fetched nearly one million dollars at auction), and its portrayal of a glamorous, safe, overwhelmingly white New York City.

Watch it as nostalgic, escapist entertainment—a mid-century American time capsule. I'm betting you'll want to re-watch it as a character study that even manages to have a "message"—and a wholesome one at that. It communicates the joys and follies of youth in America at its peak—an age of seemingly infinite potential—and the necessity of finally growing up and actually taking a stand, of actually *being* someone. It became the road less traveled.

CABARET

Bob Fosse's 1972 film *Cabaret* is supposed to be propaganda for Weimar decadence and against Nazi brutality. But the film utterly fails as propaganda insofar as it changes no minds. In fact, *Cabaret* is more akin to a diagnostic tool—like inkblot tests or gestalt images—for distinguishing between fundamentally different human types: people who love beauty versus people who love ugliness, people who love order versus people who love chaos, people who love health versus people who love decadence. Just as some see a goblet and others a pair of profiles, just as some see a duck and others a rabbit, some see *Cabaret* as a celebration of decadence and others see it as a case for National Socialism. Most of the latter, of course, do not embrace or condone National Socialism themselves. But once the movie is over, they can at least *understand* why millions of Germans did so.

This is why I include *Cabaret* in my pantheon of Goebbels Award laureates—namely Hollywood films that Joseph Goebbels would have released unaltered—including such titles as *Quiz Show, Storytelling, Miller's Crossing,* and *Barton Fink.*[1]

Cabaret is set in Berlin in the early 1930s, just before the Nazis came to power. The titular cabaret is the Kit Kat Klub, which is upheld as the epitome of Weimar culture, as indeed it is. But what do we see on stage? Is it a new image of man's highest potential? Is it a vision of a perfected society? Nothing of the sort. It is merely a parody and inversion of the existing culture and its values, including its sexual mores, martial ethos, and aesthetic standards.

The music is jazz of the most irritating type: brassy tuneless farts and raspberries over a monotonous, herky-jerky beat. The singing is tuneless and brassy Broadway caterwauling. The musicians are ugly women and female impersonators with exaggerated and grotesque clown makeup and skimpy costumes revealing sagging, ravaged flesh. The MC, played by Joel Grey

---

[1] I review *Quiz Show* and *Storytelling* below as well as *Barton Fink* and *Miller's Crossing* in *Return of the Son of Trevor Lynch's CENSORED Guide to the Movies.*

(born Joel David Katz), is leering and sexually ambiguous, with ghastly yellow teeth.

The stage shows include ugly women wrestling in mud, bondage and sadism set to music, a bawdy burlesque in which dancers in German folk costumes slap one another's asses, females and female impersonators mocking soldiers, a song about a *ménage à trois*, and a song about miscegenation in which the singer pledges his love to a gorilla but ends with the words "But she doesn't look *Jewish* at all." It is pure cultural Bolshevism from start to finish.

The main character of *Cabaret* is Sally Bowles, a singer and aspiring actress. Sally Bowles was English in Christopher Isherwood's *Berlin Stories*, the *Ur*-text of this and other adaptations. But in *Cabaret*, she is an American because, well, Liza Minnelli couldn't play her as anything else. I have not read Isherwood's original, so I can't tell if Miss Minnelli does his character justice. Let's just say that if Sally Bowles is meant to be a mediocre singer with a potato face and potato physique, such that her aspirations to be a great actress are a pathetic delusion, then Minnelli nails the part. Her attempts at glamor are laughable: an unfeminine bowl-cut, clown makeup, and gaudy thrift store rags, to say nothing of her braying speech, gawky mannerisms, and mannish gait. When we first see her on stage, she looks like a cartoon mouse pretending to be a dominatrix.

Sally's motto is "divine decadence," although that may simply be a brand of nail polish. Her philosophy is pure hedonism. Anything goes, "as long as you're having fun." She smokes, drinks, and fornicates with abandon. Her goal is to become a star, or be kept by a rich man, by sheer dint of schmoozing and whoring and faking it till she makes it. She's a phony, a social climber, and a parasite.

But under all this surely there beats a heart of gold.

No, not really. Not at all. Sally is selfish, immature, insensitive, rude, and neurotic. We are supposed to feel for her because she pines for her neglectful father. (There is no mention of a mother.) But feeling pain doesn't make you a good person. In fact, bitterness over festering wounds is the most common excuse for monstrous behavior. Strip away Sally's gaucheries, neuroses, and machinations, and you won't find a little rosebud of sweetness. You'll just find a howling void of nihilism.

Minnelli's songs all have mediocre music and lousy lyrics. Her catchiest number, "Mein Herr," is about being a hypergamous gold-digger. When she meets a nice young homosexual, who beds her out of pity, she thinks "Maybe this Time" it will last. Then there's her duet with Joel Grey, "Money, Money," which informs us that "Money makes the world go 'round," a witless ditty in which vulgar Marxism meets just plain vulgar. (By every measure, it is infinitely inferior to ABBA's "Money, Money, Money.") I'll have a few words to say about her grand finale later.

The basic plot of *Cabaret* is that a young homosexual Englishman, Brian Roberts (Michael York, looking conspicuously wholesome), comes to Weimar Berlin. He finds lodging at a rooming house full of bohemian types, including a streetwalker and a pornographer who both turn out to be Nazis, as well as Sally Bowles, who is right across the hall.

The strait-laced (though gay) Englishman meets the brash American in clown makeup, and an unlikely friendship begins. Sally introduces Brian to the Kit Kat Klub, finds him work translating pornography, offers him her room for teaching English lessons, and generally inserts herself into his life, to the point of seducing him. Brian seems to sleep with her out of pity.

Once Brian and Sally are a couple, hypergamous Sally takes up with Maximilian, a fantastically wealthy aristocrat who finds Sally and Brian entertaining. He showers them with expensive presents, dangles the prospect of an adventure in Africa, beds both of them, then loses interest.

One of the most famous scenes in the film takes place as the trio returns to Berlin from Maximilian's country estate. Maximilian has explained how the Nazis are hooligans but useful for stopping the Communists. Once the Communists are defeated, people like Max will rein in the Nazis. As they enjoy lunch at a beer garden, a handsome blond youth begins singing. It is standard German Romantic or folk fare, with stags, forests, the Rhine, babies, etc. Then we see that the young man is wearing the uniform of the Hitler Youth. The song takes on a more martial and strident air with the chorus "Tomorrow Belongs to Me," and virtually the whole crowd joins in signing. "Still think you can control them?" Brian asks Max.

The song is pure, calculated *kitsch*, the product of two Jewish songwriters, and yet it is better—and seems more sincere and real—than anything else in the film. The scene is crushingly unsubtle, an exercise in ritualistic *goy*-hatred. These Hollywood Nazis are supposed to seem sinister and repellent, but they are infinitely healthier and more appealing than the smug and decadent Max and Brian, much less anything on stage at the Kit Kat Klub.

The most wholesome love story in *Cabaret* is between the impoverished businessman Fritz Wendel and the Jewish heiress Natalia Landauer, who meet through Brian, their English tutor. Fritz pursues Natalia, but there's a hitch. Jew-gentile relations are at low ebb in Germany. But Fritz has a way out. He's actually a Jew. He was merely pretending to be a Christian, because once you are a member of the vast majority in an individualistic society, people notice you and invite you to parties and cut you in on business deals. It is a farcical distortion of the truth. Crypto Jews don't lose touch with the Jewish community. The whole point of crypsis is to enjoy the advantages of belonging to *both* communities. When Fritz admits to Natalia that he is an apostate who has lied to her and everyone else, she naturally agrees to marry him. It is supposed to be heartwarming, but morally normal people find it bizarre and repugnant.

Brian and Sally's relationship has a less happy ending. Sally is pregnant. Maybe the baby is Brian's. Maybe it is Max's. Sally wouldn't dream of asking Brian to pay for the abortion, though. She'll just pawn the fur coat that Max bought her. Brian has another idea. He proposes marriage. He doesn't care if the child might be Max's. Decadence doesn't seem so divine anymore. Berlin is hell. It is a rat race in pursuit of shallow and unsatisfying pleasures. Brian sees marriage and fatherhood as a chance for both him and Sally to escape and have a normal life. He'll teach at Cambridge. Maybe there will be other children.

Sally is touched that someone would be willing to spend his life with her. But marriage would require some changes: fidelity, for one; sobriety, for another; plus unselfishness toward babies.

It also wouldn't hurt for her to pick up some of the social virtues necessary to live in a normal community. But the biggest change would be to stop chasing her absurd dream of becoming a movie star. Sally thinks about it a bit, then skulks off and has an abortion in secret. Some viewers see a strong, independent career girl strongly and independently being strong and independent, or something. And they applaud. Healthy people see that, in the end, hedonism and individualism are just a nihilistic death cult.

Brian is horrified, of course, but probably realizes he has dodged a bullet, because Sally Bowles will never change. Besides, who would want children with her looks and personality disorders? This, in truth, is the most enlightened perspective on the matter, but the only people who would voice it in *Cabaret* are the hated Nazis.

Brian returns to England, and Sally returns to the Kit Kat Klub, where she sings her final song, "Cabaret," in which she informs us that "Life is a cabaret, old chum" and then tells the story of her old flat-mate Elsie, a whore who died of drink and pills and was the "happiest corpse she'd ever seen." Then Sally vows that, instead of having a normal life, "When I go, I'm goin' like Elsie." It is an open celebration of nihilism. It is particularly grotesque from the lips of the daughter of Judy Garland, who was found sitting dead on her toilet, aged 47, after a lifetime of abusing alcohol and downers. Liza Minnelli herself has lived to be a ripe old chum, but one wonders how many lives were cut short because of her glamorization of a death cult.

Cabaret ends with another icky song and dance from Joel Grey. The final shot is a distorted reflection of the audience, in which we see a number of Nazi stormtroopers. Are they in the audience because they are hypocrites, dipping into the fleshpots while railing against them? Or are they there to bust up the place? In truth, it was a bit of both. Of course, the filmmakers want us to mourn the passing of Weimar. But healthy viewers see something very different, a message that Goebbels himself would have approved: Weimar was a disease. The Nazis were the cure.

The Unz Review, July 7, 2019

DOWNTON ABBEY

Julian Fellowes' *Downton Abbey* is an extremely popular British period drama, set in the years 1912 to 1926, which ran six seasons (the Brits call them series) on television and is now a feature film set in 1927.

I very much enjoyed the first two seasons of *Downton Abbey*. Like many *Downton Abbey* fans, I felt an intense nostalgia for a country I had never known: George V's England, an overwhelmingly white, unapologetically Eurocentric society ruled by a glamorous aristocracy and monarchy that had not strayed too far from their founding warrior ethos. I was particularly taken with the series' treatment of the First World War, which I have always found far more moving than the Second. I especially loved Maggie Smith as the scheming, sharp-tongued dowager Countess of Grantham.

Although the series did try to inject as many modern, politically correct tropes as the story could bear, the creators of the series had the good sense not to push it too far, for they knew that absolutely nobody watched *Downton Abbey* to see black faces, just as nobody chooses to visit London today because they want to see Jamaicans or Arabs or South Asians—and many people now skip London precisely to avoid them.

Like many series, *Downton Abbey* went on a bit too long. There was a natural story arc that ended with the marriage of Lady Mary (Michelle Dockery) and Matthew Crawley (Dan Stevens) sometime in season three. It should have ended there. But they managed to drag it out for six full seasons by doling out romances and tragedies to every major and bit player, to the point of farce. I was disgusted by the end of season three. I was curious to see if the show would recover in season four, but it didn't, so I stopped watching.

I had absolutely no desire to watch the *Downton Abbey* feature film, but spending the holidays with family tends to change one's mind. And in this case, I am glad. The *Downton Abbey* film is a triumphant return to form, with all the period charm and vivid, likable characters of the best parts of the series, without the soap operatic padding and empty calories. Beyond that, the politics of the film, such as they are, are decidedly wholesome and conservative, even when it tries to be progressive.

The story is set in motion when King George and Queen Mary are on a tour and decide to stay at Downton Abbey. There will be a lunch, a parade, and a banquet, plus a ball at the nearby house of their daughter Princess Mary and her very difficult husband, Lord Harewood. Naturally, the whole estate and village are aflutter, even the most cynical hearts drawing meaning and pride from the event.

Conflicts break out between the Downton staff and the royal servants. Conspiracies are hatched. Eggs and carpets are beaten. Dresses are hemmed; suggestions are hawed. Feelings are ruffled and assuaged. Cheeks blush, eyelashes flutter, men and women whirl around dance floors. Old ladies trade barbs. The dowager Countess schemes to bring home an inheritance. A republican assassin is foiled. Unjust pretensions are deflated by just pretensions, and somehow the grand structure of pretensions is upheld.

The most touching scenes of the movie involve Lady Mary, whose son will inherit Downton. When Mary raises the possibility of selling Downton and downsizing, her maid Anna begs her not to because Downton is the center of the whole community. Later, when Mary's grandmother, the dowager Countess, tells her that she is nearing the end of her life, they have a very moving conservation about how, despite the inevitability of change, the dead live on in their posterity. It is a life-affirming and deeply conservative message.

Even the republican characters, Tom Branson and the silly scullery mail Daisy, end up being conservatives of a sort. Tom is an Irish revolutionary, but he is also the son-in-law of the Earl of Grantham. In the end, he is more loyal to his adopted homeland and family, foiling an IRA assassination plot against King George.

As for Daisy, she has no truck with kings and queens, but she takes care not to deflate the pride of the local grocer who is honored to provide provisions for the royal visit. Daisy does not tell him that the royals are bringing their own supplies.

Even the one PC subplot is somewhat conservative in the end. The Earl's butler Barrow (Robert James-Collier) is a homosexual. He is somewhat put out when, for the duration of the royal visit, his retired predecessor Carson (Jim Carter), is called back into service.

So, the night of the ball, Barrow goes into town with one of the royal servants, Ellis, who is also homosexual. The two get separated, and Barrow ends up at an underground gay nightclub dancing with other fellows — all this intercut with the ball at the Harewoods, to frankly ridiculous effect — until the police arrive and arrest the lot.

Ellis uses his position on the royal staff to get Barrow out of jail. As they walk off into the night, Ellis tells Barrow that he just needs to be a bit more discreet. Barrow remarks on how good it is just to be able to talk, one man to another. It is clearly the beginning of a relationship.

The whole sequence has the best of liberal intentions, but it is nevertheless a rejection of radical gay liberation ideology, which holds that homosexuals can never find places in existing societies, thus they must burn it all down in a disco inferno.

Since it is based upon six seasons of television, *Downton Abbey* is not exactly a stand-alone film. I am sure those who have never seen the series would be quite lost, although I had not seen the latter half of the series and had no difficulty picking up the thread.

I highly recommend *Downton Abbey* to Anglophiles, lovers of costume dramas, and people who just want a vacation from multiculturalism. It is not great drama, but it is well-crafted escapist entertainment: romantic, nostalgic, visually sumptuous, with a witty and literate script and a wholesomely conservative message.

The Unz Review, December 29, 2019

EYES WIDE SHUT

The day Jeffrey Epstein turned up dead in a New York jail cell, I decided I needed to write something about *Eyes Wide Shut* (1999), Stanley Kubrick's last and weakest movie.

Epstein has quickly faded from the headlines, so let me remind you briefly of who he was. Epstein was an American Jew who enjoyed immense wealth from unknown sources, hob-knobbed with the global elite, including Bill Clinton and Prince Andrew, and was a pervert with a taste for underage girls, meaning that he was a serial rapist. He is also accused of sharing these women with his wealthy and powerful friends, which would have implicated them in marital infidelity and rape, making them subject to blackmail.[1]

In 2006, the FBI began investigating Epstein, tracking down over 100 women. In 2007, he was indicted by the federal government on multiple counts of sex trafficking and conspiracy to traffic minors for sex. If convicted, he and his co-conspirators could have spent the rest of their lives in prison. But US Attorney Alex Acosta was told to go easy on Epstein, because "he belonged to intelligence." Epstein received a sweetheart deal. He pled guilty to two state prostitution charges and spent thirteen months at a Florida county jail with generous work release. Epstein's co-conspirators were not prosecuted at all. The records were sealed, and would have remained so, were it not for the efforts of reporter Julie Brown, whose stories led to the unsealing of Epstein's records, followed by his arrest and death in custody.

The most plausible explanation for Epstein's mysterious life and death is that he was a pimp who implicated rich and powerful men and then blackmailed them, financially and politically. If he enjoyed the patronage of "intelligence," it was most likely Israeli. When he was first arrested, he called in favors from his patrons (and probably from his victims as well), to avoid federal prosecution, which could have embarrassed many powerful people. When Epstein was re-arrested, there was no way he

---

[1] See Greg Johnson, "Jeffrey Epstein's Death Gives New Life to 'Conspiracy Theories,'" *Counter-Currents*, August 19, 2019.

could escape prosecution, so he was murdered to protect the se-crets of any (or all) of his patrons and victims.

Eyes Wide Shut is relevant to the Epstein case because at the core of the film, Stanley Kubrick—who was something of a ren-egade Jew—gives us a glimpse into how a specifically Jewish financial and political elite uses sexual perversion and anti-Christian occult rituals to promote internal cohesion and control.

Eyes Wide Shut is set in the late 1990s. Tom Cruise plays Dr. Bill Harford, the protagonist. Nichole Kidman plays his wife Al-ice. They have a seven-year-old daughter named Helena. Bill is a medical doctor and obviously does quite well for himself. The Harfords have a huge, beautifully decorated Manhattan apart-ment, nice clothes, and a spiffy Range Rover. But the first clue that something might be amiss in their marriage is the fact that they have only one child, aged seven. Did the flame go out? Does Alice no longer want to bear Bill's babies?

The movie opens with the Harfords preparing for a Christ-mas party to be held at the mansion of Victor and Illona Ziegler. Victor is played by Sidney Pollack. Ziegler is obviously sup-posed to be Jewish, so the Christmas party seems a little odd. The Harfords also celebrate Christmas, but there appeared to be a seven-branched candelabrum in their dining room. Apparent-ly, religion doesn't mean much in the world Kubrick is portray-ing.

The Ziegler mansion is immense and magnificent. They clear-ly belong to the upper one percent of the one percent. Kubrick makes it clear that that Harfords don't belong to Ziegler's social set. He has been invited because he is Ziegler's doctor. "This is what you get for making house-calls," he declares to Alice.

As soon as they arrive, Bill and Alice go their separate ways. Alice gets rapidly drunk and ends up being pursued by a Hun-garian Pepe Le Pew named Sandor Savost, who regales her with one cynical quip about marriage after another as they stand at the bar or whirl around the dance floor to "I'm in the Mood for Love."

Bill ends up strolling around arm-in-arm with a couple of models, both of them taller than him. (Come to think of it, virtu-ally every woman in the movie is taller than him, including Alice.) Cruise spends practically the whole movie grinning in a manner that seems both smug and desperately ingratiating, entitled and needy. It is bizarre and unsettling, but I am sure theater people have a word for it, as might the DSM.

Bill notices that the piano player in the band Ziegler has hired is Nick Nightingale (played by Todd Field), someone Bill knew from medical school. They strike up a conversation while Nightingale is on break. Nightingale invites him to look him up one night while he is playing at the Sonata Café.

Then Bill is interrupted by Ziegler's butler, who guides him upstairs. Now we see the kind of house-calls that account for his lavish lifestyle. We are ushered into a bathroom bigger than many New Yorkers' entire apartments. Ziegler is struggling into his clothes while a nude model sprawls unconscious on a chair. Her name is Mandy, and she has overdosed on cocaine and heroin during a quickie with our gracious host. Doctor Harford rouses her and gives her a stern talking to. Apparently, a visit to the emergency room is not required.

Ziegler is clearly a member of the inner party of the elite: ambiguously Jewish, fantastically rich, utterly degenerate. The Harfords come from a lower, outer stratum of the elite. (For instance, Bill actually knows Nightingale, who is merely someone Ziegler hires to play the piano.) Bill is a doctor. Alice used to manage an art gallery. They probably come from money. They might be faintly Jewish, or maybe just New York *goys* steeped in a Jewish atmosphere.

As soon as they enter the Ziegler party, the Harfords are bombarded with opportunities to cheat, but neither does so. The higher one climbs in the social hierarchy, the closer one approaches the inner party, the greater the degeneracy and the more ferocious the assault on marital fidelity. While something is wrong with their marriage, they are at least faithful to one another. After the party, we see them naked on the bed. Dr. Bill is feeling frisky, but Alice is not into him and looks away.

The next day, we catch a glimpse of the Harford morning and evening routines. Once Helena is tucked into bed, Alice smokes a little pot and gets paranoid and combative with Bill. The topic is sex and infidelity. Bill states flatly that he would not cheat on

Alice. He also states flatly that he thinks Alice would not cheat on him, simply because she's his wife. Alice mocks this. We are animals after all. Does Bill expect her to believe that "millions of years of evolution" can be stopped dead by Bill's fidelity to his marriage vows? Doesn't he at least *think* about cheating?

Alice is particularly incensed at how cocksure Bill is that she is faithful. Bill is a typical modern conservative. He seems to think that only men have strong sexual desires, which are still weak enough to be kept in check by vows and a sense of honor.

But women—at least the kind of women one might marry—don't face the same temptations. Without men constantly bothering them, women would be sexually inert. He's not quite sure about women like Mandy, but he probably thinks she is merely a fallen woman who sleeps around only for the money. The possibility of female promiscuity, infidelity, and hypergamy—the desire to "trade up"—is not something that he takes seriously.

"If you men only knew," Alice responds ominously. She then proceeds to red-pill her husband by telling him of her fantasies of sleeping with a handsome Naval officer who stayed at the same hotel as them the previous summer.

But Alice is careful to add that even when she fantasized about cheating on Bill, she still felt tender, sad feelings for him and found him "dearer than ever." In short, Bill is like a child to her, not a man. Apparently, after Helena was born, Alice did not need to bear a second child. She simply turned her husband into one. Which is why, of course, their marriage has fizzled.

Bill understands nothing about female psychology, and precious little about male psychology, for that matter. He does not understand that part of the sizzle of marriage is the possibility of infidelity. We all value our partners more when we see that other people want them. But we also value them more if we believe that they are capable of taking advantage of these other options.

Alice feels contempt for her husband because he is surrounded by attractive women all the time and is not tempted by them, which means that she can take him for granted, that he would never cheat, that the moral man is fully in control of the animal man. He's sexually inert, gelded.

Beyond that, she is enraged by the fact that he takes her fidelity for granted, that he thinks of her as sexually inert and incapable of pursuing other options. This is why she needles and nettles him into stammering incredulity and rage with the story of the Naval officer. She wants to make him jealous. She wants to make him angry. In her heart of hearts, she would respect him more if he blew up and hit her.

But not our Bill, who is simply aghast.

Bill is saved by the bell, literally. The telephone rings. One of his patients, Lou Nathanson, has died. (Another fabulously wealthy, presumably Jewish character with a Christmas tree in his apartment.) Bill feels he needs to go over and spend some time comforting his daughter Marion. This is the kind of house call that ushered him into high society.

The visit to the Nathanson apartment is the beginning of a series of temptations—an implausibly long series of temptations that comes to resemble an allegory like *The Pilgrim's Progress*. In an intensely awkward scene—one of many to come—Marion kisses Bill and confesses her love for him only a few feet from her father, lying on his deathbed.

After Bill departs, he sees a couple kissing. This makes him imagine Alice making love with the Naval officer. Then he passes sex shops. Then he is taunted as a faggot by a bunch of drunken frat boys. (All of them taller.) Next he bumps into a beautiful prostitute, Domino (also taller than him), who takes him back to her apartment. But Bill chickens out, pays her for her time, and flees.

Then, close to midnight, Bill arrives at the Sonata Café just as Nick Nightingale is finishing up his set. Over drinks, Nick tells Bill of a party he is going to play at starting at 2 a.m. It is a masked ball/orgy, where he plays blindfolded. But the last time he played, the blindfold was not secured, and he caught a glimpse of "such women." Bill of course wants to attend and wheedles the location and password out of Nick. The password is "Fidelio," which means "fidelity"—rather ironic, considering what he is contemplating. But as it turns out, the possibility of infidelity actually strengthens fidelity.

Bill then rushes off to the Rainbow Costume shop and rouses its owner, Mr. Milich, from his bed to rent a tuxedo, hooded

cape, and a mask. The scene is overlong, padded, and excruciat-
ingly awkward, with Cruise grinning and whipping out his
New York State medical ID card. When Milich enters the shop,
he finds his teenage daughter engaged in some sort of sex play
with two middle-aged, cross-dressing Orientals. Mercifully, the
scene eventually ends, with Bill in a cab on his way to an estate
in Long Island.

The ball/orgy is the most famous sequence in *Eyes Wide Shut*.
The scene, like the story as a whole, is based on Austrian-Jewish
Decadent novelist and playwright Arthur Schnitzler's *Traumno-
velle* (*Dream Story*). In the novel, the ball takes place at the time of
Carnival or Fasching (Mardi Gras), when traditionally people
indulge themselves and invert the Christian virtues before the
beginning of Lent.

In the movie, the ball is before Christmas, but there's nothing
Christian, or even rebelliously Christian, about this event. Indeed, it is most definitely *anti*-Christian, a profanation and inversion of Christianity. The orgy begins with a ritual to the
sound of Nightingale's spooky organ music and Romanian Or-
thodox liturgical chant played backwards. The ritual is presided
over by a masked figure dressed as a Catholic Cardinal.

In the novel, the protagonist, Fridolin, is definitely Jewish,
and the ball/orgy is represented as a gathering of members of
Austria's Christian elite. Kubrick first read the novel in 1968, and
after *2001: A Space Odyssey*, considered adapting it with Woody
Allen as the explicitly Jewish protagonist. But Kubrick later decided to tone down the Jewishness of the character. He even
considered casting Steve Martin in an explicitly comic adaptation. But when he finally made the film, he explicitly told his
Jewish screenwriter, Frederic Raphael, that Bill would be played
by a non-Jewish actor, and that the ball would be a gathering of
America's specifically *Jewish* elite.

To subtly underscore the Jewish elite nature of the gathering,
parts of it were filmed at Mentmore Towers, the country house
of Baron Mayer de Rothschild (1818–1874). In addition, some
aspects of the costumes were modeled on the famous 1972 surrealist costume ball thrown by Marie-Hélène de Rothschild
(1927–1996) at the Château de Ferrières-en-Brie.

So why would the power-elites of a society engage in group perversion? The richer a person is, the more opportunities there are for self-indulgence. After a while, though, such people get jaded and hunger for exotic pleasures, including ones that violate the rules of morality and the laws of society. It takes a highly developed sense of honor not to abuse the freedom granted by great wealth. Even when such an aristocratic ethos was cultivated, there were many spectacular failures. Moreover, today's oligarchy has dispensed with the pretenses of honor entirely.

But this is not merely another night at the Playboy Mansion. Beyond routine degeneracy, elites also use sexual perversion as a tool of control. Just as street gangs require prospective members to sully themselves with crimes to join, elites have similar rituals, the more morally repulsive the better. Pedophilia and cannibalism probably top the list. Simple rape and murder are mere vanilla.

The prospects are eager to incriminate themselves because joining the gang will bring them power. But self-incrimination also gives the gang power over its members, who must obey lest they be exposed and humiliated. And of course worse sanctions are waiting in the wings, as Jeffrey Epstein reminds us.

When Bill arrives, the ball is just beginning with a ritual, presided over by a "Cardinal" figure who is surrounded by a circle of beautiful women, whose costumes are clearly inspired by the 1940 painting *Attirement of the Bride* (*La Toilette de la mariée*) by German Surrealist artist Max Ernst (1891–1976). When the ritual ends, the strumpets, who are almost nude except for their masks and footgear, fan out and take up with people in the crowd. Then the ball/orgy gets down to business.

One woman takes up with Bill. Needless to say, she is taller than him. Then things stop making sense. Immediately, she states that Bill does not belong there and warns him to leave. He is in mortal danger, and so is she for warning him. But there's really no way that she could know this. When Bill entered, she was engaged in the ritual. There was no time for anyone to figure out that Bill was an interloper, and no way to communicate this to the woman. There was also no way that she could have figured this out on her own, for he was masked like the rest of them.

Bill strolls around the orgy, taking it all in. In one room, same-sex couples are dancing to "Strangers in the Night." In others, people are rutting with various strumpets.

Bill is then approached by one of the servants, who tells him that his driver has a question for him. He is then shown back into the ritual chamber where, somehow, everyone we have just seen *in flagrante* is waiting for him. He is then unmasked as an imposter and told to disrobe. He's really gonna get it now.

But then the tall woman who warned him speaks up. She will take the punishment for him. She is then led away by a hooded figure with a huge golden nose. Bill is released with a stern warning not to speak of anything he has seen, lest he and his family pay the price.

We later learn that Bill's unmasking had a simple explanation. He drew attention to himself by arriving in a cab, not a limousine. When he checked his coat, the pocket contained a costume rental receipt made out to someone who was not on the guest list. But this still does not explain how the woman could have known who he was. Nor does it explain how the whole party could instantaneously gather back in the ritual chamber to unmask him.

Either Kubrick's script and editing are incoherent, or he wanted the scene to have the illogic of a dream. In a dream other characters *just know things* about you because they *are* you, and events occur without any plausible transitions. Of course, the whole story is based on a novel called *Dream Story*. But there's nothing *else* about the film that would lead one to think the ball is just a dream. The rest of the film seems like real life, and in real life, the characters make references to the ball. So if the ball is a dream, the rest of the movie would have to be a dream as well. But it does not *seem* like a dream, which to me means that *Eyes Wide Shut* is simply incoherent and unworthy of Kubrick.

Next we see Bill at home. It must be very, very early in the morning. But his bad day is not over yet. Alice is giggling in her sleep. He awakens her, and she tells him about her dream. She was in a deserted city, naked and ashamed, and blamed him for her plight. The lifeless realm of artifice is her marriage. Blaming him for her nakedness and shame points to Bill's mysterious dereliction of manliness that has sapped the life out of their marriage. Bill, white knight that he is, looked upon his naked wife… and decided to find her some clothes. Millions of years of evolution, and Bill passed up a perfectly good opportunity for sex.

As soon as Bill left, however, the deserted city turned into a verdant garden, and Alice's shame and anger turned to happiness. She was still naked, though. The Naval officer emerged from the woods, looked at her, mocked her, then made love to her. (Because he knows what to do with a naked woman.) Then they were surrounded by couples coupling. Then Alice began to have sex with countless other men. She knew that Bill was watching her and started laughing at him. Then he woke her.

Dr. Bill has been through a rather long day, and I can't imagine a more humiliating bit of news to cap it all off. In a normal man, millions of years of evolution might have led to anger, even violence. But not our Bill.

If this is starting to seem like a very long story, don't worry: There's only one more hour left.

The next day, a very tired Bill runs a bunch of errands. He tries to locate Nick Nightingale, using his grin, doctor card, and lies to wheedle his hotel out of a waitress, but when he gets to the hotel, the creepy gay desk clerk describes how a visibly bruised and shaken Nick checked out in the wee hours in the company of two burly men. Then Bill returns the costume he rented (without the mask, which he has lost). He discovers that Mr. Milich is now prostituting his daughter to the Orientals — and to Bill as well, if he is interested. These scenes are all annoying padded and awkward, with plenty of Cruise's excruciating grinning.

Cut to Bill at his office, brooding over the Naval officer. Then he drives to the estate, where a bloodless, vampiric looking butler hands him a threatening note. Back at his office, Bill continues to brood. He calls Marion Nathanson, clearly hoping to hook up with her. When her fiancé answers, he hangs up the phone. Then he goes back to the prostitute Domino's place and finds her gone. Her roommate Sally (taller, etc.) lets Bill in, and he begins flirting with her intensely, grinning idiotically and repeating everything she says back to him. Sally manages to cool his jets by informing her that Domino has just tested positive for HIV, which means that Bill has dodged a bullet.

Bill then walks the streets and realizes he is being followed. Ducking into a coffee house, he glances at the evening paper. Miss Amanda Curran, a former Miss New York, was admitted to the hospital with a drug overdose. This is the Mandy at Ziegler's party and, he suspects, the woman who warned him at the orgy. Bill goes to the hospital, pretending to be her doctor, and is informed that she died at 3:45 that afternoon. When he views her body in the morgue, he seems certain that she is the woman who warned him that both their lives were in danger. And now she is dead.

At this point, Victor Ziegler summons him to his mansion. This is no ordinary house-call. Ziegler informs him that he was at the orgy the previous night. He also tells Bill that he has had him followed that day. He knows that Bill has been investigating what happened. He wants to know if Bill plans to pursue his inquiries any further. He wants to scare him into silence, so he tells Bill that he would not sleep very well if he knew who it was behind those masks.

But then Victor tries a strange gambit. What if everything that happened that night — the warnings, the threats, etc. — were just a charade to scare Bill into silence. This is impossible, of course, for reasons explained above. Beyond that, Bill asks what kind of charade ends up with someone being killed. Victor replies that Mandy simply had her brains fucked out and was sent home. The overdose was her doing. The door was locked from the inside. The police were satisfied.

Victor knows a disturbing lot of details, in short, which makes one suspect foul play. But if they intended to kill her, she would have been found dead. They would not have left her alive, to be rushed to the hospital where she might have regained consciousness. Victor sums it up glibly: "It was always gonna be just a matter of time with her," which of course makes it easier to hide foul play but less necessary to risk it.

Then Victor concludes on a jocular note, while patting Bill on the back (never in a million years would I turn my back to Victor

Ziegler): "Somebody died. It happens all the time. But life goes on. It always does . . . until it doesn't. But you know that, don't you?" A nice parting threat to Bill. It is a chilling but ambiguous scene, a bit static and draggy, but well-played by Pollack.

Bill returns home to find Alice sleeping. The mask he wore to the ball is on the pillow next to her. Is it a threat? Did she find it and place it there herself? It is never made clear, but Bill breaks down in tears. Waking her, he says he will tell her everything. They seem to spend the rest of the night talking. Once Helena is up, they take her Christmas shopping. Frankly, under the circumstances, I would not have let Helena out of my sight. But once she runs off to look at toys, Bill asks Alice what they should do.

Alice thinks they should be grateful that they survived their little adventures, whether they were dreams or real. Bill insists that a dream is not just a dream, which Alice acknowledges. Alice also acknowledges that a person cannot be judged by what he does in a single night. Both of them can accept the situation.

Then Alice says, "We're awake now—and hopefully for a long time to come." They are awake regarding their relationship. They are also awake regarding their own psychological motivations. Finally, they are awake to the dangers of the world—and they realize that things may be a little dicey, hence the "hopefully for a long time to come" line.

This element of threat also throws light on Kidman's lines that bring this movie to its thudding and vulgar end: "But I do love you, and know that there is something we need to do as soon as possible—fuck." Because Bill has strayed, Alice respects him again. She wants him again. Beyond that, however, his little adventure has revealed that their world is a much stranger and scarier place than either of them imagined. So it is natural that a wife would cleave to her husband for protection.

Eyes Wide Shut was Kubrick's last film. He died six days after showing his final cut to Warner Brothers. Of his mature films, it is definitely the weakest, but it still has some virtues. The sets, costumes, locations, and photography make it a gorgeous film to look at. The music is well chosen. It also contains fine performances by Sidney Pollack and Todd Field.

The main weaknesses are a flabby script, overly long scenes, and intensely annoying performances by Cruise and Kidman. I could forgive them if they were supposed to start as unlikable characters who then grow deeper and more sympathetic through their trials. But they don't. If that was Kubrick's intent, then we have to judge this movie a failure. The first time I heard Nichole Kidman say "fuck," fade to black, I felt such revulsion and rage that I would have pushed a button and blown the whole film to hell.

But for all its faults, *Eyes Wide Shut* has two important messages to which today's Dissident Rightists are particularly receptive. It dramatizes important truths about man-woman relationships and displays how sexual perversion is a tool of elite control. If you already know the score on these matters, however, you might not want to suffer through two hours and forty minutes of Cruise and Kidman.

The Unz Review, October 1, 2019

FAR FROM THE MADDING CROWD

John Schlesinger's 1967 adaptation of Thomas Hardy's 1874 novel *Far from the Madding Crowd* should be a universally recognized cinema classic. But although it received generally positive reviews and did well in England, today it is virtually unknown, even among my friends who are film buffs.

I am going to comment on the movie only, not the book, which I have not read. I am told, however, that the film is a fairly faithful adaptation. Since the film is more than fifty years old, there will be spoilers.

Far from the Madding Crowd is set in the West Country of England in the 1860s. A young shepherd, Gabriel Oak (Alan Bates at his handsomest), proposes marriage to Bathsheba Everdene (Julie Christie at her loveliest), who is apparently an orphan living with her aunt on a neighboring farm. They would make a handsome couple. Gabriel is clearly intelligent, hard-working, and responsible. He pleads his case well. But Bathsheba declines, because she does not "love" him, and to her mind, it is as simple as that. One has to wonder, though, what exactly she means by love, and why it features so prominently in her decision, since rural farm folk tend to be very pragmatic about such matches. She even urges Gabriel to think pragmatically and find a woman with some capital.

Soon Bathsheba moves away, and Gabriel tries to put her out of his mind. But when Gabriel's flock is killed in a ghastly accident, he is forced to up stakes and seek employment on another man's farm. In his search, he comes across a farm where a fire is sweeping through the hayricks. The farmhands are ineffectual in fighting the fire, so he takes charge and saves the farm. He then discovers that the farm belongs to Bathsheba. Her uncle, a wealthy farmer with no children of his own, has willed it to her, and she is now wealthy. She recognizes Gabriel's value and employs him.

When Bathsheba fires the farm's bailiff for thievery, she decides that she will manage the farm herself. She is, in short, one of those "headstrong, independent women" that every year ad-

vertisers and journalists tell us are *brand new*, not like the shrink-
ing violets and clinging vines of yesteryear. Apparently, this
radical break with the past has been happening every year at
least since 1874, when the novel first appeared.

However, unlike today's strong, independent woman stories,
Far from the Madding Crowd is not a feminist morality play. Quite
the opposite. Hardy shows that Bathsheba's independence is
actually a source of great suffering for herself and the people
around her. As an orphan, Bathsheba has nobody to look out for
her, especially to give her guidance in matters of the heart. Her
aunt did try to care for her—deflecting Gabriel's advances,
which strikes me as a bad choice. But she might have expected
her niece to become wealthy and thus to be able to aim higher.

However, once Bathsheba leaves her aunt and is installed as
mistress of a large and valuable farm, she has no economic necessities that might prompt her to make a pragmatic match,
which allows her to let her feelings decide. Moreover, she has no
family or friends of her station who can tell her unpleasant
truths that she needs to hear. In one scene, for instance, he basically orders a servant girl to lie to her about the history of a cad
with whom she becomes infatuated, leading to disaster.

The basic message of *Far from the Madding Crowd* is that empowering a person who lacks wisdom and maturity is a bad
thing. Indeed, empowering such people actually cuts them off
from the sources of wisdom and maturity that they need. But it
is not just an anti-feminist message, although in this case the
primary victim is a woman. It is an anti-individualist message,
for the whole thrust of individualism is to empower people to
make their own decisions, regardless of wisdom and maturity.

Gabriel settles in on the farm, where he consistently demonstrates manly self-discipline, conscientiousness, and technical
mastery. He is, in truth, a natural leader—an alpha male—and
slowly Bathsheba gives him more powers and responsibilities.
He's a rock. He's always there for her. And apparently there's
nothing the least bit loveable or sexy about it from her point of
view.

One spring day, Bathsheba finds an unused valentine in her
dead uncle's papers. (It is odd that a childless old man had a

valentine to begin with, but it makes sense it was never used.) On a whim, Bathsheba writes "Marry Me" on it and sends it to Mr. Boldwood, the even wealthier farmer next door.

Boldwood, brilliantly played by Peter "I'm as mad as hell, and I'm not going to take it anymore" Finch, is a bachelor in his late forties who is instantly smitten with the beautiful Bathsheba and of course wants to marry her. He too would be a fine catch. A bit old, but fit and good-looking, with extensive resources and proven skills in farming and business. One imagines Bathsheba's old aunt would have pleaded Boldwood's case.

But none of that seemed to occur to Bathsheba. The proposal was only a joke. She cannot marry him because she does not love him. Boldwood, however, presses her not to refuse him outright but to give him her decision at harvest time. Out of weakness, Bathsheba agrees, stringing the poor man along for months while he hopes in vain that she will become a bit more pragmatic or perhaps even grow to love him.

It was, of course, wrong for Bathsheba to send the proposal in the first place. Her old aunt would have quashed the idea immediately, and Bathsheba would probably have assented. But her only peers at the time were farmgirls who worked for her and would not have felt comfortable giving her advice even if they had known better. A mature and sensitive woman would never have trifled so callously with the old bachelor's heart.

Bathsheba was also wrong to string Boldwood along. A more mature woman would have admitted her mistake, apologized sincerely, and flatly refused him. But then again, a more mature woman would not have made the mistake to begin with.

But Boldwood too was at fault. He was too smitten to grasp Bathsheba's immaturity and simply would not take no for an answer. Like Gabriel, he should have simply tried to put her out of his mind.

Still, Bathsheba might well have ended up marrying Boldwood were it not for the appearance of cavalry sergeant Francis Troy, played by Terence Stamp. Although his face entirely lacks beauty or character, the fact that he is tall, dashing, and wears a uniform makes him irresistible to women. Troy, however, is a cad, with a full suite of what the manosphere calls "Dark Triad" traits—narcissism, sociopathy, and manipulativeness—which women commonly mistake for healthy alpha male traits. Troy's lines are among the most brilliant in the script, and Stamp is superb at bringing this loathsome character to life.

Before Bathsheba came on the scene, Troy had seduced, impregnated, and then abandoned one of the farm girls, Fanny Robin. He actually agreed to marry her. But it was an impromptu affair, and when she went to the wrong church at the appointed time, his vanity was so inflamed that he broke the engagement. Fanny mysteriously disappears, and later we learn it was not just due to being jilted but also to hide the shame of being pregnant.

In any case, Troy soon had a much richer and prettier prospect: Bathsheba herself, whom he proceeded to woo with flattery, teasing, and dangerous displays of swordsmanship. The swordplay scene is utterly ridiculous, but Christie is entirely believable in communicating her character's hopeless, irrational infatuation with Troy. She truly does "love" him. (The film credits include a folk song consultant, a sword master, and a horse master, so of course I found it irresistible.)

In one of the best scenes of the film, Boldwood tries to bribe Troy into marrying Fanny and leaving Bathsheba to him. Troy toys with Boldwood, then announces that he is too late, for he has married Bathsheba that very morning. Boldwood is crushed.

The honeymoon does not last long. Troy has apparently left the military. He is immediately accepted as lord of the manor, but he has no knowledge of farming or interest in responsibility. In a scene that beautifully illustrates his character—or lack of it—he regales the adoring farmhands with bawdy military songs while drinking them under the table. Meanwhile, a storm brews up, and when Gabriel tries to get some of the farmhands away from the party to secure the hayricks from being blown away, he is rebuffed by Troy who does not want to lose his audience. It is classic narcissist behavior. So Gabriel and Bathsheba herself struggle in the storm, soaked to the bone, to save the farm from loss while Troy's revelries continue.

Troy also enjoys gambling over cockfights, and his narcissism makes it easy for his opponents to keep raising the stakes, lest he lose face. It isn't *his* money that he is losing anyway.

Another extravagance is a large musical clock, which features a trumpeter in the same cavalry uniform as Troy wore. The design of the clock does not seem to fit with the style of the period, cleverly suggesting Troy's essential childishness and lack of taste.

Bathsheba is willing to suffer quite a lot because she is "in love" with Troy. But things come crashing down when a very pregnant Fanny Robin shows up at the farm asking for Troy's help, then promptly dies in childbirth. When the coffin is brought to the farm for burial, Gabriel hides the fact that it also contains a baby. But Bathsheba opens the coffin and discovers it. Troy then walks in, and his behavior is utterly galling. Suddenly, he seems to be filled with love and remorse for Fanny, kissing her dead face as Bathsheba looks on in horror, then demands that he kiss *her* instead. Troy leaves the farm but erects an expensive tombstone for Fanny in the manor's churchyard. The grave is below a gargoyle waterspout, and the first rains of fall turn it into a mud pit, brilliantly underscoring the true nature of Troy's behavior. He is simulating love and dejection merely to spite Bathsheba. Troy then goes to the ocean, undresses, and swims out to sea.

Bathsheba is at the corn exchange when she is told that her husband has apparently drowned, his body swept out to sea. She faints dead away, but her ever-faithful orbiter Boldwood is there to catch her. After a decent period of mourning, Boldwood begins courting her again. Because there is no body, Bathsheba must wait six years before she is free to marry again. Boldwood tells her he will wait. Again, Bathsheba wants to say no, but he again pressures her to wait until Christmas to decide.

As Christmas approaches, Boldwood prepares a lavish party, confident that he will be announcing his engagement. He seems positively giddy, and it is impossible not to feel for him. But then disaster strikes. After Bathsheba has accepted his ring, but before they can announce their engagement, Troy reappears. He has faked his death. But having heard of Bathsheba's prospective engagement, he returns out of spite to assert his marital rights. Bathsheba is shocked and refuses to follow him. So Troy begins to manhandle her. Then we hear a shot. Troy falls dead on the stairs. Boldwood stands with a rifle.

Then we witness one of the most wrenching tragic climaxes since Sophocles. Bathsheba does not fly to Boldwood's side to thank him for rescuing her. She breaks down in tears over her beloved Frank. Now Boldwood sees the terrible truth. By showing up at the party, Frank revealed to everyone that he was a complete monster. But that did not matter, because Bathsheba "loved" him. Boldwood is a genuinely noble man, but it doesn't matter, because she didn't "love" him. Justice doesn't enter into this at all. Boldwood looks on, in utter horror, at the abyss of irrationality into which he has flung his life. For he will hang for this, for a love that was entirely one-sided and illusory.

Two men—one noble, the other base—end up dead, all for a woman of genuine beauty and goodness who was empowered to make catastrophic decisions that destroyed two lives and brought misery to her own.

But Bathsheba eventually recovers. She buries Frank in the same mud pit as Fanny and adds his name to the tombstone. She still has a large and prosperous farm, surrounded by people who feel genuine affection for her, including her ever-faithful and reliable Gabriel, who is there to help her run the place.

But instead of wasting away in Bathsheba's friend zone, Gabriel decides to move to America. Only then does Bathsheba truly appreciate him. For she can only really love a man who is independent of her. She rushes to stop him. Gabriel says he will stay under one condition. Then, in a gesture that will pierce even the most cynical hearts, he repeats word for word his vision of married life that she had rejected at the beginning of the film. But this time she says yes. It was the right choice. They will raise beautiful children on a happy and prosperous farm.

The movie ends with Gabriel and Bathsheba settling into married bliss. But then the eye of the camera strays over to Troy's clock, focusing on the soldier in the tower, like a *memento mori* to remind us that the Troys of the world and the irrational romanticism they evoke will always threaten marriage and family life.

The Unz Review, April 2, 2019

FIGHT CLUB

These are notes for a lecture on *Fight Club* given on October 25, 2000 in an adult education course called "Philosophy on Film." For a fuller interpretation of *Fight Club*, see Jef Costello's "*Fight Club* as Holy Writ."[1]

What's philosophical about *Fight Club*? *Fight Club* belongs alongside *Network* and *Pulp Fiction*[2] in an End of History film festival, because it beautifully illustrates ideas about human nature, history, and culture from Hegel and Nietzsche—especially as read through the lenses of Alexandre Kojève and Georges Bataille.

Prehistoric society is relatively egalitarian and focuses on the cycles of nature and the necessities of life. Hegel held that linear history begins with men risking death in duels over honor, which spring from the demand that one's sense of self be recognized by others.

The struggle over honor has winners and losers. Its outcome reveals two kinds of men. The master values honor above life. The slave values life above honor. In terms of Plato's division of the human soul into reason, spiritedness (*thumos*), and desire, the master is ruled by spiritedness, which is intrinsically connected with honor, whereas the slave is ruled by desire.

The struggle over honor gives rise to class structures and class struggles. The ruling class enjoys leisure, which gives rise to the whole realm of high culture, which is driven by the quest for self-knowledge.

The truth about man, though, is somewhat anticlimactic. Mankind has created art, religion, and philosophy—and endured untold suffering in uncounted wars and revolutions—only to discover that . . . we are all free and equal, which is basi-

---

[1] In Jef Costello, *The Importance of James Bond & Other Essays* (San Francisco: Counter-Currents, 2017).

[2] I review *Network* below and *Pulp Fiction* in *Trevor Lynch's White Nationalist Guide to the Movies*, ed. Greg Johnson (San Francisco: Counter-Currents, 2012).

cally how we lived before history.

When we learn the truth about ourselves, history and culture are no longer necessary. When we are all free to pursue our own aims, history and culture will be displaced by mere consumption, the satisfaction of desire, which in a sense is a return to prehistory. Thus the end of history in Hegel's sense brings about the rise of Nietzsche's "Last Man," who believes that there is nothing higher than himself and his petty pleasures.

The protagonist of *Fight Club*, played by Edward Norton, is a man with no name. (He is called Jack in the script, but Jack is a name he adopts from a series of pamphlets about diseases.) He is Everyman. He is the Last Man. He works at a sociopathic corporation. He lives in a condo. He has no apparent religious convictions or cultural interests. He buys clothes and furniture, always with the question, "What does this say about me as a person?" He is single and appears to be celibate. He's free, equal, and has plenty of money to buy stuff. But he feels empty inside. He can't sleep at night, and you know how crazy that can make you.

Everyman seeks out meaning by attending support group meetings under fake names and false pretenses. He doesn't seem to have much truck with the forms of spirituality these peddle, but he does find opportunities for genuine emotional catharses, which help him sleep at night. Unfortunately, another faker has the same idea: Marla Singer (Helena Bonham Carter). Her presence causes our hero to freeze up.

Marla's intrusions drive Everyman to take refuge in an all-male support group. This is significant. History begins not just with isolated men battling for honor, but with bonded male groups, *Männerbünde*, fighting over honor.

Unfortunately, this particular group is called Remaining Men Together. It's for testicular cancer survivors. Emasculated men hugging each other and crying will not restart history. In fact, the group is pretty much a microcosm for everything wrong with the modern world, which would prefer that all men be emasculated, weepy huggers. But it does point to the next step Everyman needs to take.

On one of his business trips, Everyman meets Tyler Durden

(Brad Pitt in his most charismatic role). Everyman is a prisoner of the modern world, but he feels above it. He is like a cow shuffling down a chute in a slaughterhouse who feels he is the master of the situation because he keeps up a constant stream of ironic smart-assery. Tyler is genuinely free of the producer-consumer system: He buys his clothes from thrift stores (at best), squats in an abandoned building, and has his own business (he manufactures and sells soap).

Everyman, however, is a Consumer in the hands of an Angry Author. And the Author dictates that Everyman be stripped of all his worldly possessions, because "The things you own, they end up owning you." Then he must be delivered to Tyler Durden, for a new beginning. First, Everyman learns that his luggage has been seized and destroyed because it vibrated. Then, he returns home to find that his condo has been incinerated. He needs a place to stay. Fortunately, he has Tyler's number.

Cut to Lou's Bar, where Everyman and Tyler are drinking and bonding. At the end of the evening, Tyler asks Everyman to hit him. It is a rather shocking suggestion. Neither man has ever been in a fight. Neither man has been tested. Neither man knows how far he would go to win. Would he risk life itself for victory? If so, he is what Hegel called a master. If he is willing to accept dishonor to avoid death, he is a slave. Of course at this point, neither man is willing to risk death. Until now, they haven't even been willing to risk a bloody nose.

After they fight, Tyler and Everyman enjoy a kind of post-coital bliss, then retire to Tyler's place: a crumbling mansion where he squats. It is as if fighting is an initiation into a new world where bourgeois values of comfort and security no longer matter.

Tyler and Everyman have their fights in front of other men, who naturally want to join in. That's how Fight Club is formed. Fight Club is a *Männerbund*. It is structured as a secret, initiatic society. It produces a change of consciousness. "Who you were in Fight Club is not who you were in the rest of your world. You weren't alive anywhere like you were alive at Fight Club. But Fight Club only exists in the hours between when Fight Club starts and when Fight Club ends."

Fight Club also transforms values. "After a night in Fight Club, everything else in your life gets the volume turned down. You can deal with anything. All the people who used to have power over you have less and less." Fight Club breaks the hold that bourgeois society has on us, which springs from a willingness to endure routine forms of dishonor and degradation in exchange for comfort and security.

Not every initiation in Fight Club involves combat, but all of them involve risking death. For instance, one rainy night, Tyler lets go of the wheel of a stolen car, crashing it. When he and the rest of his party crawl out of the wreckage, he declares, "We just had a near-life experience." One cannot really live until one puts aside the fear of death and the desire for comfort, security, and control that are at the foundation of bourgeois society.

As Tyler puts it, "Self-improvement is masturbation. Self-destruction is the answer." The self that must be destroyed is the bourgeois self, the rational producer-consumer. That self must be destroyed so that a higher self may be born, which is, of course, self-improvement in a deeper sense.

Tyler understands that an encounter with death forces one to take life seriously. Modern society is masterful at reducing risks and keeping death at bay. Thus it deprives people of opportunities to really come to grips with their mortality, shed illusions, and live life more seriously.

One night, Tyler demonstrates this by pulling a gun on a convenience store clerk and telling him he is going to die — unless he stops wasting his life as a convenience store clerk. It is an utterly brutal and terrifying encounter, but Tyler thinks he is doing the man a favor: "Tomorrow will be the most beautiful day of Raymond K. Hessell's life" — because of his brush with death at the hands of a gun-toting maniac.

Tyler practices similar tough love with his own friends. One day, he kisses the back of Everyman's hand then dumps lye on it, causing an excruciating chemical burn. Again, his motive is to force a transformative confrontation with death: "First you have to give up. First, you have to know — not fear, know — that someday, you're gonna die. It's only after we've lost everything that we're free to do anything."

When the ordeal is over, Tyler says "Congratulations. You're a step closer to hitting bottom." This is the language of Twelve Step programs. Addiction is sustained by self-deception. Hitting bottom is when the consequences of addiction are so catastrophic that one can no longer evade the reality of one's situation. One confronts it in a moment of clarity, at which point one may embark on the road to recovery.

One of the illusions Tyler is concerned to dispel is the idea of divine providence: "You have to consider the possibility that God doesn't like you. He never wanted you. In all probability, he hates you. This is not the worst thing that can happen . . . We don't need him. Fuck damnation. Fuck redemption. We are God's unwanted children. So be it!"

Tyler's rationale for this line of attack is explained earlier, when he says "Our fathers were our models for God. And, if our fathers bailed, what does that tell us about God?" If God is just another absent father, then belief in his providence is just another excuse for not taking responsibility for one's life and engaging in self-parenting — or creating a *Männerbund*. (I wonder if Tyler's burning chemical kiss was inspired by the "box" in Frank Herbert's *Dune*. If so, the aim is very different.)

Now I want to discuss two questions. Is Fight Club fascist? And: Is Fight Club gay?

Yes, Fight Club is fascist. After all, Tyler Durden makes his soap out of human fat. That's a joke, but with that detail, the author of the original novel, Chuck Palahniuk, is telling us something. Fight Club is clearly anti-liberal, anti-consumerist, anti-bourgeois, and anti-capitalist. It is also populist, because it empowers ordinary men against the establishment. The only question is: Does Fight Club reject liberalism from the Left or from the Right?

The best way to answer that question is with another question: Does Fight Club admit women? No. Therefore, Fight Club rejects the essential premise of liberalism: human equality. Fight Club is populist, but it is not egalitarian. Fight Club is open to men of all social classes, not because it rejects hierarchy as such, but merely because it rejects the existing hierarchy and wants to create a new one, in which men who are willing to risk combat rule over those who don't. But that's also true of the Nazis and Fascists.

The Unabomber's Manifesto spends a good deal of time critiquing Leftism from a loosely Nietzschean "vitalist" perspective, meaning the idea that a good society gives expression to the life force, thus any institutions that constrict it must be thrown aside. Leftists recoil in fear from such talk, because equality requires leveling and constricting, domesticating and socializing the life force. Leftism is over-socialization. *Fight Club* offers essentially the same critique, but it focuses specifically on *masculine* vitality. Leftism isn't just over-socializing, it is also emasculating.

If Fight Club does not admit women, does that mean it is gay? The Catholic priesthood does not admit women. Does that mean it is gay? Uh-oh. There may be a point here. We can at least say that the movie *plays* with this question.

Fight Club is a bunch of men rolling around half naked and punching each other. Some people find that . . . suggestive. Tyler declares: "We're a generation of men raised by women. I'm wondering if another woman is really the answer we need." Everyman seems to be sexually jealous when Tyler hooks up with Marla. He resents Marla for intruding on his relationship with Tyler. He also clearly feels jealousy of Tyler's affection toward Angel Face, which sends him into a psychotic rage. (Chuck Palahniuk revealed that he is gay in 2004.)

But in a deeper sense, the answer is obviously no. Tyler and Everyman are both heterosexual. Beyond that there is a matter of principle: It does not make men gay to want to work or socialize with one another while excluding women. Women have a great deal of power in pre-historic and post-historic societies because they are relatively egalitarian. Women have a great deal of power over children in all societies. Thus if boys are to mature into men, at a certain point they need to separate themselves from their mothers. They need male-only spheres for that. This is much easier, of course, when they have fathers. But when fathers are absent, they can find father substitutes. One such substitute is the *Männerbund*. Or, in less fancy terms, the gang.

Bonded male groups are not just necessary for the healthy

maturation of boys. They are what create and sustain human history and culture. Almost every important institution until quite recently was sex-segregated. Institutions probably work best that way. Feminists, of course, want to break down those barriers, and one of their techniques is to insinuate that any institution that excludes them must be somehow "gay."

Yes, progressive women are not above exploiting "homophobia" to get their way. If they were consistently progressive, they would be saying that men should not think being gay is a stigma at all. Men should not let themselves be manipulated like this. Maybe men should demand that they be allowed into all-female spaces, so that women can absolve themselves of the suspicion of lesbianism. Or better yet, both sexes could call a truce to this childishness. But men are the ones on the retreat, so things will only turn around if they assert themselves.

Fight Club has a cell structure. Fight Clubs can and do pop up everywhere. Fight Club meets once a week and exists only between certain hours. Then Tyler started handing out homework assignments. This is the speech he makes before the first assignment:

Man, I see in Fight Club the strongest and smartest men who have ever lived. I see all this potential. And I see it squandered. God damn it, an entire generation pumping gas and waiting tables; or they're slaves with white collars. Advertising has us chasing cars and clothes, working jobs we hate so we can buy shit we don't need. We're the middle children of history, man, with no purpose or place. We have no Great War, no Great Depression. Our Great War is a spiritual war. Our Great Depression is our lives. We were raised by television to believe that we'd be millionaires and movie gods and rock stars—but we won't. And we're slowly learning that fact. And we're very, very pissed-off.

Tyler's homework consists mostly pranks and acts of vandalism. But they too are initiations, preparing the way for the next phase.

If the bonded male group is the origin of history, then we should expect Fight Club to go political. Thus Fight Club morphs into Project Mayhem. At that point, Tyler starts building bunkbeds, because Project Mayhem is a full-time commitment.

Project Mayhem is a cross between a goon squad and a Zen monastery. (But, then again, Zen is the religion of the samurai.) The members of Project Mayhem dress alike, submit to a charismatic leader, chant his cant like robots, and seem ecstatic at the prospect of immolating themselves for the cause. Freedom, equality, individualism, and creature comforts aren't what they want. They want to be "space monkeys" who give their lives for the common good. As Nietzsche said, "Man does not strive for happiness; only the Englishman does that."

The ultimate goal of Project Mayhem is to collapse industrial civilization and start history over again. Tyler envisions going back practically to the stone age:

In the world I see you are stalking elk through the damp canyon forests around the ruins of Rockefeller Center. You'll wear leather clothes that will last you the rest of your life. You'll climb the wrist-thick kudzu vines that wrap the Sears Tower. And when you look down, you'll see tiny figures pounding corn, laying strips of venison on the empty carpool lane of some abandoned superhighway.

Phase one of collapsing civilization is blowing up the headquarters of the major credit card companies, erasing people's debts. This is easy for Tyler, because if you know how to make soap, you know how to make dynamite.

We never learn what phase two is.

Indeed, near the end, *Fight Club* takes a psychological turn for the worse and becomes as anticlimactic as history itself. It is upsetting, because one really wants to *like* Tyler. But the modern media can't convey profound anti-modernist messages without putting them in the mouths of madmen.

What is the lesson of *Fight Club*? The End of History in modern liberal-egalitarian consumer society is good at satisfying our desires for comfort, security, and long life. But we're not satisfied with satisfaction. There's more to the human soul than that. In modernity, masculine *thumos* is, for the most part, unemployed. In fact, it is regarded as a disturber of the peace. But idle hands do the devil's work, and unemployed *thumos*, if mobilized by a charismatic leader and properly directed, can overthrow the modern world and start history over. Maybe next time, we will get it right.

The Unz Review, June 12, 2020

THE *GAME OF THRONES* FINALE

I loved the *Game of Thrones* series when it first got started. I watched it on the recommendation of Greg Hood's *Counter-Currents* reviews of Season One and Season Two.[1] I was so taken with it that, when I ran out of episodes, I actually picked up George R. R. Martin's books to see how the stories continued, which is very unusual for me, since I don't have time for contemporary fiction.

I like the idea of fantasy as a genre, but in truth, I only care for Tolkien. Martin does, however, have a remarkable imagination, and I appreciate his twist on the genre: depicting a world of magic in which most people are too vulgar, petty, and flat-souled to see it. I also liked Martin's emphasis on Machiavellian *Realpolitik*, his strong psychological realism, and his firm grasp and application of the logic of pre-modern religion- and honor-based societies, which even at their most decadent and cynical are very different from modern liberalism.

Of course, Martin has lots of flaws. He's needlessly coarse and vulgar, traits only magnified in the TV series. He's laughably repetitive, although in his mind he probably thinks his prose is musical. The repeated themes of castration and incest are distasteful, and the violence and cruelty he relates become farcical after the *n*th repetition. I read one of his novels, then half of the sequel, then tossed it aside in disgust.

I eventually came back to the series, though, just to keep an eye on one pop-culture franchise the continued popularity of which frankly bewilders me.

Based on my limited reading of Martin's books, I thought the series was a creditable adaptation. Yes, a lot had to be left out, and some characters and plotlines were amalgamated. But the surgery was skillfully done. Yes, a lot was vulgarized for television. And when the series ran out of Martin novels to adapt, I came to appreciate Martin much more, for it was clear

---

[1] Gregory Hood, reviews of *Game of Thrones*, Seasons 1 and 2, *Counter-Currents*, April 2, 2012 and April 2, 2013.

that the producers were not capable of maintaining the integrity of Martin's universe and characters or of extending and resolving his byzantine plot. Instead, the series increasingly depended on cool-looking set pieces and effects—often just ripping off elements of Peter Jackson's *Lord of the Rings* movies— and vulgar pandering to contemporary ultra-Leftist values, as if Martin's novels were not already subversive enough, with their swarms of marginal anti-heroes.

Watching the final three seasons was like losing a loved one to dementia. They look the same on the outside, but increasingly *they just aren't there anymore*. Matters were not helped by the fact that the younger cast members all aged rather badly. In fact, I take back the senility metaphor. GOT became like a bad marriage, in which one's spouse becomes both physically repulsive and psychologically alien with the passage of time.

Frankly, I am just glad the whole thing is over, and the final episode was so dumb and dramatically flaccid that it made it really easy to say goodbye to Westeros forever. As a cheat and disappointment, the *Game of Thrones* finale rivals the end of *Lost*.

In the penultimate episode Daenerys Targaryen, who claims the Iron Throne of Westeros once occupied by her father, led armies of racial aliens and Westerosians to lay siege to the usurper Queen Cersei in King's Landing. Cersei's allies and armies were defeated. Her defenses were breached. The city surrendered. And then Daenerys did something shocking: She and her single surviving dragon reenacted the firebombing of Dresden, incinerating the city and countless innocents whose terror and suffering are depicted with great pathos.

Daenerys is the supreme avatar of Left-wing feminist white savior fantasies. She is a heroine of the SJW Left. Indeed, quite a few cats—and perhaps even a few human babies—have been named after her. But in the end—as if I had managed to sneak in and write the script myself—she reveals herself to be an egalitarian humanist mass murderer, just like Stalin, Roosevelt, and Churchill.

Countless feminists were so triggered that their pussyhats shot clean off their heads. There was much screeching and

Tweeting to have the episode re-shot. Since some of these protests issue from the same Left-wing quarters where Bomber Harris is praised, one wonders about their motives. Perhaps this plot twist revealed too much, too soon, to too many.

The one person who predicted Daenerys' behavior and could have prevented it was Lord Varys, who wanted to put Jon Snow on the Iron Throne instead. Snow would be a better ruler, and he also has a better claim to the throne, as he is actually Aegon Targaryen, the son of Daenerys' older brother Rhaegar. But the dwarf Tyrion Lannister, the Hand of the Queen, betrays Varys to Daenerys, who has him killed.

Before Varys is killed, however, there is a conversation between Varys and a kitchen girl that strongly hints that he is trying to poison Daenerys. Based on my reading of the characters, I expected in the next episode that Tyrion would try to persuade Jon Snow to overthrow Daenerys, but since Jon Snow is an effeminate, waffling modern anti-hero, his face perpetually rumpled in confusion and self-doubt, I predicted that he would not have it in him. And while Tyrion argued and Snow dithered and an increasingly paranoid and megalomanical Daenerys plotted to kill them both, the kitchen girl would set things right by poisoning the dragon queen. And why not? She probably had people in King's Landing. I think this would have been a much more satisfying story than what we were served up.

At the beginning of the finale, Daenerys assembles her troops before the ruins of the Red Keep. The racial aliens, the Dothraki and the Unsullied, who were pretty much killed off a couple episodes back, are somehow present in vast numbers. Daenerys addresses them in their native tongues. The war, it seems, is not over. For now Daenerys will go on to "liberate" all of mankind by conquering them and bringing them under her rule.

The staging is clearly meant to call to mind *Triumph of the Will*, which means that GOT is staking out the broad "liberal" political center by declaring that the far Left—including its legions of adoring SJW fans—and the far Right are essentially the same in their evil.

Disgusted by the slaughter at King's Landing and appalled at the prospect of endless wars of liberation, Tyrion tenders his resignation as Hand of the Queen and immediately is given the "Seize him you fools, he's getting away" treatment. Amazingly, though, Jon Snow is allowed to visit him in the dungeon, where Tyrion naturally tries to enlist him in treason. Also amazingly, nobody was appointed to listen in and report this to the Queen.

Jon Snow visits Daenerys to try to reason with her. She treats him to more megalomanical global liberation talk. She knows what is right and will incinerate any city that resists her in order to liberate it. Jon replies with modern liberal mush: What if you're wrong? What if they don't want that? Then he stabs her in the heart. Which came as some surprise, because it simply isn't in his character.

Then we're treated to a few minutes of manipulative suspense as Daenerys' dragon finds her body. Will he get angry and melt Jon Snow? Or is Jon immune to dragon fire anyway? But then, for no apparent reason—except that the directors thought it would look cool—the dragon decides to melt the Iron Throne instead. Then the dragon picks up Daenerys' body and flies away, *leaving Jon Snow free to make up any story he wanted.* Besides, he's the rightful king, so who would challenge him?

Flash forward a few months. It turns out that Jon Snow didn't come up with a good story or assert his right to the throne. Somehow, he has gotten himself thrown in the dungeon of Obama, the alien commander of the Unsullied. The lords of Westeros and their armies have surrounded King's Landing, and a parley takes place. At this point, if we were still in the world of medieval fantasy literature, they would negotiate the king's ransom with Obama. After all, Jon Snow is the rightful king, being held prisoner by a racial alien. The logical thing would be to strike a deal to get him out of prison, and to get the alien off the soil of Westeros.

But for some reason, Obama does not make terms. Instead, Tyrion is marched out of the dungeon, still in chains, to address the assembled lords (and strong, independent ladies).

Apparently, after eight seasons of savage wars, all premised on the idea that legitimacy flows from dynastic succession, they have suddenly had an attack of collective amnesia. Apparently, Jon Snow is no longer their king, simply because Obama strenuously objects. (Why come there at all, then?) Sure, placate Obama by listening to his objections. Get Jon out of the dungeon and Obama out of Westeros. Then put him on the throne where he belongs. But no.

So Tyrion suggests that Jon be packed off to the Knights Watch (which has nothing to guard against, since the White Walkers are dead and the Wildlings are now in Westeros).

He also suggests that they appoint a new king themselves, from one of their number. (The suggestion that everybody be allowed to choose is laughed off.)

When Edmure Tully stands to speak, we learn that deliberations will follow the progressive stack. Sansa Stark simply orders him to "Sit down, uncle." Because hierarchy isn't real, manners don't matter, and men don't have a sense of honor, he meekly complies. So the future of Westeros will be decided by a dwarf, a cripple, and some strong, independent ladies.

The dwarf suggests that the best king would be Brandon Stark, a crippled boy who can sire no heirs, thus guaranteeing somewhere down the road a crisis—perhaps even eight seasons of bloody civil war—as rivals vie for the succession. But nobody thinks of that, and nobody objects, because they all have amnesia or are afraid to mansplain.

Brandon, we are told, has the best story, and that qualifies him to rule. Except he doesn't have the best story, but nobody objects to that. And why is having the best story a qualification to rule anyway? But nobody objects to that either. Beyond that, Brandon is possessed by a figure known as the Three-Eyed Raven, who seems to know everything, especially about the past. But knowledge is not wisdom, and even wisdom is not leadership. So while Bran might be useful to keep around for information, he is not qualified to be king. But nobody thinks of this, and nobody objects.

In fact, the only objection comes from Sansa Stark, Brandon's sister, who says that the North wants to remain an independent kingdom. She'll be the queen, of course. To which there are no objections either. So it is all decided. Of course, if all it takes to secede from the Seven Kingdoms is to ask, then why didn't any of the other kingdoms follow suit?

If the lords and ladies of Westeros are this agreeable, why exactly were there eight seasons of civil war?

Wasn't it all caused by the desire of the North to secede in the first place?

And this gets us basically to the midpoint of the episode. The rest is occupied by long, sentimental leave-takings, perhaps setting us up for any number of spinoffs. Like the parley, the look (but not the substance) of many of these scenes was simply adapted from Peter Jackson's *Lord of the Rings* movies. So we get Councils of Elrond, things being summed up with quill pens in big books, and departures from the Gray Havens, because they looked cool, and they worked in the originals, and maybe viewers won't notice they are being manipulated by derivative, cynical schlockmeisters coasting on nostalgia for better stories. Hey, it works for J. J. Abrams, right?

Every life is but a knife edge, the twinkling of an eye bounded by two eternities, one in which we didn't exist, another in which we will exist no more. Yet countless millions of human beings choose to spend untold hours of their fleeting and irreplaceable lives watching crap like *Game of Thrones*: derivative, manipulative dramas filled with toxic propaganda. We pay people who hate us to pollute our minds with filth. It is utterly shameful.

But am I throwing away even more time by writing about it? Not if I can inoculate even a few people against the next *Game of Thrones* to come along. Not if I can help create a better culture, with better stories, for future generations.

That would truly be a happily ever after.

GATTACA

Gattaca (1997) is a dystopian science fiction movie set some-time in the mid-twenty-first century. Humans are doing a lot of manned space exploration. Genetic engineering and zygote se-lection have eliminated major and minor genetic problems, from mental illness to baldness. As a smiling black man who works as a eugenics counselor explains to a pair of prospective parents, the children produced by these techniques "are still you, just the best of you."

In the world of *Gattaca*, everyone is attractive, clean-cut, and dressed in elegant business suits. They drive cool, retro-looking electric cars, listen to classical music, dine in fine restaurants, and live in multi-million-dollar lofts and beach houses in Marin county. The space agency, called Gattaca, is headquartered in Frank Lloyd Wright's Marin County Civic Center building, which will look futuristic even centuries from now.

It sounds pretty utopian to me. But writer-director Andrew Niccol wants to convince us that it is a totalitarian hell.

Gattaca is the story of Vincent Freeman (Ethan Hawke), whose name could only be more symbolic if they just called him Victor Freeman. Vincent is the guy who is going make free will triumph over determinism.

Vincent is a naturally conceived child in a world in which such births have become rare. As soon as Vincent is born, a blood sample is taken, and his parents are informed that he will likely suffer from various mood disorders and die of a heart at-tack by the age of thirty. It is a bit heavy to lay on a woman who has just gone through labor, but Niccol wants us to hate these people.

From the moment of birth, Vincent is treated as an invalid. In fact, the whole society is constructed around the distinction be-tween the genetically Valid, namely the engineered, and In-Valid—get it? get it?—namely, those conceived naturally. The Valids are privileged, and the In-Valids are oppressed. Vincent's mother coddles him and doesn't want him to play outside. His father tells him not to dream about going into space with a bum ticker. Both parents also invest more emotionally in their younger son, Anton, who was genetically selected and tweaked before birth.

Okay, let's pause here for a moment to let this sink in. For a society that values intelligence, there's something rather stupid about this.

First, the idea of a caste system between Valids and In-Valids makes no sense. A society that values eugenics values science and objective merit. Such a society would know that among the so-called In-Valids, you would find superlative intelligence, health, beauty, creativity, and other excellences among naturally conceived people *at pretty much the rate that we find them today.* Thus the idea that In-Valids would be subjected to crass discrimination and oppression is simply an attempt to brand eugenics as an arbitrary, evil form of discrimination, like "racism" against black people (which isn't that unreasonable either, to be honest, but White Nationalists prefer racially homogeneous societies where such discrimination is made impossible.).

Second, there's no doubt that genes determine our potentials. And, as the Director of the Gattaca space agency, played by Gore Vidal, says, "Nobody exceeds his potential. If he does, it simply means we did not gauge it accurately to begin with." This is true. Our potential is what we can do. What exceeds our potential is what we can't do. We can't do what we can't do.

But there are several factors being left out here.

Our potential is the outer limit of what we can do. But how many people get anywhere near those outer boundaries? Thus knowing potentials is not the same as knowing life outcomes.

Our genes aren't the only things that determine our potential. You might have genes to make you a star athlete, but you don't have the potential to do that if you are paralyzed in a car accident.

Why are these people so cocksure that they can gauge people's potential accurately? In *Gattaca*, Vincent, the Director, and Vincent's love interest Irene (Uma Thurman) all do things that they "can't" do, which means that their potential has not been gauged accurately. But a society that values science and objective merit would not permit such smugness and the injustices and waste of resources that would inevitably follow.

In the society of *Gattaca*, genetic testing has basically elimi-nated the job interview, the *curriculum vitae*, and the letter of rec-ommendation—as if your genes are your only qualification, re-gardless of the maturation, education, experience, and character that you have acquired over your lifetime.

Granted, one can weed out some applicants based on genetic grounds. The lame, the halt, and the blind can't do certain jobs. Astronauts can't have weak hearts. Surgeons can't be blind. Conductors can't be deaf.

But once you eliminate gross disabilities, other factors beyond genetic potential become relevant. For instance, some people who *can* do a job may not *want* to. A society that overlooks such factors is stupid, not smart—scientistic, not scientific.

Let's look at the case of Vincent. Vincent is apparently highly intelligent, but he is told that he is fit only for manual labor be-cause of—get this—his weak heart. *Yes, it is that stupid*. In the real world, of course, a highly intelligent young man with a weak heart might be shunted into the precise job that Vincent ended up in: a programmer at the space agency.

If Vincent really had a bad heart, no amount of training could fix it. In fact, such training could kill him. But one has to wonder: Wouldn't the world of *Gattaca* also have the technology to fix heart defects or simply replace defective hearts with lab-grown transplants?

No matter how much Vincent dreams of going into space, he can't be an astronaut if he has a bad heart. That is not an unrea-sonable or tyrannical requirement. Astronauts have to deal with enormous stress. An astronaut who dies of heart failure may cost the lives of his fellow crewmen. Astronauts are also very expensive to train.

Vincent, however, decides that he is going to cheat his way into space. We are supposed to think this is inspiring, but it is deeply unethical. Vincent buys the identity of Jerome Eugene (get it?) Morrow, played by Jude Law. (Two years later, Law's identity is simply stolen in *The Talented Mr. Ripley*.) Eugene is genetically Valid. He has a stratospherically high IQ and is a phenomenal athlete. Or at least he was until a botched suicide attempt left him paraplegic. Jerome is now a self-pitying drunk.

Jerome had a much better genetic hand dealt him than Vincent, but he played it poorly. Vincent had a worse hand, but he plays it well. Of course, how well we *can* play our cards is also, arguably, a genetic card that is dealt us. But how well we *actually* play them is another thing. No matter how comprehensive and fine-grained genetic determinism may be, I see people exercising more or less agency, more or less wisdom, in making something out of what nature makes them into. And as for those who think they can predict those results with a blood test, well, something in my blood tells me we would be fools to believe them.

To pass himself off as Jerome, Vincent needs to go to ridiculous lengths, because the world of *Gattaca* is a Kafkaesque police state. Vincent can't just get a fake ID, because one's genes are one's ID. When Vincent walks into work every day, he doesn't swipe his lanyard. His finger is pricked and his DNA analyzed. (Sounds unsanitary.) Vincent also has to worry about leaving hair and skin flakes at his desk, for apparently these are collected and analyzed as well. (Sounds insane.) Then there are the urine tests. Thus Vincent needs a constant supply of Jerome's hair, skin, blood, and urine. Every morning, he has to put blood into false fingertips and strap bags of urine to his leg before going to work.

Would he have given up if they had started requiring stool samples?

The world of *Gattaca* is an idiocracy, not a meritocracy, eugenics as viewed by the dysgenic. We're supposed to find it chillingly dystopian, and just because it is stupid, it doesn't mean it's implausible. Communism was quite stupid too, after all, but it reliably produced dystopias all over the globe.

Aside from its ludicrous dystopian elements, *Gattaca* does put its finger on a deep human truth that has real dramatic potential. The society of *Gattaca* is really quite bourgeois, meaning that everyone operates on the assumption that the best life is a long and comfortable one, and the worst thing possible is a short life, especially if one meets a violent end.

In more heroic ages, such a mentality was disdained as worthy only of slaves. In terms of Plato's psychology, bourgeois man is ruled by his desires, meaning that desire wins out when it conflicts with other motives, such as honor. Heroic man, by contrast, is ruled by *thumos*—the part of the soul that responds to honor and seeks adventure and even conflict—so that when *thumos* conflicts with desire—even the desire for self-preservation—*thumos* wins out.

Vincent is told that he will live a short life and thus should take it easy, whereas he concludes that he needs to up life's intensity. Vincent and his brother Anton play chicken by swimming out into the ocean. The chicken is the first one who turns back. Anton is engineered to be a superior athlete. He is confident that he will always win, and he always does, until one day Vincent beats him. Then, armed with a new confidence, Vincent runs away from home to fulfill his dreams.

Years later, Vincent meets his brother again and explains how he won: When he swam out, he did not save anything for the trip back. In other words, he was willing to risk death for victory. Their game of chicken was a reenactment of Hegel's image of the beginning of history: the struggle to the death over honor.

Even though Vincent did not save anything for the trip back, he still made it back, because there's a difference between our objective limits and our subjective sense of what those limits are. We usually can do more than we think we can, but we learn that only by disregarding what we—and others—*think* our limits are. Doing so requires risk, sometimes mortal risk, sometimes merely risking other people's disapproval. But the possibility of dying should be a small thing compared to the certainty of never really living if we don't try.

Not saving anything for the journey back also explains Vincent's desire to go into space, heart condition or not. He wanted to get out there. He wasn't concerned with coming back.

I will say no more about *Gattaca*'s plot, save that there's a whole lot more dumbness for you to discover if you are curious, including a number of completely pointless scenes and plot twists.

Gattaca may be dumb, but it is beautiful. The cast, clothes, cars, music, sets, and production design are all first rate. I especially loved the scene in which Vincent and the rest of his crew enter their rocket ship dressed in elegant business suits.

Even though *Gattaca* is crude anti-eugenics propaganda, it probably didn't do much harm. The movie was pretty much a flop, so few people saw it. Moreover, it is so dumb that it could only convince dumb people of dysgenics, and dumb people already practice dysgenics.

Beyond that, *Gattaca* also had eugenic effects. Co-stars Ethan Hawke and Uma Thurman met on the set, and their roles might have gotten them thinking. Not only are they good-looking, they are highly intelligent and descend from elite families. They married in 1998 and had two good-looking kids. For eugenicists, breeding well is the best revenge.

The Unz Review, April 27, 2020

THE GENTLEMEN

Guy Ritchie's *The Gentlemen* is his best movie since his first two feature films, *Lock, Stock, and Two Smoking Barrels* (1998) and *Snatch* (2000), largely because it is a gentrified return to their crime caper format.

Ritchie at his best is a kind of British Quentin Tarantino, with his underworld settings, non-linear storytelling, colorful and witty dialogue, and gleeful political incorrectness (because criminals don't think and talk like SJWs would like them to)—but without Tarantino's sprawling, self-indulgent running times.

Ritchie at his worst? Well, imagine what Tarantino would turn out if he were in indentured servitude to Disney.

The Gentlemen has a great deal of star power. Matthew McConaughey plays the protagonist, Mickey Pearson, an American who ends up at Oxford on a Rhodes Scholarship but drops out to become a drug kingpin. Some twenty years later, he has leveraged his Oxford connections into a pot-growing empire, tucked away on the country estates of aristos who are hard up for cash to maintain their stately homes.

Mickey, however, wants to retire and offers to sell his operation for $400 million to a bland, prissy American Jewish crime lord Matthew Berger, played by Jeremy Strong. But, as he finds out, the underworld is a jungle, and it is dangerous for the king of the jungle to retire, for it signals weakness, and the jackals come running.

Mickey, however, is fortunate in his friends. Charlie Hunnam (*Sons of Anarchy*, *The Lost City of Z*) plays Raymond, Mickey's loyal right-hand man. Michelle Dockery (*Downton Abbey*) plays Mickey's steely wife Rosalind. Colin Farrell is hilarious as a mixed martial arts coach with small-time gangster connections.

He also lucks out with his enemies. Hugh Grant is brilliant as Fletcher, a sleazy private eye and would-be blackmailer who narrates the whole tale. Then there are Berger and the Chinese narcotics mafia, led by Lord George (Tom Wu).

I won't say much about the plot, because I actually want you to see *The Gentlemen*, but I do need to reveal some elements to comment on the controversy it has generated.

Like *Lock, Stock, and Two Smoking Barrels* and *Snatch*, *The Gentlemen* has been accused of being "racist" and "anti-Semitic," both for its language and also for the plot conflicts. For instance, throughout *The Gentlemen* Jews are characterized as Jews, and this being a crime drama, none of them are good Jews. The Colin Farrell character also explains to a black fighter that he should not take offense at being called a "black bastard" because it happens to be true. The gangster Dry Eye is described as a "Chinese James Bond," complete with "ricense to kill." One of Dry Eye's henchmen is named "Phuc," suffers from asthma, and dies hilariously. I saw this film in a packed theater, and the audience laughed heartily in all the "wrong" places.

Beyond that, the main conflicts in the movie break down along racial and ethnic lines—whites vs. Chinese and whites vs. Jews (Berger and his Mossad bodyguards, which he calls "crabs")—and, boy, do the whites ever win. The whites, moreover, are in the pot business, and pot doesn't kill anyone, while the reptilian Chinese sell heroin and coke, which are "destroyers of worlds"—something made graphically clear as the film unwinds.

When the Jew, Berger, double-crosses Mickey Pearson—and don't whine about a spoiler here, because as soon as you see Berger's face, you know he will be a double-crosser—Mickey tells him that he can go free only after he makes financial restitution then cuts a pound of flesh from his own body. And, unlike Shylock, Mickey Pearson is not going to let himself be stopped by a technicality.

Moreover, there are a number of black bit players, most of them rapping, tumbling buffoons. All of them more or less take orders from whites.

But Ritchie has some plausible deniability on the racism charges. First of all, all the people who say bad things are criminals, so Ritchie can say that he's just being realistic when he has bad people say bad things. Second, there are also some minor white antagonists, in the form of a Russian oligarch (who is also ex-KGB) and his hired guns.

Beyond that, Guy Ritchie can probably say that some of his

best friends are Jews, given that he and ex-wife Madonna were deep into Kabbala. Furthermore, Ritchie allegedly speaks some Hebrew, and he actually named his three children with Jacqui Ainsley (who does not appear to be Jewish) Rafael, Rivka, and Levi. (Ritchie also adopted an African child, David, while married to Madonna, as well as fathering her son Rocco.) Given these kinds of dues, I think Guy Ritchie is entitled to talk about Jews like they talk about themselves.

I highly recommend *The Gentlemen* if you are looking for a grown-up, politically incorrect comedy about colorful rogues. There's a bit of violence but nothing too distasteful. The script is witty, the plot has some surprising twists and turns, the performances are excellent, and the pacing never fails. Although there really aren't any good guys in this story, at least the white guys win in the end.

The Unz Review, February 20, 2020

HIGH & LOW

Like most Westerners, I got to know Akira Kurosawa through his classic samurai films: *Seven Samurai, Throne of Blood, The Hidden Fortress, Yojimbo, Sanjuro, Kagemusha,* and *Ran.* Thus I was surprised to discover that fully half of his thirty films are actually set in contemporary Japan over the stretch of Kurosawa's long lifetime (1910–1998). *High and Low* (1963) is one of the best of these films, along with *Drunken Angel, Stray Dog,* and *Ikiru.*

Many of Kurosawa's most important Japanese films are actually based on stories by Western writers: Shakespeare, Dostoevsky, Tolstoy, and Gogol chief among them. In the case of *High and Low,* however, the source is a hard-boiled American crime novel: *King's Ransom* by Ed McBain (born Salvatore Lombino), who under the name Evan Hunter was also the screenwriter for Hitchcock's *The Birds.*

The Japanese title of *High and Low* is *Tengoku to Jigoku,* which literally means "Heaven and Hell." But *High and Low* is a good title, because the movie is constructed around the contrasts between a modernist mansion of Kingo Gondo (Toshiro Mifune) which stands alone on a high bluff overlooking Yokohama, and the crowded, chaotic city below.

There is also a contrast between high and low class, understood here as rich and poor. From the point of view of the poor people of Yokohama, however, it is easy to think of Gondo's lofty mansion—isolated, spacious, starkly modern, and cooled by breezes—as heaven compared to the cramped, noisy, sweltering hell they inhabit. (Kurosawa loves to portray people sweating, fanning themselves, and huddling by electric fans. He must have hated hot weather.)

But these contrasts are not setting you up for a Marxist narrative about the virtuous poor and their wicked capitalist exploiters. Quite the opposite. *High and Low* is a portrait of a virtuous industrialist who is targeted for destruction by a nihilistic criminal who hails from the professional rather than the working class and is motivated not by need but by envy and pure malice.

Kingo Gondo is not a steel baron or oil tycoon. He is an executive at National Shoes, which makes women's footwear. But it
turns out there is a heroic and manly way to make women's
shoes. Gondo has worked his way up from being an apprentice
shoemaker to being a shareholder and executive. He is hosting
some of his fellow executives, who wish to enlist him in a corporate coup against the "old man" who founded the company and
is stuck in a rut of making unfashionable "army boots." Gondo's
colleagues wish to manufacture flashy shoes that are cheaply
made. Gondo wants to make more fashionable products, but he
feels that selling shoddy merchandise is dishonorable and eventually dresses down his colleagues, then tosses them out.

Gondo then explains to his assistant that he has been planning his own takeover of National Shoes, mortgaging himself to
the hilt buying up chunks of stock. All he needs is to complete
one last purchase. But before he can dispatch his assistant with a
check for fifty million yen, he receives a phone call informing
him that his son Jun has been kidnapped and demanding thirty
million yen in ransom. (This is thirty times higher than the highest recorded ransom.) But when Jun walks into the room, Gondo
concludes that the the the call was a sick prank. It turns out, however, that the kidnappers have snatched Jun's playmate, Shinichi,
the son of Aoki, who is Gondo's driver.

This creates a great moral dilemma. Gondo's first reaction is
that he will not pay. It is not *his* child, after all. Instead, he will
complete the deal that he has staked everything on. Surely the
kidnapper will be reasonable and let the poor child go. But no, if
Gondo does not pay, the child will die. It is an agonizing choice.
If he does pay, the child may still die, the money may never be
recovered, and Gondo will almost surely be ruined. Eventually,
though, Gondo is persuaded by his wife, his driver, and the police to pay the ransom. It is the compassionate thing to do.

At this point, the movie was nearly half over, and it suddenly
dawned on me that *the film had not yet left Gondo's house*. Most of
it has been shot in his vast and sparsely-furnished living room.
Thus far, *High and Low* has been, in effect, a filmed stage play.
But Kurosawa is so virtuosic at creating dramatic tension and
coaxing out compelling performances that the result is not static

at all. *High and Low* is not just a well-crafted crime drama that was wildly popular with Japanese moviegoers. It is also an *avant garde* cinematic experiment—in fact a whole series of them—a fact that most viewers are too enthralled to even notice. It really sneaks up on you.

The ransom sequence takes us from the spacious and static setting of the Gondo mansion to a cramped passenger car on a high-speed express train. Yes, the Japanese had them even in the early-1960s. It is an amazingly tense and dynamic action sequence.

The film then switches gears again into a quasi-documentary about the police's attempts to find the kidnapper and recover Gondo's money. At this point, some people might feel the movie drags, but I found the meticulous rationality of the detective work fascinating. From the police's first appearance at Gondo's house—disguised as delivery drivers in case the house is under surveillance by the kidnapper—they are impressive in their intelligence, sensitivity, camaraderie, and teamwork. It is a wonderful portrait of what is possible in a homogeneous, high-IQ, high-solidarity society—everything whites have lost by embracing diversity. The kidnapper is the police team's stark antipode: also highly intelligent, but a solitary, sadistic sociopath.

In the last scenes of *High and Low*, as the police close in on their quarry, the film shifts style yet again into pure German Expressionist horror, then into post-war Existentialism. Caligari meets Camus. This film is truly a descent from heaven into hell.

The ending is happy but haunting. In this case, justice has triumphed, but at great cost. Evil and chaos will always threaten order and goodness. They will always need to be quelled by brave and rational guardians of public order.

High and Low is clearly an anti-Marxist film. Gondo is a self-made man, who rose to his position due to hard work. He was not born to wealth and privilege. His wife does come from a privileged background, and her dowry certainly helped matters, but he had to win *her* through hard work and character as well. (Her dowry gives her some clout in the deliberations about whether to pay the ransom.) Gondo puts the integrity of his products above the simple pursuit of profit. He is also willing to court financial ruin when he is convinced that paying the ransom is the right thing to do.

The kidnapper is not driven by want, but merely by resentment. His goal is not simply to take Gondo's money but to humiliate and destroy him. It is clear that his malice is so deep and irrational that no social reform will ever banish it. In fact, the Leftist rhetoric he spouts is simply a tool by which these monsters gain the power to murder millions.

This being a Kurosawa film, vestiges of Japan's feudal traditions crop up throughout the story. Gondo's driver Aoki acts like a cringing, servile feudal retainer. This makes Gondo angry. After all, this is modern Japan. Both men come from humble backgrounds. They simply have a business relationship. Why shouldn't they be on terms of social equality?

But the men are not equal, and the deepest inequality is not financial but a matter of character. Gondo risks his fortune to save the child of his driver. Risking oneself to protect one's retainers is, of course, the foundation of feudal obligation. Did Aoki understand Gondo better than Gondo understood himself?

The police are faultlessly professional in their dealings with Gondo. One of them confesses a personal prejudice against the rich. But as the detectives observe Gondo's character—his decision to pay the ransom, his courage, his intelligence, and his unpretentiousness (mowing his own lawn, breaking out his shoemaker's tools to help modify the briefcases for the ransom)—they are won over, and by the time the ransom has been paid, they have been transformed by sheer admiration into feudal retainers fighting to save their lord from social and financial ruin.

High and Low's portrayal of a heroic businessman plagued by an envious villain, as well as its celebration of the rationality of the police detectives, could almost spring from the pen of Ayn Rand. Gondo and the detectives represent the highest virtues of bourgeois modernity, whereas the kidnapper represents its deepest vice.

But the film's depiction of how the charisma of leadership springs from the willingness to risk personal ruin for what is right takes us into the entirely different moral realm of aristocratic honor culture. In truth, Gondo's argument with his colleagues over lowering the quality of their shoes and then his struggle with himself over whether to pay the ransom are versions of Hegel's primal duel that stakes life itself over matters of honor and sorts men into two types: masters and slaves.

Kurosawa sees truth in both value systems and uses the tension between them to create powerful drama. He uses the same tension to great effect in 1948's *Drunken Angel*, the first of his sixteen films with Toshiro Mifune. Kurosawa uses the conflict between samurai honor culture and Buddhist compassion to similar dramatic effect in *Rashomon*.[1]

High and Low is a masterful fusion of compelling drama, technical virtuosity, and artistic daring. By bringing in deep, serious—ultimately world-shaking—value conflicts, Kurosawa makes high art out of the otherwise low genre of detective fiction. It is one of Kurosawa's finest works.

The Unz Review, June 29, 2020

---

[1] Trevor Lynch, "*Rashomon* and Realism," *Return of the Son of Trevor Lynch's CENSORED Guide to the Movies* (San Francisco: Counter-Currents, 2019).

INTERSTELLAR

In 2010, Christopher Nolan released one of the greatest science fiction films of all time, *Inception*. *Inception* is stunningly artful and imaginative, as well as dramatically gripping and emotionally powerful.[1]

Then, four years later, Nolan released *Interstellar*, which is almost as good. It may seem silly not to want to "spoil" a film that has been out for six years, but if you haven't seen it, I want you to see it. Thus I am going to talk about the basic story and themes while skirting large chunks of the plot.

Interstellar is set sometime late in the late twenty-first century. Global technological civilization has undergone a collapse. There has been war, famine, and technological regression. And it is only getting worse, because some sort of blight is destroying plant life all over the globe. Those who do not starve will suffocate as the blight destroys the oxygen supply.

But the ultimate end is a closely guarded secret. Official policy in what remains of the United States is that things will get better, but the current generation are caretakers. They need to hold on, produce food, and have children to repopulate the earth. School textbooks teach that the moon landing was a hoax, while NASA still exists, working in secret on a way to perpetuate the human species on other planets. Plan A is to save the people on Earth by finding them a new home. Plan B is to send human embryos to a new world.

Nearly fifty years before the events of the film, a wormhole appeared near Saturn giving mankind a path to a new galaxy. NASA managed to locate twelve potentially habitable worlds on the other side. Ten years before the film's present, they dispatched scientists to those worlds. They called them the Lazarus missions, after a man who came back from the dead. Most of the scientists were never heard from again. But some promising data came back. Now they need to send a follow-up mis-

---

[1] I review *Interstellar* in *Trevor Lynch's White Nationalist Guide to the Movies*.

sion, which will be headed by Joseph Cooper (Matthew McConaughey).

Three planets show the most promise, named for the scientists who were sent to them: Miller, Mann, and Edmunds.

Miller's planet is near a black hole. It is covered with shallow water, but the gravitational forces create mile high waves that relentlessly sweep its surface. There is no life. Because of its proximity to the black hole, time passes at different rates on the planet in orbit above it. The landing team is gone only three hours, but for the rest of the universe, twenty-three years have passed. The scientist who remained on the ship has grown old, and the families of the landing party have, of course, changed dramatically. The children they left behind have become adults and have had children of their own, while people in their parents' generation have died. The whole sequence is enormously imaginative and deeply moving.

The next planet was explored by Dr. Mann (Matt Damon), who claimed that it was habitable. We never see the surface of the planet, because Dr. Mann has made his base on a cloud. The planet is surrounded by layers of solid frozen clouds, which is again highly imaginative and surprising. Mann's world is not, however, habitable. Dr. Mann has gone mad in his solitude. He sent back false data simply because he wanted someone to rescue him. He was willing to risk the future of the whole human race out of sheer selfishness.

Only Edmunds' planet is left. But the crew does not have the fuel to get there. Much of it had been burned up in the twenty-three years they orbited Miller's world. So Cooper takes the ship back to the black hole, hoping to use its gravitational force to sling the ship to Edmunds' planet. But Cooper has to stay behind. He detaches his small lander and falls into the black hole while the ship speeds its way to Edmunds' planet. Their encounter with the black hole has taken only a few minutes, but fifty-one years have passed back on Earth.

After being sucked into the black hole, Cooper is deposited back our solar system, near Saturn. He discovers that in the last half century, humanity has built an armada of vast space ships that will eventually pass through the wormhole to Edmunds' planet, which will be humanity's new home.

In an incredibly moving final sequence, Cooper meets Murphy, the ten-year-old daughter he left behind, now an aged woman surrounded by her vast brood of children and grandchildren. As a child, Murphy begged her father to stay and resented him for years after his departure. But she is at peace, because he helped save her and the entire human race. She tells him that he should not stay around and watch his own child die. He needs to go back out there, to Edmunds' planet, where Dr. Amelia Brand (Anne Hathaway) is waiting in hibernation; he needs to find her, awaken her, and help prepare humanity's new home.

Interstellar, like all of Nolan's movies, is a deeply serious work. There are four themes that are especially poignant.

The first is the tension between rootedness and exploration. The world of *Interstellar* has officially given up on space exploration. They are pledged to be caretakers on a planet that is becoming uninhabitable. Their political and educational system is dedicated to constricting people's horizons. Caretakers live within their limits. Explorers go beyond and set new limits. Cooper used to be a NASA pilot, but now he is a farmer, and he hates it. He wants to be among the stars, not scraping a living from the dirt. As *Interstellar* shows, however, on a dying Earth, one can't be a caretaker unless one is an explorer. To survive, one must aim at more than survival. But, then again, the ultimate goal is a new place to put down roots.

The second theme is the difficulty of saying goodbye, especially when Cooper leaves his children behind on a mission from which he may never return. A great deal of *Interstellar*'s emotional power derives from the pain of separation, exacerbated by the time differentials. (One of the best traits of James Gray's *Ad Astra* was its meditation on what traits of character and beliefs would be necessary to sustain such explorers.)

The third important theme is the role of lies in society. The school system teaches that the Moon landing was a hoax, but it funds NASA in secret. The ultimate fate of the Earth is top secret. Amelia Brand's father, Professor Brand (played by Michael Caine), claims to be working on Plan A, but has concealed the fact that he has failed to solve the "gravity problem" that will allow mankind to leave the Earth *en masse*. He lied to give people hope. The robots have an honesty setting, because it is understood that perfect honesty dissolves society. This a theme in *The Dark Knight Trilogy* as well.

Finally, *Interstellar* is about racial survival, which is a particularly poignant issue for whites, since we are on the path to extinction. When faced with extinction, the feminist idea that having a career grants higher status than motherhood is quietly forgotten. Plan B presupposes that women will bear enough children to make exponential growth possible. And although Cooper's daughter Murphy plays a very important role in saving all of humanity, she also has a large family surrounding her at the end of her life. (The adult Murphy is played by Jessica Chastain. The aged Murphy is played by Ellen Burstyn.)

Interstellar is not flawless. For some reason, McConaughey insists on speaking with a twangy, mush-mouthed accent that none of his other family use, so it just seems fake. Time travel and an almost literal *deus ex machina* also play important roles, which I found annoying. I have no scientific quibbles because this is science *fiction*, so the jargon only has to *sound* good. And it does.

But the virtues of this film are immense. The story is gripping, the script brilliant, and the acting is uniformly excellent. This is my favorite McConaughey role. Michael Caine, Matt Damon, Jessica Chastain, and Ellen Burstyn are all outstanding. The sets, equipment, and special effects are also quite dazzling.

Special mention is due Hans Zimmer. Frankly, I am not a fan, but this is his best score. To my ears, it sounds like he took the organ pedal from the opening fanfare of Richard Strauss's *Also Sprach Zarathustra* and turned it into a minimalistic but often emotionally shattering accompaniment.

I've said quite a lot about this movie, but I guarantee that if you watch it for the first time, it will still be filled with surprises. *Interstellar* is a masterpiece: imaginative, enthralling, inspiring, and cathartic.

The Unz Review, April 12, 2020

JOKER

One of the great things about Heath Ledger's Joker in Christopher Nolan's *The Dark Knight* is that he does not have an origin story. Or, actually, he tells two contradictory origin stories, neither of them probably true. But the police can't find a single shred of information on his real identity: who he was, where he came from, and how he got those scars.

Todd Phillips' much-anticipated *Joker* is an origin story starring Joaquin Phoenix as Arthur Fleck, who becomes the Joker. Frankly, both of Ledger's origin stories are more interesting.

The question on everybody's mind is: How does Joaquin Phoenix's Joker compare to Heath Ledger's? The answer is: There is no comparison. Phoenix's Joker isn't even as good as Jared Leto's in *Suicide Squad*. There is no question that Phoenix is a fine actor, but the character he brings to life simply isn't compelling. He's just a repulsive loser.

Traditionally, the character of the Joker has drawn upon the Romantic idea that madness can be entwined with genius, charisma, psychological depth, and creativity. Phoenix's Joker is much closer to the sad truth: The vast majority of crazy people are not deep, creative, or interesting. They are just pathetic, shambling, vacant defectives who repeatedly betray and disappoint the people who are unfortunate enough to love or take care of them.

Ledger's Joker has a Nietzschean and Heideggerian philosophy, which he articulates with striking words and deeds. Phoenix's Joker doesn't have a nihilistic philosophy. He's just a depressive. When we first see him, he is holding a sign reading "Everything Must Go." Yeah, it's for a going out of business sale, but it's also *symbolic*. Phoenix's Joker does not "stand for" nihilism as a worldview. As he says later on, he doesn't stand for anything. He has no worldview. He's just a tortured soul, and a banal one at that.

All the other Jokers—Ledger, Leto, Nicholson, even Cesar Romero, ferchrissakes—have some charisma. They are commanding presences. Phoenix's Joker has no charisma at all. He's a physically repulsive stick insect of a man: unkempt, unhealthy, and slightly effeminate, reeking of cigarettes and low self-esteem. You'd want to squash him like a bug, if you'd deign to notice him at all.

There are a few flashes of a steely-eyed social competence when Arthur rehearses his appearance on the *Murray Franklin Show*, but it went nowhere, so it struck me as breaking character.

Ledger's Joker launched a million memes, both because of his character and his lines. Phoenix's Joker will have no such influence. He's a pathetic nobody with nothing to say.

Judging from the technology and social trends, *Joker* is set in the early 1980s: There are no desktop computers or cell phones. Dem programs are being cut for the mentally ill, and drunken Wall Street yupsters are an annoyance on the subway.

Arthur Fleck lives with his mother Penny Fleck, who seems to be bedridden. Arthur brings in money as a clown, but he's not that funny. Arthur suffers from mental health problems. He has been committed, he sees a counselor, and he is taking seven different medications. But because of budget cuts, the counselor and drugs are disappearing, and commitment will probably not be an option either. Soon there will be only the street.

Arthur is beaten up by some "teens" (read: brown people) so one of his colleagues at the clown agency (surely there must be clown agencies, right?) gives him a revolver for protection. When the gun falls on the floor during one of Arthur's clown shows in a children's cancer ward, he is fired.

Then, still wearing his clown makeup, Arthur is roughed up by some black hoodlums on a night train, pulls out his gun, and shoots them dead. No, wait, that was Bernard Goetz. Arthur was harassed by Wall Street yuppies and shoots three Patrick Batemans dead with seven bullets from what appears to be a .22 pistol (but who's counting?).

This inspires a Leftist uprising of black and brown people—and some white dirtbags—who begin to wear clown masks to show how sick and tired they are of being terrorized by stockbrokers on the subway.

Oh, and billionaire Thomas Wayne (Brett Cullen), who is going to run for Mayor of Gotham, says that people like him, who have made something of their lives, think that all of life's losers look like clowns. Of course there is only one politician in America today who would say something so unpolitic. Is he supposed to be Donald Trump?

At this point, given the obvious anti-white, Bolshevik slant here, perhaps I should mention that director Todd Phillips and his co-screenwriter Scott Silver are both Jewish. However, to their credit, the entire film is not cast against type. Arthur is first assaulted by non-whites, and sullen black women play prominent unsympathetic roles, subtly underscoring that Arthur's alienation is in part that of a poor white man in a society in which the lower classes and those who provide services to them are increasingly non-white.

As much as I feared that Arthur Fleck was going to be turned into a sympathetic victim, it is really impossible to like him. When Arthur learns that his mother believes Thomas Wayne is his father, he goes to the Wayne estate to talk to Thomas Wayne and ends up physically assaulting Alfred Pennyworth in front of young Bruce Wayne.

Then he stalks and confronts Thomas Wayne. Wayne explains that he never had sex with Penny Fleck, that Arthur was in any case adopted, and that she was committed to Arkham State Hospital for mental illness and also for endangering Arthur. When Arthur steals his mother's file from Arkham and confirms Wayne's story, he does not apologize to Wayne. Instead he smothers his mother with a pillow.

Arthur also savagely murders the colleague who gave him the gun. I found this scene so distasteful that I almost walked out. But then I thought of my duty to you, dear reader, and stayed to the end.

One of the obvious influences on *Joker* is Martin Scorsese's *The King of Comedy* (1983), a dark comic masterpiece that almost reaches *Fawlty Towers* levels of pure cringe. Robert De Niro plays Rupert Pupkin, a deranged man who wants to be a standup comic and is obsessed with successful comedian and talk-show host Jerry Langford (brilliantly played by Jerry Lewis).

Like Rupert, Arthur lives with his mother (although there is some suggestion that Rupert's mother is dead and that, like

Norman Bates, he has only an imaginary relationship with her).

Both Rupert and Arthur have imaginary relationships with talk-show hosts whom they eventually meet in real life. In Arthur's case the host is Murray Franklin who, to tighten the connection between the films, is played by Robert De Niro.

Yet another connection is that both Rupert and Arthur have black romantic interests. When white men date non-whites, the natural presumption is that they are dating down out of insecurity, which makes sense given that both characters are losers. (In De Niro's case, he actually had a child with Diahnne Abbot, the actress who plays his love interest. De Niro has fathered five children with three black women. One could be considered an accident, etc.) In Arthur's case, his relationship with his neighbor, single mother Sophie Dumond, is imaginary.

Both movies also have a cartoonish scene in which we see Rupert and Arthur from a distance chased back and forth by security personnel.

The climax of *Joker* is when Murray Franklin invites Arthur on his show. At this point, Arthur is wearing clown makeup and wishes to be introduced simply as "Joker." This is Arthur's big break, but he is not interested in actually entertaining anyone. In truth, he lacks both the talent and the interest. Arthur's laughter is merely a syndrome, a mechanical tic, unconnected to a sense of humor. The only laughs he gets on the show are by being socially awkward.

Arthur is entirely absorbed in self-pity. He confesses to killing the three yuppies and claims to find it funny. Murray Franklin is appalled but challenges him to defend himself. Heath Ledger's Joker could have said something interesting and plausible. But this Joker has only inarticulate bitterness and rage. Then he shoots Franklin in the head and shambles away, allowing himself to be taken into custody.

The dénouement of the film takes place in the immediate aftermath of the Joker's arrest. The Leftist clown mask protests have turned into city-wide rioting. The police car transporting the Joker to jail is rammed by an ambulance driven by a clown protester. The injured Joker is lifted from the back seat and laid on the hood of the police car in a pose clearly drawn from Andrea Mantegna's *The Dead Christ and Three Mourners*. Then the Joker/Christ regains consciousness/resurrects, stands up on the hood of the car, and draws a smile on his face with his own blood to the acclaim of the crowd. Our savior.

A comic genius (who may or may not be Paul Waggener) summed it up best: *The Passion of the Christ* for Juggalos.

The movie ends, however, with the Joker in Arkham, explaining himself to another unsympathetic black social worker, then dancing down a sterile hallway, leaving bloody footprints, followed in cartoonish pursuit by orderlies.

But the last half of the movie might actually be one of Arthur's fantasies, because at one point, Arthur empties out his mother's refrigerator, climbs inside, and closes the door. Can people open refrigerators from the inside? Is the whole latter half of the movie a dying man's fantasy? Is this another giant jerk-job like *Lost*? Is the joke on us, the audience?

I pray there is no sequel.

As a purely technical achievement, I would rate *Joker* 9/10. It is well-acted, well-directed, and well-paced. The urban settings are utterly hellish. The music by Icelandic composer Hildur Guðnadóttir is highly effective.

But as a compelling story, I would rate *Joker* 6/10. What is this movie, exactly? It is no superhero or supervillain movie in any conventional sense. Nor it is an unconventional one like M. Night Shyamalan's *Unbreakable*. Is it supposed to be a psychological thriller? If so, it is not thrilling. Is it supposed to be a dark comedy? It is not that funny. Is it supposed to be social satire? If so, it is entirely lame and conventional.

The simple truth is that *Joker* is a boring movie about a disgusting loser. Although there's no accounting for taste or madness, I think those who fear *Joker* will incite incels to go on shooting sprees are wrong. I'm betting that the most savage thing *Joker* inspires is this review.

THE LEOPARD

Luchino Visconti's masterpiece is his 1963 historical epic *The Leopard* (*Il Gattopardo*, which actually refers to a smaller spotted wild cat, the serval, which is the heraldic animal of the princes of Salina in Sicily). Visconti's film is a remarkably faithful adaptation of the 1958 novel of the same name by Giuseppe Tomasi di Lampedusa. *The Leopard* became the best-selling Italian novel of all time, carrying off many critical laurels as well. In its beauty of language, philosophical depth, and emotional power, *The Leopard* is one of the greatest novels I have ever read, and Visconti's film does it full justice. Both are works of genius.

Set during the Risorgimento, the unification of Italy into a modern nation-state, *The Leopard* is sometimes called "the Italian *Gone with the Wind*," which is an apt comparison, although *The Leopard* is better both as a book and a film. Like *Gone with the Wind*, *The Leopard* is a historical romance set against the backdrop of a war of national unification in which a modern, bourgeois-liberal industrial society (the Northern Kingdom of Piedmont and Sardinia, ruled from Turin by the house of Savoy), triumphs over a feudal, agrarian aristocracy (the Kingdom of the Two Sicilies, encompassing Sicily and Southern Italy and ruled from Naples by the house of Bourbon). Even the time period is basically the same. The novel *The Leopard* is set primarily in 1860–62, and the film takes place entirely in this time frame.

The story begins in May of 1860, when Giuseppe Garibaldi, a charismatic nationalist general, raised an insurgent force of 1000 volunteers and landed in Sicily to overthrow the Bourbons. The Garibaldini fought for no king or parliament. They fought for the nationalist idea. They fought for a unified Italy that did not yet exist.

Garibaldi fought his way to Palermo, declared himself dictator, then raised new troops to take the fight to the mainland, where he overthrew the last Bourbon king, Francis II. Then Garibaldi handed the kingdom over to King Victor Emanuel of Piedmont and Sardinia and retired into private life. Plebiscites were held throughout Italy, except in Venice, which was under

Austrian rule. All of Italy, save the Papal States, agreed to unification under the house of Savoy. In 1862, Garibaldi raised an army to march on Rome and forcibly incorporate the Papal States, but he was stopped by troops loyal to the new unified kingdom.

Lampedusa was a Sicilian aristocrat and a partisan of aristocracy. As a study of classical aristocratic virtues, *The Leopard* can be placed alongside Aristotle's *Nicomachean Ethics*. As a meditation on the decline of aristocracy into oligarchy, it can be placed alongside Plato's *Republic*. Visconti, however, was both an aristocrat and a self-professed Communist. Thus his adaptation also highlights other aspects of the novel, dramatizing how the revolutionary energies unleashed by the ideas of the sovereign people and a unified national state were coopted by the old Italian aristocracy and corrupted by the rising middle classes. Although I am a national populist, not a Marxist, there is much truth in Visconti's depiction.

The hero of *The Leopard* is Don Fabrizio Corbera, Prince of Salina, the head of an ancient Sicilian noble family. In the film, he is played by American actor Burt Lancaster, which is perfect casting, for Don Fabrizio is described a hulking blue-eyed blond. Visconti's casting of the whole Corbera clan is remarkable. Princess Maria Stella, played by Rina Morelli, perfectly fits her description in the book, and the couple's children all resemble their parents and their siblings.

Another important character is the prince's nephew and ward, Tancredi, the orphaned and impoverished prince of Falconeri, whom Lampeusa describes as blue-eyed, dark-haired, and rakishly handsome. Tancredi is brought to life on film by Alain Delon. Tancredi is an adventurous lad who has fallen in with liberals, nationalists, and revolutionaries. When Garibaldi lands, Tancredi rushes to join him.

Tancredi is described as charming, ambitious, and somewhat unscrupulous. Thus it is never clear how deep his commitment to the Risorgimento actually is. When he speaks to his uncle, the prince of Salina, he tells him that everything must change so that everything can remain the same. The revolution will ultimately pass away, and Sicily's immemorial customs and ancient aristocracy will quietly reassert themselves. It is never clear if this rather cynical view is accepted by Tancredi himself or simply crafted for his uncle's consumption. But as the story—and especially the film—unfolds, it becomes increasingly clear that if Tancredi ever believed in the ideals of the Risorgimento, he eventually dropped them.

The prince of Salina uses Tancredi's connections to Garibaldi and his wealth and prestige to insulate himself and his family from the chaos of the revolution. With sublime indifference to current events, the family departs Palermo on its annual retreat to the village of Donnafugata, where they have inherited an immense palace.

Visconti's portrayal of their journey and welcome is remarkable. The family arrives, emerging from the enclosed sweatboxes of their carriages, their elegant clothes white with dust from the unpaved mountain roads. Greeted ceremoniously by their retainers and the village notables, they immediately attend a church service. Visconti's camera slowly pans the prince and his family, all of them studies of dignity and decorum although drenched in sweat and caked with filth. Only after thanking God for their safe journey do they retire to their palace and freshen up.

The dignified arrival of the Salinas stands in sharp contrast to Visconti's farcical treatment of the local plebiscite presided over by Don Calogero Sedàra, the mayor of Donnafugata. Sedàra is a strong proponent of the new order. He makes no pretense of partiality. After the prince votes, he proposes a toast with a liqueur in the three colors of the new Italian flag. The prince, who straddles the worlds of the Bourbons and the Savoyards, chooses the Bourbon white, drinks, and winces at the cloying taste.

When Don Calogero reads the results, a brass band continually interrupts him. As it turns out, he has cooked the books. Of the 512 votes cast, 512 are yesses. In truth, the plebiscites were widely fraudulent. The new order had not even legitimated its power, and it was already abusing the public trust.

Who is Don Calogero Sedàra? He is the man of the future. Just as the prince of Salina represents the best of the aristocracy, Sedàra represents the virtues and limitations of the rising middle classes. Sedàra is a man of humble birth but outsized ambition and avarice, which he pursues single-mindedly with boundless intelligence and energy. Now, like the prince, a man of around fifty, Sedàra has amassed a large fortune, become mayor, and is the leader of the revolutionary forces in his district. Sedàra is described as a "beetle of a man," and his portrayal by Paolo Stoppa is of limited success. Stoppa aptly communicates Sedàra's avarice and gaucheries but not his intelligence and hard work.

Sedàra's wife is never seen. She is reputed to be a woman of great beauty but bestial manners, probably due to mental illness. Her father was one of the prince's peasants known as Pepe Cowshit. They have only one child, their daughter Angelica (Claudia Cardinale, almost perfect casting, although she lacks Angelica's green eyes), who has inherited her father's intelligence and ambition as well as her mother's beauty, which—reinforced by her father's wealth and a bit of polishing at a Florentine finishing school—makes her a formidable force.

On the night of his arrival in Donnafugata, the prince holds a dinner for the local notables, including Don Calogero. In the novel, it is explained that the prince does not wear formal evening clothes at this dinner because he knows the villagers don't have them. It is a magnanimous gesture, designed to make class distinctions less onerous on the dignity of the villagers.

But in comes Don Calogero, in white tie and tails, a gesture that in the prince's eyes is more significant than the revolution itself. Indeed, it *is* the revolution itself. Although ill-tailored and ill-shaven, Sedàra's clothes put him above the prince and his family, at least to those who reckon by appearances. Those who know the truth, however, understand that this outcome has occurred only by virtue of the prince's magnanimous condescension and Sedàra's social climbing. (In the film, the prince's magnanimous gesture is not communicated, so the Salinas' surprise at Sedàra being overdressed comes off as mere snobbery, when the truth is precisely the opposite.)

All is forgotten, however, when the radiant Angelica appears. Tancredi is instantly smitten. But this presents a problem. Earlier that very day, the family's Jesuit chaplain father Pirrone told the prince that his eldest daughter, Concetta, wished to marry her cousin Tancredi and believed the feeling to be mutual. The prince, however, dismissed the idea because the timid and submissive Concetta is not a suitable bride for an ambitious man like Tancredi, who needs an equally ambitious wife and a far larger dowry than he could afford to provide Concetta. Angelica, however, is a perfect match, because she is beautiful, intelligent, a wealthy only-child, and a dedicated social climber.

One of the most interesting characters in *The Leopard* is Ciccio Tumeo (played by Serge Reggiani), the local church organist and the prince's hunting companion. Tumeo is an intelligent and thoughtful commoner. He is also a far more zealous guardian of the traditional order than the prince. Tumeo is a Bourbon loyalist because of the patronage and kindness extended to his family by the deposed king's ancestors. He was educated at royal expense, and when his family was in need, they petitioned the court for aid and received it. In his essentially feudal view, this patronage binds and obliges him to the Bourbons. Thus he voted "no" in the plebiscite and was incensed that his vote was changed by Sedàra, whom Ciccio regards as a dishonorable opportunist.

Tumeo tells the prince of Sedàra's bestial wife and her father, Pepe Cowshit. When the prince informs Tumeo that on that very evening he is going to tell Sedàra of Tancredi's proposal of marriage to Angelica, he thinks the match is not appropriate because of Angelica's background. Furthermore, the prince off-handedly informs Tumeo that to prevent him from leaking news of the engagement, he and his hunting dog Teresina will be locked in the prince's gunroom until the deal is struck.

The prince obviously values Tumeo's judgment and companionship. So why doesn't he simply swear Tumeo to silence? Probably because the prince thinks that Tumeo's oath is worthless, because he is not a gentleman. This casual condescension appears earlier in the film as well, when upon his arrival in Donnafugata, the prince greets Teresina before he greets her master. (Actually, such behavior is common among "dog people" of all classes, and nobody takes it personally.)

The final sequence of the film is set two years later at a grand ball in Palermo in which Angelica and Don Calogero are introduced into Sicily's high society. It seems a rather long wait, but the setting is determined by the politics of the times. Garibaldi's attempt to march on Rome has been defeated by troops loyal to the new king in Turin. The house of Savoy is firmly in control. The revolutionary energies stirred by the Risorgimento's idea of a sovereign Italian people in a united nation-state have been largely coopted and corrupted by the glamor and prestige of the old aristocracy and the avarice of the bourgeoisie.

The aristocracy, however, is doomed to slow displacement. They have expensive tastes and, like Tancredi's father, the prince of Falconeri, are often very bad at managing money. In the past, great aristocratic fortunes could be replenished every few generations by the loot of a victorious war. But in the nineteenth century, the usual route was to marry the daughters of the rising oligarchy, who crave the status and lifestyle of the aristocracy and are better at making and managing money.

We see the process of corruption from the very beginning of *The Leopard*. When Tancredi and two of his fellow Garibaldini visit the prince near Palermo in their dashing red uniforms, a young Northerner, Count Cavriaghi (Terence Hill), addresses the prince as "excellence," an honorific abolished by Garibaldi. An aristocrat himself, with tastes in poetry, music, and painting, Cavriaghi is dazzled by the Salina palace, especially its magnificent frescos. Later, after Tancredi's engagement, Cavriaghi pays court to the prince's daughter Concetta. Later when Tancredi and Cavriaghi appear in Donnafugata, they wear the Prussian blue uniforms of the national army. They have accepted demotions in rank from Garibaldi's forces for a rise in social status.

The aristocracy magically softens Don Calogero's revolutionary fervor as well, to the point that he buys a title for himself. When he informs the prince of this at the end of their engagement negotiations, both the prince and father Pirrone walk away as if he has said nothing. Later, when the prince turns down an invitation to join the senate in Turin, he recommends Sedàra instead, dryly remarking that "his family is an old one, or soon will be."

By the ball, the process of corruption is complete. The leaders of the new army and the jumped-up bourgeoisie like the Sedàras are fêted by the old aristocracy. Colonel Pallavicino, who defeated Garibalidi's last insurgency at Aspromonte, is an especially honored guest. They feast and dance till dawn. Then, in a detail added to the movie, Pallavicino goes off to execute deserters who went to Garibaldi's side at Aspromonte. Tancredi and Sedàra, the former revolutionary now dressed in top hat and tails, approve. It is time for law and order. It is time to get down to business.

At the ball, the prince meditates on mortality. He is in decline. His family is in decline. His class is in decline. After the party, the prince chooses to walk home. Seeing a priest on his way to administer someone's last rites, he kneels and crosses himself, then looks up to Venus, as the morning star, and prays to be delivered from the realm of change. A mathematician and astronomer, the prince is essentially a Platonist. He sees numbers as unchanging and the heavens as a realm of eternal, cyclical change. The prince is both perfectly Catholic and perfectly pagan.

Three chapters of the novel were not adapted to the screen.

Chapter V, "Father Pirrone Pays a Visit," tells of the priest's 1861 excursion to his home village. However, the best lines of the chapter, where Pirrone discourses on the nature of the aristocracy to drowsy peasants, were incorporated into the film, in a scene during the Salinas' journey to Donnafugata.

Chapter VII, "Death of a Prince," narrates the prince's last days in 1883, emphasizing the pagan themes intimated at the end of the ball. The prince has two visions of Venus, at a train station as he returns to Palermo, and on his deathbed, where she appears to guide his soul to the unchanging realm. This chapter is utterly heartbreaking. I wish Visconti had included it in his film.

Chapter VIII, "Relics," is set in 1910 and narrates the total ruin of the great house of Salina, whose prestige and substance have been squandered by the high living and bad business decisions of the prince's male heirs and the superstitious pieties of three of his four daughters, who have become old maids (apparently, they could not find a place in the new order). Angelica, now widowed, seems to have flourished, although there is no mention of any children to carry on the Falconeri name. It is fitting, then, that the last word of the novel is "dust."

The Leopard is obviously a deeply pessimistic meditation on the decline of aristocracy and the rise of the middle classes. Written by the last prince of Lampedusa, whose adopted son inherited his property but not his title, the novel was rejected by both publishers to which it was submitted. Then, before he could submit it to another publisher, the author died of cancer, aged sixty. But *The Leopard*'s pessimism is somewhat belied by its spectacular posthumous success, both as a novel and a film. Because of books like *The Leopard*, we can at least hope that healthy archaic values and institutions can someday return and that, by understanding the seeds of decay, we can perhaps avert it.

Lampedusa was a reactionary and an advocate of aristocracy. I am not. In my view, Garibaldi's only flaw was unifying Italy as a monarchy, not a republic. Although I cannot help but admire the prince of Salina's virtues and magnificent way of life, his political instincts were entirely wrong.

The prince never should have married Tancredi to Angelica or contemplated any alliance with the Sedàras of the world. He should have married Tancredi to Concetta, who because of his cynicism ended up an embittered old maid. He should have taken a seat in the new senate, not ceded it out of cynicism to the likes of Don Calogero Sedàra.

Furthermore, just as the prince was too willing to ally himself with the middle classes, he was entirely too dismissive of improving the lot of the common people, in violation of the feudal ethos that bound the most decent man in the whole book, Ciccio Tumeo, to the deposed Bourbons. Sicily today is objectively better off with paved roads, running water, sewers, and other improvements airily dismissed by the prince.

In short, the best outcome for Italy would have been a marriage of the feudal-warrior ethos of the old aristocracy with a progressive national populism, cutting out the rising oligarchy altogether. This position is actually represented in *The Leopard* by Cavalier Chevalley di Monterzuolo (played by Leslie French), the Piedmontese functionary who asks the prince to join the new senate. In the twentieth century, this synthesis was finally realized by Mussolini, only to be reversed by the Second World War, with some help from the dried-up husk of the house of Savoy.

When the prince bids Chevalley goodbye, he says, "We were the leopards, the lions. Those who will take our place will be jackals, hyenas. And all of us—leopards, lions, jackals, and sheep—we'll go on thinking ourselves the salt of the earth." An accurate prophecy—but a self-fulfilling one. It was the dereliction of men like the prince of Salina who made it so.

The Leopard's depiction of the corruption of Garibaldi's national-populist revolution offers many lessons to national populists today. We should count ourselves fortunate that the old monarchies and aristocracies of Europe are pretty much dead, and those that remain are pretty much politically irrelevant. National populists believe that political sovereignty resides in the nation, not in dynasties. Political legitimacy flows from representing the common good of the people, not from dynastic descent. Social and political hierarchies are justified only by the common good of society, not by divine right or hereditary caste. Monarchy and aristocracy have a seductive glamor, but they are at best imperfect images of just political hierarchies.

However, national populists should emulate the honor-centered warrior ethos of the old aristocracies, as well as their feudal sense of social responsibility, which are the necessary correctives to bourgeois materialism and individualism.

Lampedusa makes clear that the material magnificence of the old aristocracy springs from essentially spiritual and anti-materialist values. Aristocracies arise by subordinating material interests, including the instinct of self-preservation, to the pursuit of honor. Aristocracies transmute material wealth into spiritual values like honor and prestige through munificence and the creation of beautiful and useless things, such as the entire realm of high culture.

But *The Leopard* also shows how high living combined with an ethos of generosity leads to the ruin of great estates and the rise of oligarchy. Oligarchs can better maintain the opulent lifestyles of the aristocracy because they are materialists, individualists, and fundamentally selfish. The bourgeois ethos subordinates honor and culture to self-preservation and commodious living. Obviously, a cash-poor revolutionary movement like national populism needs to adopt the warrior ethos of the aristocracy, but we can't afford aristocratic pretensions in the material realm. We need to be revolutionary ascetics if we are to free ourselves from the trammels of oligarchy.

Everything about this movie is superb: the directing, casting, acting, costumes, camerawork, sets, and Nino Rota's ravishing Romantic score. I have one reservation. Not a criticism so much as a reservation. *The Leopard* is a short novel but a very long movie, clocking in at 185 minutes in its definitive version. The ball sequence alone occupies the last fifty minutes. I resisted watching for years, simply because of the time investment. But there is something magical about this movie. When the ball started, I no longer felt I was watching a movie. I felt I was *in* it. And it made such a strong impression that it was all I remembered about the movie when I re-watched it after more than a decade to write this essay. Buy the Blu-ray and watch it in installments if you must, but you must watch it.

Visconti's film will especially appeal to lovers of historical costume dramas, romances, and comedies of manners. If you like Jane Austen adaptations, you will find *The Leopard* especially appealing, for like Austen, Lampedusa is a student of classical virtue ethics and creates very subtle character portraits. Thus I highly recommend *The Leopard*, the novel and the film. They are two twentieth-century masterpieces that can be appreciated both as escapist entertainment and as profound meditations on politics, morals, and the human condition.

The Unz Review, August 25, 2019

LOOK WHO'S BACK

"Whenever there is a decline of righteousness, and the rise of unrighteousness, then I come back to teach dharma."
— *Bhagavad Gita*, Chapter IV, Verse 7

"Nobody can stay mad at Hitler forever."
— *Look Who's Back*

David Wnendt's 2015 film *Look Who's Back* (*Er ist wieder da*) is based on Timur Vermes' 2012 novel of the same name about Adolf Hitler being mysteriously transported to modern Berlin and becoming a viral media sensation. *Look Who's Back* is a fascinating and funny film, but its intended message is hard to fathom. Is the movie a satire of modern society, a satire of the modern media, a warning against recrudescent fascism? If it is entirely satire, it is too broad and all-encompassing so that one does not know where the filmmaker stands, and for what.

As I see it, however, the net effect of this film is to make Hitler seem like a much more rational and compelling figure than the carpet-chewing madman to which we are accustomed. This, in turn, undermines the film's attempt to smear National Populists like Marine Le Pen and Geert Wilders by linking them to Hitler. But surely this was no part of the Wnendt's or Vermes' intentions.

Look Who's Back strikes me as a strange mashup of Jerzy Kosinski's only good story, *Being There* — in which a mysterious cipher rides other people's projections into a position of power — and *Network*, Paddy Chayevsky's brilliant satire of television, in which an ambitious and unscrupulous female producer exploits Howard Beale, a TV-anchor turned mad prophet and tribune of populist rage. Only in this case, the cipher is invisible not because he is unknown but because he is overexposed, supposedly dead, and people refuse to believe their lying eyes.

The basic story of *Look Who's Back* is quite simple. Through some miracle, Adolf Hitler (Oliver Masucci) has been transported from April 1945 to 2014. He wakes up in a Berlin apartment complex near the site of the old Chancellery. He then has the sort of comic misadventures one would expect of a guy dressed as Hitler wandering around present-day Berlin. Naturally, nobody thinks *he* has come back. Instead, they take him to be a Hitler impersonator, i.e., a madman or a clown. People want to take selfies with him and do the Hitler salute. Parts of the film are presented as unscripted interactions with real people. If this is true, it seems remarkable how few negative reactions he receives. Frankly, I think it is all fake.

Hitler befriends a newsstand owner and begins to catch up on the last seventy years. He is horrified to learn that Poland still exists, and on German territory no less. Hitler regards Angela Merkel with contempt and regards her party as a pale imitation of National Socialism. But he puts a great deal of stock in the Greens.

Hitler then teams up with Fabian Sawatski (Fabian Busch) who is a bit of a loser, living with his mom and dreaming of being a director while relegated to delivering mail and making coffee at the offices of the MyTV network. Fabian is convinced that this Hitler impersonator will be a huge success and wants to come along for the ride.

Criss-crossing Germany in Fabian's mother's car, Hitler talks to ordinary Germans about the evils of immigration and race-mixing and the sham of liberal democracy. He finds many receptive listeners. Again: Is this for real or just a morality play? Is it a warning that even the slightest deviation from the liberal democratic consensus will lead straight to You Know Who?

If this is the intended message, then why does the filmmaker portray Hitler as level-headed, reasonable, and even humorous? Why not just use the ranting TV Hitler we have seen a thousand times before? Vermes and Wnendt know that this image of Hitler was constructed by extracting the impassioned climaxes from what were often long lectures filled with facts and arguments. Vermes, by the way, is quite masterful at capturing Hitler's voice and style, as ably discussed by *Counter-Currents'* own James O'Meara,[1] and this is carried over into the

---

[1] James J. O'Meara, *Look Who's Back, Counter-Currents*, May 5, 2014

film with hilarious effect even when Hitler encounters such minor modern oddities as granola bars.

Hitler hits the big time when Katja Bellini (Katja Riemann) takes over MyTV. She thinks Hitler will be sensational, but her resentful underling, Christoph Sensenbrink (Christoph Maria Herbst) thinks he can oust her by engineering a public backlash against putting Hitler on a TV satire show. Sensenbrink urges the writers to come up with the most offensive jokes possible. (Example: Q: What did the Jewish pedophile say? A: Want to buy some candy?)

But Hitler's monologues are not the rantings of a genocidal madman. Nor are they comedy routines, although they have a biting wit. Instead, they are candid and heartfelt meditations on the banality of modern culture, the failure of liberal democracy, and the need for meaning in life. Hitler is a hit.

But then footage of Hitler shooting a small dog that attacked him comes to light. This turn of events is deeply implausible, as Hitler was a dog lover. But it is used to great effect. The audience turns on him. Hitler is *kaput*. Bellini and Sawatski are *aus*. Sensenbrink takes Bellini's job.

But then . . . Hitler comes back. Hitler is, after all, a best-selling author. So Hitler holes up at Sawatski's mom's apartment and writes his second bestseller, *Look Who's Back*. In a hilarious satire of the modern image makeover, Hitler donates money to animal charities, appears on talk shows, and even manages to get beaten up by skinheads.

Meanwhile, the network's profits plummet without Hitler, which sets up a scene in which Sensenbrink does a parody of Hitler's famous *Downfall* tirade. (It is notable that the only ranting in the movie is not Hitler's but Sensenbrink's.) One of the idiots at the network suggests hiring Hitler back, because "Nobody can stay mad at Hitler forever." Surely Jews would disagree.

Which brings us to another aspect of this film that strikes me as dishonest: Jews are mentioned from time to time, but always in ways that make them seem essentially powerless and in need of protection. They are readily dismissed when they start going on about the dangers of resurgent Hitlerism. Bellini wants Hitler's assurance that Jews will not be mocked, but Hitler takes her to mean that Jews are "no laughing matter." A protest from a Jewish organization is laughed off. When an elderly Jewish woman recognizes that Hitler really is Hitler, it is dismissed as dementia. Germans, in short, regard Jews as weak: weak enough to be pitied but also weak enough to be ignored.

This strikes me as a complete inversion of the truth. A huge amount of modern politics in the West consists of placating "deeply concerned" Jews, even when they are transparently neurotic and manipulative. For instance, *steps had to be taken* lest space aliens be triggered into anti-Semitic pogroms when it was discovered that trees in Germany and buildings in America look like swastikas from above.[2]

The film ends with Hitler, Sawatski, and Bellini making a movie of *Look Who's Back*. The worst-case scenario of someone realizing that Hitler is actually, you know, *Hitler*, is acted out in the movie and disposed of with a diagnosis of mental illness. The movie completed, Hitler and Bellini ride through the streets of Berlin in an open limousine while Hitler monologues on the rise of nationalism, populism, and xenophobia around Europe to a montage of images of demonstrations and politicians like Marine Le Pen and Geert Wilders. This, he claims, is an ideal environment for him to come back.

We are supposed to feel chills, but I felt rather angry at the attempt to stigmatize sensible European National Populism by equating it with Hitler. Want borders? You're no better than Hitler! Want standards? What is this, Nazi Germany? Of course, America was not Nazi Germany before 1965, when we opened our borders; or before the cultural revolutions of the 1960s which declared war against all reigning norms and values.

Look Who's Back is a highly entertaining film, but it is deeply fake. The premise that Adolf Hitler could return to modern

---

2 See the "Forest Swastika" entry on *Wikipedia* as well as Dan Glaister, "Navy agrees to camouflage 'swastika' base," *The Guardian*, September 27, 2007.

Germany, become a TV star, and then perhaps return to politics is meant as an insult to the German people, many of whom are shown to be receptive to his message, and those who disagree are generally polite and rational. But surely there is no shortage of people in Germany who would hasten to indulge in sadistic, self-righteous ranting, cloaked in the banner of anti-fascism if Hitler really did return.

I suspect the truth would be closer to what we have been going through in America over the last few years when a real-life TV star became President. Donald Trump is no Hitler, but a large portion of the US population has been gaslighted into thinking Trump is Hitler's second coming and has reacted accordingly. And Trump Derangement Syndrome is the merest shadow of the *oy veying* that would rend the very fabric of the universe if Hitler actually did come back.

Nevertheless, I highly recommend *Look Who's Back*. Oliver Masucci is a compelling Hitler, although they should have given him blue contact lenses. Katja Riemann is simply regal. Indeed, the entire cast is good.

Again, it is hard to determine the film's actual message. But liberals find it deeply disturbing, and Right-leaning individuals who are supposed to be scared away from national populism by an association with Hitler might have exactly the opposite reaction. I have never believed that the triumph of national populism—which is based upon universal, objective reality, not mere historical contingencies—requires the rehabilitation of Hitler, but taking some of the sting out of the *reductio ad Hitlerum* can't hurt either. Try showing this film to normies and see how they react.

The Unz Review, December 4, 2019

"DEATH MY BRIDE"
LOST HIGHWAY

Lost Highway is probably not a lot of people's favorite David Lynch film. I would rank it in the lower rungs of his canon. But it is still a masterful film that draws me back again and again.

The big question about *Lost Highway* is what actually happens. This movie has a plot that you can fully summarize without really spoiling it, because the meaning is never really given away.

There are only two real options for interpreting *Lost Highway*. Either the story is a delusion (a dream or a psychotic waking dream), or it is set in a real world. If *Lost Highway* a dream, like much of *Mulholland Drive*, where does the dream begin or end? In *Mulholland Drive*, there is a break between dream and reality, but no such break is clear in *Lost Highway*.

Fred Madison, the protagonist of *Lost Highway*, is clearly somewhat deranged. The song over the opening and closing credits is David Bowie's "I'm Deranged," one of the finest creations of his late career, both highly accessible and utterly *avant garde*. But derangement itself is a real thing, existing in the real world. Fred and his derangement are depicted *in* the film. The film is not in Fred's head. Fred's head is in the film.

If, however, *Lost Highway* is set in the real world, then we have to conclude that supernatural events and powers are real as well. I am partial to this interpretation, for the supernatural is "real" in all of Lynch's other major works.

One of the clues to the meaning of *Lost Highway* is a comment by the protagonist, Fred Madison (Bill Pullman), who says that he does not own a video camera because he likes "to remember things my own way. Not necessarily the way they happened."

Fred, however, is followed by a shadowy figure, the Mystery Man (Robert Blake), who documents the things he would prefer to forget, including the murder and dismemberment of his wife Renée (Patricia Arquette), which Fred does not even remember having done until he is confronted with the video.

The idea of doing terrible things and only learning of them later, from an external viewpoint, in which one is an object, is deeply unsettling.

This establishes that in *Lost Highway*, video/film is an objective medium—and since *Lost Highway* is itself a film, I think we should at least try to give it a realist interpretation. *Lost Highway* depicts a series of events that take place in a real world, albeit one in which magic takes place, as opposed to a dream or fantasy world, subject to the distortions of subjectivity, such as lapses of memory, repression of memory, wishful thinking, etc.).

But if *Lost Highway* shows us what really happened, then . . . what really happened?

The movie falls into three parts.

In the first part, Fred Madison kills his wife Renée, whom he suspects is cheating on him. Fred is sentenced to die, but disappears from his cell and is replaced by Pete Dayton (Balthazar Getty).

In the second part, Pete meets Alice Wakefield, a dead-ringer for Renée Madison (also played by Patricia Arquette). Alice is the girlfriend of Dick Laurent/Mr. Eddy (Robert Loggia), a gangster and porn producer with a really bad temper.

In the third part, Pete disappears, and Fred takes his place. Fred has apparently taken on Pete's body to get out of jail and has now discarded it. Alice disappears, but Renée reappears, no longer dead. Fred tracks down and kills Dick Laurent/Mr. Eddy, who is sleeping with Renée. The movie ends with Fred in Mr. Eddy's Mercedes being pursued by police. In the last few seconds of the film, Fred begins to morph into another person, perhaps Pete, but more likely someone else who will let him again escape the consequences of his actions.

The film's publicist suggested the story was a "psychogenic fugue." This is not strictly true. A psychogenic or dissociative fugue is a form of temporary amnesia in which the subject loses his personal identity but then regains it. When Fred murders Renée he has no recollection of it until he sees the video. This could be a dissociative fugue or just a blackout. But the switch from Fred to Pete back to Fred is not simply amnesia. It is presented as Fred somehow stealing Pete's skin, using it as a disguise to escape prison and uncover the mystery of Renée's past, and then discarding it when it is no longer necessary.

Lynch reportedly liked the phrase "psychogenic fugue," but focused more on the musical metaphor. In a fugue, a theme is played (Fred and Renée), then a counter-theme comes in (Pete and Alice), followed by the return of the original theme. In a particularly well-constructed fugue, the counter-theme is foreshadowed in the main theme, and the main theme is echoed in the counter-theme. Lynch does this systematically in *Lost Highway*, both with the script and with the soundtrack.

The first part of *Lost Highway* is my favorite. Lynch is masterful at creating an atmosphere of brooding suspicion and menace.

The film opens with Fred Madison sucking on a cigarette and looking a bit worse for wear from the night before. Somebody hits the door buzzer, and when he presses the "listen" button, he hears the words "Dick Laurent is dead." He looks out the windows, but nobody is there.

That night, Fred is packing his saxophone for a gig at the Luna Lounge (where all the lunatics play), when Renée makes her first appearance, emerging from the dark to tell Fred she doesn't want to go to the club with him that night. She wants to stay home and "read." Fred is naturally suspicious. With her tight dress, sultry pose, and highball in her hand, she's not exactly dressed to stay home and read. Their whole interaction seethes with tension and concealment.

And there is something about Renée's cool manner that invites suspicion. Her dowdy brunette bangs stand in stark contrast with her tight, chic dresses, giving the impression that she is wearing a wig, inviting us to wonder what else she might be concealing.

Fred is soft-spoken and soft-faced, the kind of guy who bites back on his anger and broods. But his music is menacing, ugly, and unhinged, a window into his inner turbulence. (In the second part of the film, Pete Dayton hears Fred's music on the radio, finds it intensely annoying, and turns it off.) When Fred calls Renée on a break, there is no answer, which makes him suspicious. When he arrives home, he enters their bedroom. There are red drapes, which is one of Lynch's visual signatures of the uncanny or supernatural, featured most prominently in his various *Twin Peaks* projects, but also in *Blue Velvet* and *Mulholland Drive*, and perhaps in *Eraserhead* as well, although it is shot in black and white. Renée is asleep in a bed with dark red and black sheets. She invited Fred to wake her up when he got home. (Presumably for sex.) But there is no sign that he did.

The next morning, Renée goes out to fetch the newspaper and sees an unmarked envelope on the steps. Inside is an unmarked VHS tape. She is somewhat furtive about the tape. Later we learn that she did porn before meeting Fred. Perhaps she fears someone is reaching out from her past to mess with her marriage. Fred sees the tape and insists on watching it. It is just a few seconds of video of the front of their house. It makes no sense. Visibly relieved, Renée suggests that maybe it was left by a real estate agent.

That night, Fred lies in bed brooding. He recalls seeing Renée at the Luna Lounge with a suspicious character named Andy. Renée enters, disrobes, and slides into bed. The following sex scene is one of the creepiest in world cinema, simultaneously surreal and hyper-realistic. To *détourn* a phrase from Enoch Powell, it depicts the sober truth that every sex life — like every political career — ultimately ends in failure. Fred and Renée's lovemaking is rank with tension and estrangement.

Then there is a flash of light and the motion slows — in Lynch's cinematic language, signs of supernatural influences intruding into the realm of nature. Then we hear a bit of This Mortal Coil's "Song to the Siren," which features prominently in the second part of the film. (This is a fugue-like foreshadowing of a prominent element of the second part.) Fred seems desperate to break down Renée's icy emotional reserve. When he climaxes — or fails to climax, or climaxes too soon without her (the failure is not clear) — she pats him reassuringly on the back, saying "It's okay, it's okay," causing Fred to disengage and recoil slowly in humiliation and horror.

Renée stares off into space emotionless as an anguished Fred tells her of a dream he had. Renée is in the house, calling Fred's name, but he couldn't find her. There is a roaring fire on the hearth. White smoke creeps through the house, another one of Lynch's signatures of the uncanny. Fred enters the bedroom, passing the red drapes. We see Renée in bed from his point of view. (The movie camera is often Fred's point of view.) Fred says "It looked like you, but it wasn't." Then he rushes at her, and she screams. Then he wakes up from a dream. He was dreaming he was telling her of a dream. But, now awake, he momentarily sees her with the face of a wizened old man, and it scares the bejeezus out of him.

This dream raises an important theme in the movie: Renée's identity. Fred thinks she is hiding something in her past, as well as sneaking around behind his back in the present. The dream also foreshadows what will happen the very next night—as does the hallucination that Fred has after waking up. In the universe of *Lost Highway*, dreams and visions can foretell the future.

The following morning, Renée finds another video tape. This time, the video continues inside their house. The camera goes down the hall to their bedroom. The last thing we see before the video cuts out is Fred and Renée asleep in their bed. Naturally, they are terrified and call the police.

That evening, Fred and Renée attend a party hosted by the rich and sleazy Andy (Michael Massee), an old friend of Renée that Fred regards with suspicion. Fred looks across the room and sees a face on the stairs that he recognizes but maybe can't place. It is the face he saw superimposed over Renée's the night before. The man approaches and the music dies away, suggesting that there is something supernatural about him, that in some way this is an encounter outside of normal time. This is the Mystery Man, played by Robert Blake. The conversation they have is one of the best scenes in the movie:

MYSTERY MAN: We've met before, haven't we?
FRED (smugly): I don't think so. Where was it that you think we've met?
MYSTERY MAN: At your house. Don't you remember?
FRED: No, no I don't. Are you sure?

MYSTERY MAN: Of course. In fact, I'm there right now.

At this point, the Mystery Man hands Fred a cell phone and tells him to call his house. Fred complies and hears the man standing in front of him answer the phone in his house. Being two places at the same time is, of course, not a natural ability, so Fred is alarmed. He thinks this may be the guy who taped him last night in his sleep.

FRED: How did you get into my house?
MYSTERY MAN: You invited me. It's not my habit to go
    where I'm not wanted.
FRED: Who are you?
MYSTERY MAN: (laughs)

Who is the Mystery Man? First of all, he is the man with the camera, recording the things that Fred prefers to forget. He is the guy who puts things on your permanent record. But he is not an instrument of karmic or cosmic justice. In fact, he helps people escape their just desserts. He has supernatural powers, but he apparently cannot interfere in people's lives without their consent. His favors presumably come at some cost. Fred has invited him into his house without even knowing it, probably through his suspicion and jealousy.

When the Mystery Man leaves the music returns. Fred points him out to Andy, asking who he is. Andy doesn't know his name, but believes he is a friend of Dick Laurent. This turns out to be correct. Fred replies, "But Dick Laurent is dead, isn't he?" Andy doesn't believe Laurent is dead and seems alarmed at the suggestion. Clearly there is a connection between them.

Fred and Renée leave the party. Fred asks Renée how she knows Andy. The story she tells is suspiciously vague. When they return home, Fred searches the house but finds no one. As Renée prepares for bed, Fred wanders through his dark house. He broods, looking in a mirror. Renée calls to him exactly as in the dream. Then we see two shadows crossing the living room. One is Fred. The other is the Mystery Man. Then Fred emerges from the darkness. At this point, I expect that things occurred as in the dream. Fred lunges toward Renée in bed, who screams.

The next morning there is another tape. Fred puts it in and watches it. The images are same as the first two, but when they get to the bedroom, the bed is awash in blood, and Fred is frantic, surrounded by Renée's dismembered and disemboweled corpse. He has tried to overcome their estrangement by literally opening her up, turning her inside out, and tearing her apart. He is horrified and calls for her in the next room. He has no recollection of his crime.

Fred is convicted and sentenced to death. In prison, he begins to suffer headaches. A huge bruise appears mysteriously on his forehead. One night in his cell, racked with pain, Fred looks at the wall of his cell. We hear "Song to the Siren," and he has a vision. It is as if curtains are raised on a stage. He sees a cabin exploding and burning in reverse. Time moving backwards is a sign of the supernatural. Then the Mystery Man appears at the door of the cabin, looks at Fred, and goes back inside. ("Song to the Siren" foreshadows its usage at the cabin at the climax of the film.)

Fred's cell is bathed in flickering blue light, another of Lynch's signatures of the supernatural. We then see Pete Dayton by the side of a road. People scream to him not to go. We see smoke. A figure writhes on a bed. There is screaming and tearing, then we see something that I can only describe as what it would look like to pull a new skin over one's face. Then there is just a blurry blob of skin.

The next morning, Fred Madison is not in his cell. He has been replaced by Pete Dayton, an auto mechanic who shares Fred's general size and hair-color, as well as his soft build and face. He also has a huge bruise on his forehead. Later, we manage to piece together the following story. Pete came home with a man his parents and girlfriend Sheila had never seen before. It was the Mystery Man. Pete left with this man, for reasons unknown, and his parents and girlfriend witnessed something profoundly disturbing. At the very least, Pete simply vanished.

I believe the Mystery Man offered Pete something in exchange for, basically, *his skin*. Pete was spirited away and somehow wrapped around Fred, as a disguise. Since Pete Dayton does not belong in prison, he is released, and Fred goes with him. But the police tail him to find any possible clues about what took place.

Pete returns to work after a few days. He then becomes romantically involved with Alice Wakefield, Renée's dead-ringer, although Alice is blonde. As the film unfolds, we discover that Alice and Renée are the same person.

This story, of course, reminds many people of Alfred Hitchcock's *Vertigo*, in which Jimmy Stewart's Scottie Ferguson falls in love with Kim Novak's icy blonde Madelaine Elster, loses her to death, then finds her brunette dead-ringer and slowly learns they are the same person. But the mystery of *Vertigo* has a perfectly mundane explanation, whereas no such explanation is possible in *Lost Highway*.

Alice is the truth about Renée: a more real, less concealed version of Renée. She's a bottle blonde, but instead of wig-like bangs, we see her roots, so we know it is her natural hair if not her natural color. Alice stars in porn. Alice is the girlfriend of gangster and porn producer Dick Laurent/Mr. Eddy, who hires Pete as a mechanic. When Mr. Eddy begins to suspect their affair and threatens Pete, Alice hatches a plot. They will rob Andy, one of Laurent's associates in the porn industry, and run off together. But things don't go exactly as planned. Andy attacks Pete and ends up killing himself in a gross but genuinely funny way.

When they are robbing Andy's house, Pete sees a picture of Andy, Dick Laurent/Mr. Eddy, Alice, *and* Renée. Pete asks "Is that you? Are both of them you?" Of course both of them really are the same person, but which one is more real? Alice points to the blonde and says "That's me," which sends Pete into agony, including a nosebleed (another Lynchism, this one standing for bad news), which I interpret as Fred's shock at finally getting to the truth about Renée.

In the third part of the film, Alice and Pete both disappear, and Renée and Fred both return. The police at the crime scene look at the same group photo, and it contains only Renée. When Fred asks the Mystery Man "Where's Alice?" and is informed that her name is Renée, and if she told him her name was Alice, she was lying.

Both Fred and Pete desperately want to *possess* Renée/Alice, both sexually and spiritually. But they also want to *know the truth* about her, the real her. Fred is so frustrated by her essential mystery and aloofness that he literally turns her inside out. But woman, like earth, can be torn apart, and still each part will clamp down on, close up, and preserve an essential mystery and otherness.

Lost Highway is Fred's quest for the truth about Renée. Fred is essentially a truth seeker. But like many truth seekers, Fred is so focused on his object that he remains a mystery to himself. Fred is an extravert, a modern man who seeks infinite knowledge/ power over the external world (Renée in particular) while not knowing himself. Self-knowledge is a classical virtue connected with another classical virtue: temperance, self-limitation, self-liberation from ceaseless striving for knowledge/power in the external world.

To seek truth, Fred needs power. Knowledge requires power. Knowledge gives power, and power makes it possible to acquire more knowledge. Enter the Mystery Man. The Mystery Man is evil, but he also represents self-consciousness. With his video recorder, he tapes the things that Fred prefers not to remember and confronts him with the truth about himself. Fred uses the Mystery Man but disowns him at the same time. At the party, Fred recognizes him but doesn't know from where. Fred has already invited him into his house but represses the memory. In his cell, Fred sees him before his transformation into Pete, which will get him out of jail and give him a new life so he can continue to pursue the truth about Renée. In the third part of the film, the Mystery Man confirms that Alice was really Renée. Then he points his video camera at Fred and asks him who he really is. But Fred doesn't really know the answer to that question, so he flees.

If Fred is Faust (= fist, the outward-focused power of grasping = objectification, subjugation, appropriation), then the Mystery Man is his Mephistopheles. Fred will sell his soul for power, because he is such an extravert—obsessed with power/knowledge in the material realm—that he doesn't know himself. So why would he value his soul?

The Mystery Man, however, knows the value of a soul because he is the principle of self-knowledge and self-limitation and ultimately of freedom from striving.

Which raises the question: Why does he enable Fred's ceaseless quest for knowledge/escape from himself and from personal responsibility? When the Mystery Man clothes Fred in Pete's skin, he is helping him evade responsibility. When Fred begins to morph in the car at the end of the film, the police will find someone else when they pull the car over, and Fred will escape punishment yet again.

Perhaps the Mystery Man follows William Blake's principle of allowing the fool to persist in his folly long enough to become wise. As I will argue, this strategy actually works, for Fred does attain self-knowledge and even some wisdom by the end of the film. But we can't really blame him if he still doesn't want to end up back on death row.

If *Lost Highway* is a search for the truth about Renée, then the climax takes place when Pete (Fred) learns the final truth about Alice (Renée). Pete and Alice ransack Andy's house, take his car, and go into the desert to the cabin of a fence. It is the cabin that Fred saw burning and exploding in reverse before his transformation.

The fence is not there. They will have to wait. They make love in the desert, in the sand, in the headlights of Andy's red Ford Mustang, to "Song to the Siren." Pete repeats, with increasing desperation, "I want you. I want you." To which Alice finally replies: "You'll *never* have me." Sexually, there is no climax, but musically there is. Also, dramatically speaking, this is definitely the climax of the movie.

Alice walks into the cabin and disappears. Pete disappears as well. It is Fred who stands up in his place, illuminated by the headlights. If the purpose of Pete was to get Fred out of jail and learn the truth about Renée, then he has served his purpose and can be discarded. (One wonders where Pete ends up.)

There is, however, another form of knowledge—namely, self-knowledge—and thus another, subsidiary climax in the third part of the film. When Fred enters the cabin he sees the Mystery Man, who confirms the truth about Renée and then asks Fred who he is. But self-knowledge is not Fred's strong suit. With the Mystery Man in pursuit, Fred rushes to Andy's car, whose headlights are now dying. It is the dying of outward directed consciousness as the Mystery Man tries to force Fred inwards. But Fred manages the start the car in the nick of time and speeds away.

Fred ends up at the Lost Highway Hotel where he finds Renée and Mr. Eddy/Dick Laurent having a tryst. After Renée departs, Fred abducts Eddy/Laurent, throws him in the trunk of his own Mercedes, and takes him to the desert. When Fred opens the trunk, Mr. Eddy lunges for his throat. It looks hopeless until Fred makes a conscious leap of faith. Instead of using both hands to fight off the guy strangling him, he reaches out. Someone puts a knife in his hand, and he slashes the throat of Mr. Eddy.

Mr. Eddy looks up and asks "What do you guys want?" Two men are standing above him. It was the Mystery Man who came to the rescue. The Mystery Man, as keeper of one's permanent record, hands Mr. Eddy a tiny TV. In his dying moments, Mr. Eddy is going to see his life flash before his eyes on a Sony Watchman. We see Mr. Eddy, Andy, and Renée in Andy's living room, watching a porn film in which Renée stars. As the porn morphs into a horror/snuff (?) film, we see Renée and Mr. Eddy with their hands all over each other as they watch. This is the full truth about Mr. Eddy and Renée, now revealed. The Mystery Man takes back the TV.

Mr. Eddy looks at his former friend, who has now betrayed him, and says "You and me, mister. We could really out-ugly them sumbitches, couldn't we?" Then the Mystery Man shoots Mr. Eddy with Fred's gun, a gun stolen by Pete from Andy's house. The Mystery Man whispers something in Fred's ear, imparting some sort of knowledge. We see an extreme closeup of Fred's face. When the camera pulls back, only Fred remains, with the gun thrust in his pants. Fred has gone from being unconscious of the Mystery Man to consciously asking for his help to becoming one with him.

Outwardly directed knowledge can be represented as an arrow of intentionality, a beam of light sweeping back and forth like headlights illuminating the external world. This is represented by Lynch's footage of a nighttime highway. The lost highway is Faustian man rocketing ever forward in the dark, ever searching for power/knowledge, ever fleeing self and responsibility. Thus the Lost Highway Hotel is a suitable location for two hedonists' endless pursuit of pleasure.

Self-knowledge, which turns back to its source, can be represented as a circle. Fred has learned the truth about Renée. But has he gained any truth about himself? Yes. For after merging with the Mystery Man, Fred returns to his house, presses the buzzer, and says "Dick Laurent is dead." The first time he hears these words, it is not his voice. Who said it and why remain mysteries. But by circling back to the beginning, the movie shows us that Fred has achieved self-consciousness.

How is merging with the Mystery Man equivalent to gaining self-consciousness? Fred's obsession with Renée and Pete's obsession with Alice are all about wanting to overcome *mystery*. And not just mundane biographical mysteries but sexual and ultimately metaphysical *otherness*. Faustian Fred's whole problem is that he *rejects* mystery. But in rejecting mystery, he rejects the finitude of the world and knowledge of his own finitude. A world without finitude is a world without boundaries to our knowledge and power.

But that's a grandiose fantasy, and the world tends to push back, creating greater and greater frustration and finally murderous rages. By embracing mystery, Fred embraces both the finitude of the world and his own finitude. By accepting that there are some things we can't know or do, Fred actually gains self-knowledge and self-control, i.e., real freedom.

Whereas the ancients abided by the Stoic maxim, "There are some things we can control and some things we can't," thus they could rest in the face of necessity, moderns follow the maxim "There are some things we can control and some things we can't control *yet*," which means ceaseless striving for knowledge and power.

Does this mean that the Mystery Man was part of Fred all

along? That strikes me as a reductive psychological interpretation. The Mystery Man is real. Fred merely comes to self-consciousness of their relationship. Lynch ends the film as he begins it: rocketing down a nighttime highway to Bowie's "I'm Deranged." But by ending and beginning in the same place, Lynch encloses the restless intentionality of modernist Faustian striving within the circle of classical self-consciousness and self-limitation. So we return to the beginning with a difference.

Fred's achievement of self-consciousness is arguably more important than learning the truth about Renée, but realizing that truth is still the climax of the film, whereas Fred's self-awareness is relegated to the dénouement.

So what is the truth about Renée? How is it possible for Alice to be Renée if Renée is dead? How is it possible for Alice to simply disappear and for the dead Renée to be alive again in the third part of the film? These are the toughest questions for a realist interpretation of *Lost Highway*. Here is my reading. Either Alice and the revenant Renée are dreams/hallucinations — or they are real but defy the laws of nature, i.e., they are supernatural. I wish to suggest the latter.

Fred and Pete are desperate to overcome the gulf, the mystery that lies between them and Renée/Alice. But this gulf can never be bridged, because Renée/Alice is not a natural being. What is she? She's obviously a *femme fatale* of some sort. Hence, during one of Pete's freakouts, Lynch shows us a black widow spider creeping up a wall and moths in their last convulsions around a lightbulb. But if Renée can cheat death, if Alice can simply pop in and out of existence, we are dealing with no ordinary *femme fatale*. She has a supernatural dimension.

Perhaps she's a succubus, a demon in female form, who drags men to their doom. Or, what amounts to basically the same thing, perhaps she is a siren, another supernatural female entity who lures men to their deaths — as made crashingly clear by the music that plays both times Fred and Pete try in vain to sexually break down the distance between them and Renée/Alice, This Mortal Coil's version of Tim Buckley's "Song to the Siren." These are the lyrics, including This Mortal Coil's changes:

On the floating, shapeless oceans
I did all my best to smile,
'Till your singing eyes and fingers
Drew me loving to your isle.

And you sang, "Sail to me, sail to me
Let me enfold you.
Here I am, here I am
Waiting to hold you."

Did I dream you dreamed about me?
Were you here when I was forced out?
Now my foolish boat is leaning
Broken lovelorn on your rocks
For you sing, "Touch me not, touch me not
Come back tomorrow."
O my heart, O my heart
shies from the sorrow.

Well I'm as puzzled as the newborn child
I'm as riddled as the tide:
Should I stand amid the breakers?
Or should I lie with death my bride?
Hear me sing, "Swim to me, swim to me
Let me enfold you
Here I am, Here I am
Waiting to hold you."

In the end, when Fred reappears, standing in the headlights of the car, he is choosing to stand alone in the breakers, with all their terrors, rather than to embrace death, his bride. He embraces life, and by embracing the Mystery Man, he might just get away with it all in the end. Decency does not allow us to describe this as a happy ending, but that is probably Lynch's intent.

Like the human soul itself, *Lost Highway* is deep and dark. It is hard to take its measure. But it remains one of Lynch's most unsettling and rewarding works of art.

The Unz Review, November 19, 2019

THE MANDALORIAN

"Help us, Dave Filoni. You're our only hope."

On December 20th, 2019, J. J. "Death Star" Abrams and Disney Corp. will complete the destruction of the *Star Wars* saga
that many of us have loved since childhood, while raking in
untold millions by cynically exploiting nostalgia for the mythos
they are desecrating. So pass the popcorn, because I'll be right
there, dear readers, to review it for you.

But the Disney-*Star Wars* marriage has not been entirely
fruitless. Seventy-five percent—soon to be eighty percent—of
their movies have been disasters, but *Rogue One* is a pretty
good film.[1]

And now we have *The Mandalorian*, the first live-action *Star
Wars* TV series, which is a collaboration between Dave Filoni—
the producer of the two excellent animated *Star Wars* series, *The
Clone Wars* and *Star Wars: Rebels*—and John Favreau, director of
such movies as *Elf, Iron Man, Iron Man 2, Cowboys and Aliens,*
and the recent remakes of *The Jungle Book* and *The Lion King.*

Both Filoni and Favreau are pretty much creatures of the
modern mass media. They probably believe all the tenets of
political correctness. But in Filoni's animated series, his love of
Star Wars and geek/bro energy pretty much kept the worst ex-
cesses of SJWism at bay. Favreau is the wild card here, for he is
half-Jewish and pretty much a Disney Corporation insider.
Let's hope the Force triumphs over the Schwartz, lest *The Mandalorian* be reduced to another Disney-*Star Wars* farce.

The Mandalorian is basically a Space Western, which is a fantastic tack but also a dangerous one because the bar has been
set impossibly high by Joss Whedon's *Firefly,*[2] which is not just

---

[1] See my review of *Rogue One* in Return of the *Son of Trevor Lynch's
CENSORED Guide to the Movies.*

[2] See my review of *Firefly* in *Son of Trevor Lynch's White Nationalist
Guide to the Movies,* ed. Greg Johnson (San Francisco: Counter-
Currents, 2015).

a Space Western but one of the best science fiction series of all time.

The Space Western is a good fit for the *Star Wars* franchise, because the original *Star Wars* drew upon elements of Akira Kurosawa's *The Hidden Fortress*, and samurai and cowboy films are easily convertible, since the underlying warrior ethos is the same (*Seven Samurai* = *The Magnificent Seven*, *Yojimbo* = *A Fistful of Dollars*).

The title character is the Mandalorian with No Name played by Chilean-born actor Pedro Pascal (Oberyn Martell in *Game of Thrones*), with a low, husky, ultra-cool Clint Eastwood voice. The Mandalorian people were introduced as early as *The Empire Stikes Back*. At least Boba Fett wears Mandalorian armor. But they were developed extensively in Filoni's two animated series as a people with a warrior-aristocratic ethos and a loose, feudal form of government. In the new series, we learn that they suffered greatly under the Empire, were scattered around the galaxy, and have adopted crypsis to survive. (Favreau's fingerprints?) They follow a tradition and an honor code ("This is the way"). Like ronin (masterless samurai) and American gunslingers, they work as freelance wielders of violence (mercenaries, bounty hunters).

The Mandalorian with No Name is a bounty hunter, a profession introduced in the first trilogy. Here we learn that it is governed by a guild with its own code of conduct and technologies (bounty chips, which are basically wanted posters, and tracking fobs).

The first season of *The Mandalorian* has eight episodes, five of which have aired at the time of this writing. The opening three-episode story arc is utterly compelling, introducing the lead characters and their universe, and hooking us in. The story takes place shortly after the fall of the Empire, when law and order have broken down in the galactic rim (the Wild West), and both criminals and bounty hunters thrive.

The Mandalorian with No Name accepts a particularly lucrative unofficial bounty from a former high imperial officer (Werner Herzog, whose accent departs from the British norm for the Empire) guarded by a contingent of Storm Troopers, their armor somewhat worse for wear. After a series of trials, the Mandalorian with No Name captures the bounty, which turns out to be an adorable Yoda baby—meaning a baby of the same species as Yoda. The Mandalorian delivers the baby and collects his bounty. But then he has second thoughts. The baby is strong with the Force, but he is obviously not a criminal, whereas Imperials are clearly up to no good. So the Mandalorian returns, shoots up their base, rescues the baby, and they embark upon some *Lone Wolf and Cub*-style adventures. It is great television.

The fourth episode, however, is a big letdown. The Mandalorian lands on a planet where he promptly gets his ass whooped by a strang, independant, Xena-warrior princess badass wahman. But then he teams up with her to protect Diversity Village (there's even a blonde child) from a band of marauders. It is basically a ripoff of *Seven Samurai*. I say "ripoff" rather than "homage," because *Star Wars* already paid homage to *Seven Samurai* in a much better episode of *The Clone Wars*.

The fifth episode is much better but still rather light stuff, leaning heavily on nostalgia. The Mandalorian visits Tattooine, specifically Mos Eisley, and yes, even that specific cantina, where he asks around for work. He meets a rookie bounty hunter played by Jake Cannavale, who looks exactly like his father Bobby without any visible input from his mother, Jenny Lumet, who boasts of being the daughter of Jewish director Sidney Lumet (*Network*) and the grand-daughter of black(ish) singer Lena Horne. Their bounty is an assassin played by Ming-Na Wen. The highlight of the episode is Amy Sedaris as a ship mechanic with a strong maternal instinct for the little green fellow. The plot is quite predictable.

The Mandalorian is off to an erratic but promising start. I like the basic premise of a Space Western. I like the character of the Mandalorian with No Name. I like the fact that it is set in the *Star Wars* universe. But I especially like how *different* this series is in style from the rest of the *Star Wars* canon.

Lucas's films are extremely busy, and with the development of CGI, they only got busier. The same is true with Filoni's animated series and the Disney movies. *The Mandalorian* is not so busy, which adds a sense of realism when one bumps into a droid or an alien monster. Even the Mos Eisley cantina is not so crowded. The special effects are also quite outstanding.

Another important stylistic change is the music. It is not John Williams, or imitation John Williams. Instead, Swedish composer Ludwig Göransson has created quintessential Space Western music by simply melding Ennio Morricone and electronica. His score is tasteful, tuneful, and catchy, with moments of deep feeling and epic grandeur. He even incorporates Williamsesque themes without ever sounding like Williams. I love John Williams' *Star Wars* scores, but if Williams had scored this series, even he would have used a completely different sound.

I also liked the color palate of the first three episodes, which leaned heavily on chrome, magenta, and dark greens, like something went wrong in the Technicolor lab.

When Death Star Abrams's new technological terror is unleashed this month, I am predicting a huge flop. It may be the last big-screen *Star Wars* we get for a long time to come. So let's hope *The Mandalorian* becomes the great series hinted at in the first three episodes. It is nice to know that at least part of the *Star Wars* saga is in the hands of Dave Filoni, a talented storyteller guided by a genuine love of Lucas's vision and a demonstrated talent for carrying it forward—as opposed to envious mediocrities like Jar Jar Abrams and Rian Johnson, whose transparent aim is to mechanically repeat Lucas's original trilogy, this time as farce.

The Unz Review, December 11, 2019

NETWORK

Written by Paddy Chayefsky and directed by Sidney Lumet, *Network* (1976) is a sardonic, dark-comic satire of America at the very moment that its trajectory of decline became apparent (to perceptive eyes, at least).

Network has an outstanding script and incandescent performances, which were duly recognized. Chayefsky won the Oscar for Best Screenplay. Peter Finch won the Oscar for Best Actor for his portrayal of TV anchorman Howard Beale. Faye Dunaway won Best Actress for playing the reptilian, cynical career girl Diana Christensen. William Holden turns in a warm and credible performance as TV news executive Max Schumacher. Beatrice Straight plays Schumacher's wife Louise. She won Best Supporting Actress for basically one scene, where she denounces her cheating husband, a measure of the talent this movie lavished on even minor roles. Robert Duvall is a convincingly loathsome corporate creep named Frank Hackett. Marlene Warfield is electrifying and utterly hilarious as my favorite character, Laureen Hobbs, who introduces herself as a "bad-ass commie nigger."

Remarkably, *Network* has no film score, and it is not really missed. The script and performances stand on their own. We don't need violins to tell us what to feel.

Network is a serious movie of ideas. What's more, these ideas are objectively Right-wing, even though that was surely not the intention of Chayefsky and Lumet.

Network offers a scathing tableau of the cynicism, corruption, and propagandistic agenda of the mainstream media, one of the cultural citadels of the Left. *Network* offers a particularly dark portrait of a scheming, sociopathic career woman (Faye Dunaway's Diana Christiansen) who sleeps with a married superior.

Network also portrays the sixties generation, then rising into positions of influence, as cynical and decadent—disdaining the morals and basic decency of their parents' generation as mere sentiment. Indeed, *Network* portrays the Marxist-terrorist fringe of the Sixties Left as clownish hysterical thugs who instantly sell out when offered a TV contract.

But *Network*'s Right-wing themes that resonate the most to-day center around the conflict between nationalism and populism on the one hand and globalism and elitism on the other.

The plot of *Network* is fairly simple. Howard Beale (played by Peter Finch) is the evening news anchor at America's fourth television network, UBS, which stands for Union Broadcasting System, but it sounds like "You BS," which means something very different. Beale has been declining personally and professionally for some time, and finally, his old friend Max Schumacher (William Holden), the head of the News Division, was forced to fire him. The two got roaring drunk, and when Howard tells Max he plans to kill himself on the air, Max playfully suggests that it would get a hell of a rating. Then he reels off a whole list of equally lurid shows, which at the time seemed like an obscene parody, but seem like old hat to today's generation, who have easy online access to terrorist and cartel murder videos.

Of course, Max was not serious, and he did not dream that Howard would actually go through with it. But Howard really does go on the air the next day and announce that he will kill himself on live television. The network, of course, cuts the camera. But the stunt garners enormous attention.

Howard begs to go back on the air the next day to say a more dignified goodbye, but when he broadcast goes live, he launches into a tirade about having run out of "bullshit." (This is "You BS," after all.) The broadcast is a hit, but both Max and Howard are canned by the UBS brass, who think gutter language is beneath the dignity of their television network. (Those were the days.)

Enter Faye Dunaway's character Diana Christensen, who is in charge of entertainment programming. She, along with fellow young cynic Frank Hackett (Robert Duvall), persuade UBS to bring back Beale (and Schumacher) for much-needed ratings. (UBS is struggling in fourth rank.) As Diana puts it, "Howard Beale is processed instant God, and right now it looks like he may just go over bigger than Mary Tyler Moore."

What sends Beale into ratings heaven is his famous "Mad as Hell" tirade, which seems even more poignant in the age of Trump and Brexit and at the brink of a global depression.

I don't have to tell you things are bad. Everybody knows things are bad. It's a depression. Everybody's out of work or scared of losing their job. The dollar buys a nickel's worth, banks are going bust, shopkeepers keep a gun under the counter, punks are running wild in the streets, and there's nobody anywhere who seems to know what to do, and there's no end to it.

We know the air's unfit to breathe, and our food is unfit to eat, and we sit and watch our TVs while some local newscaster tells us today, we had fifteen homicides and sixty-three violent crimes, as if that's the way it's supposed to be. We all know things are bad. Worse than bad. They're crazy. It's like everything's going crazy.

So we don't go out anymore. We sit in the house, and slowly the world we live in gets smaller, and all we ask is please, at least leave us alone in our own living rooms. Let me have my toaster and my TV and my hair-dryer and my steel-belted radials, and I won't say anything. Just leave us alone.

Well, I'm not going to leave you alone. I want you to get mad—I don't want you to riot. I don't want you to protest. I don't want you to write your congressmen, because I wouldn't know what to tell you to write. I don't know what to do about the depression and the inflation and the defense budget and the Russians and crime in the street.

All I know is first you've got to get mad. You've got to say: "I'm mad as hell, and I'm not going to take this anymore. I'm a human being, goddammit. My life has value." So I want you to get up now. I want you to get out of your chairs and go to the window. Right now. I want you to go to the window, open it, and stick your head out and yell. I want you to yell: "I'm mad as hell, and I'm not going to take this anymore!"—Get up from your chairs. Go to the window. Open it. Stick your head out and yell and keep yelling . . .

There is a deep political truth here. Before we can have any political change at all, we need to get angry. But to get angry, we need to be assertive. And to be assertive, we require self-esteem. It is an amazingly dramatic sequence. If you don't find it stirring, check your pulse, because you might be dead.

In her bid to take over Beale's show, Diana begins an affair with Max Schumacher, who is old enough to be her father and married to boot. Max, however, is disgusted by the desire to exploit Howard Beale, who has obviously gone insane. (Howard shows clear signs of mania.) Eventually, however, Christensen and Hackett team up to fire Schumacher. Then Christensen turns the UBS news program into *The Howard Beale Show*, a grotesque variety program featuring Howard as "The Mad Prophet of the Airwaves."

Diana argues that Howard is popular because he is "articulating the popular rage." She wants a whole new slate of angry, anti-establishment programming. Diana, mind you, doesn't want to *change* society to make people *less angry*. She simply wants to exploit popular discontent and channel it into ratings and money. She wants to make it into a commodity. This is brought home brilliantly in Howard's first speech on *The Howard Beale Show*.

> Edward George Ruddy died today! Edward George Ruddy was the Chairman of the Board of the Union Broadcasting Systems — and woe is us if it ever falls in the hands of the wrong people. And that's why woe is us that Edward George Ruddy died. Because this network is now in the hands of CC&A, the Communications Corporation of America.
>
> We've got a new Chairman of the Board, a man named Frank Hackett, now sitting in Mr. Ruddy's office on the twentieth floor. And when the twelfth-largest company in the world controls the most awesome goddamned propaganda force in the whole godless world, who knows what shit will be peddled for truth on this tube?
>
> So, listen to me! Television is not the truth! Television is a goddamned amusement park; that's what television is! Television is a circus, a carnival, a traveling troupe of acrobats and story-tellers, singers and dancers, jugglers,

side-show freaks, lion-tamers, and football players. We're in the boredom-killing business! If you want truth, go to God, go to your guru, go to yourself because that's the only place you'll ever find any real truth!

But, man, you're never going to get any truth from us. We'll tell you anything you want to hear. We lie like hell! We'll tell you Kojak always gets the killer, and nobody ever gets cancer in Archie Bunker's house. And no matter how much trouble the hero is in, don't worry: just look at your watch—at the end of the hour, he's going to win. We'll tell you any shit you want to hear!

We deal in illusion, man! None of it's true! But you people sit there—all of you—day after day, night after night, all ages, colors, creeds—we're all you know. You're beginning to believe this illusion we're spinning here. You're beginning to think the tube is reality, and your own lives are unreal. You do whatever the tube tells you. You dress like the tube, you eat like the tube, you raise your children like the tube, you think like the tube.

This is mass madness, you maniacs! In God's name, you people are the real thing! We're the illusions! So turn off this goddamn set! Turn it off right now! Turn it off, and leave it off. Turn it off right now, right in the middle of this very sentence I'm speaking now—

Then Howard collapses in a dead faint. The camera dollies forward and looms up over him. Cue music. Cue applause. The audience goes wild. Thus television turns a critique of television into more television. And, arguably, Chayefsky and Lumet are turning their own critique of the media into more media. A critique of the media becomes just another media experience, which might resonate for a bit but is eventually ousted by yet another media experience. Thus the critical impetus never meshes with anything real; it poses no threat to the existing system.

Howard Beale is like the philosopher in Plato's Allegory of the Cave. He has climbed out of the world of shadows and seen the truth of things. But once he returns to the cave, he is not rejected by the cave-dwellers but instead embraced and turned into one of the dancing shadows that bemuse them.

Howard's speech centers around an important distinction between friendship and flattery. A friend tells you what you *need* to hear, namely the truth, whereas a flatterer tells you what you *want* to hear. Any truth we don't want to hear is basically bad news. But we need to hear bad news. We need to know about problems if we are to overcome them. Bad news about ourselves is usually about personal failings and inadequacies. Friends force us to confront them, which is a necessary condition of growth. Television, however, is a flatterer, not a friend. It dispenses comforting illusions that, at best, promote complacency, but usually promote corruption.

Another important distinction is *edification* versus *pandering*. To edify means to build up: to build up a person's knowledge, character, tastes, and ultimately his individuality. To pander is to stoop down, to cater to a person's existing knowledge, character, and tastes, no matter how inadequate and immature.

Human beings are not blank slates, but we are born ignorant, amoral, crude, fearful, and weak. As Thomas Sowell once put it, every new generation is an invasion of barbarians. We have to civilize them, or civilization will perish. The purpose of education and high culture is to edify: to turn barbarians into civilized men.

The culture industry, however, has the diametrically opposite agenda. Its goal is to make money by appealing to people's "given preferences": the given preferences of barbarians. No matter how ignorant, tasteless, immoral, or undifferentiated you may be, you will always find people who will cater to your preferences because they want to separate you from your money.

But the culture industry does not just breed complacency. It also encourages corruption. Having a developed personality—including tastes and morals—means that certain things are beneath you. There are things you will not do, things you will not look at or listen to, things you will not buy. Thus, to sell us more things, the culture industry has to break down the inhibitions of morality and taste that forbid certain pleasures. Edification breeds discrimination. The culture industry wants us to be less discriminating, because that means we are willing to consume more. Thus the culture industry has an incentive to dissolve all standards of morals and taste in the acid of cynicism. Civilization can't compete with barbarism in the "free market," which means that capitalism will slowly liquidate civilization, unless education and high culture are preserved from market forces.

Howard's commodified discontent is a hit. It entertains all and threatens none. The big lines kept going up. But then Howard made a speech that actually changed something, something big, something *important*:

All right, listen to me! Listen carefully! This is your goddamn life I'm talking about today! In this country, when one company takes over another company, they simply buy up a controlling share of the stock. But first, they have to file notice with the government. That's how CC&A—the Communications Corporation of America— bought up the company that owns this network. And now somebody's buying up CC&A! Some company named Western World Funding Corporation is buying up CC&A! They filed their notice this morning!

Well, just who the hell is Western World Funding Corporation? It's a consortium of banks and insurance companies who are not buying CC&A for themselves but as agents for somebody else! Well, who's this somebody else? They won't tell you! They won't tell you, they won't tell the Senate, they won't tell the SEC, the FCC, the Justice Department, they won't tell anybody! They say it's none of our business! The hell it ain't!

Well, I'll tell you who they're buying CC&A for. They're buying it for the Saudi-Arabian Investment Corporation! They're buying it for the Arabs! . . . We know the Arabs control more than sixteen billion dollars in this country! They own a chunk of Fifth Avenue, twenty downtown pieces of Boston, a part of the port of New Orleans, an industrial park in Salt Lake City. They own big hunks of the Atlanta Hilton, the Arizona Land and Cattle Company, the Security National Bank in California, the Bank of the Commonwealth in Detroit! They control AR-

AMCO, so that puts them into Exxon, Texaco, and Mobil oil! They're all over—New Jersey, Louisville, St. Louis, Missouri! And that's only what we know about! There's a hell of a lot more we don't know about because all those Arab petro-dollars are washed through Switzerland and Canada and the biggest banks in this country! . . . And there's not a single law on the books to stop them!

There's only one thing that can stop them—you! So I want you to get up now. I want you to get out of your chairs and go to the phone. Right now. I want you to go to your phone or get in your car and drive into the Western Union office in town. I want everybody listening to me to get up right now and send a telegram to the White House. By midnight tonight I want a million telegrams in the White House! I want them wading knee-deep in telegrams at the White House! Get up! Right now! And send President Ford a telegram saying: "I'm mad as hell, and I'm not going to take this anymore! I don't want the banks selling my country to the Arabs! I want this CC&A deal stopped now!"

This is pure red-meat national populism. From a nationalist point of view, it makes no sense to allow crucial industries to fall into the hands of foreign powers, especially global rivals. For instance, the coronavirus crisis has brought home the folly of outsourcing most of our pharmaceutical and medical supply manufacturing to China. Of course, our global business elites see things differently, which is where populism comes in. It is the American masses who have to rise up, shove aside the elites, and mobilize the government to intervene in the economy in the national interest.

Howard's speech is a great success. Within hours, the White House was awash in millions of telegrams—six million, to be precise—and the Saudi acquisition of CC&A was halted. It was a glorious outpouring of democracy.

But the head of CC&A, Arthur Jensen (played by Ned Beatty), is not amused. CC&A is deep in debt, and they need the Saudi money badly. So Mr. Jensen calls Howard into this office, with the goal of selling him on globalism rather than national-ism. After ushering him into the CC&A boardroom with the words "Valhalla, Mr. Beale," Jensen closes the curtains and sets the stage for a Mephistophelean harangue:

You have meddled with the primal forces of nature, Mr. Beale, and I won't have it, is that clear?! You think you have merely stopped a business deal—that is not the case! The Arabs have taken billions of dollars out of this coun-try, and now they must put it back. It is ebb and flow, tidal gravity, it is ecological balance! You are an old man who thinks in terms of nations and peoples. There are no na-tions! There are no peoples! There are no Russians. There are no Arabs! There are no Third Worlds! There is no West! There is only one holistic system of systems, one vast and immane, interwoven, interacting, multi-variate, multi-national dominion of dollars! Petro-dollars, electro-dollars, multi-dollars! Reichsmarks, rubles, rin, pounds, and shekels! It is the international system of currency that determines the totality of life on this planet! That is the natural order of things today! That is the atomic, subatom-ic, and galactic structure of things today! And you have meddled with the primal forces of nature, and you will atone!

Am I getting through to you, Mr. Beale? You get up on your little twenty-one-inch screen, and howl about Ameri-ca and democracy. There is no America. There is no de-mocracy. There is only IBM and ITT and AT&T and Dupont, Dow, Union Carbide, and Exxon. Those are the nations of the world today. What do you think the Rus-sians talk about in their councils of state—Karl Marx? They pull out their linear programming charts, statistical decision theories, and minimax solutions and compute the price-cost probabilities of their transactions and invest-ments just like we do.

We no longer live in a world of nations and ideologies, Mr. Beale. The world is a college of corporations, inexora-bly determined by the immutable by-laws of business. The world is a business, Mr. Beale. It has been since man crawled out of the slime, and our children, Mr. Beale, will live to see that perfect world in which there is no war and famine, oppression and brutality—one vast and ecumenical holding company, for whom all men will work to serve a common profit, in which all men will hold a share of stock, all necessities provided, all anxieties tranquilized, all boredom amused. And I have chosen you, Mr. Beale, to preach this evangel.

Howard is thunderstruck: "I have seen the face of God!" To which Jensen replies, "You just might be right, Mr. Beale." It is a brilliant scene, but Beatty's delivery verges on parody.

Jensen's speech is a stunning encapsulation of modern political thought and its ultimate telos: what Alexandre Kojève called the "end of history" in a "universal homogeneous state." Modern political philosophy seeks to build a stable social and political order on the broad, low foundation of something shared by all men, namely desire: desire for the necessities of life, desire for comfort and security, desire for a long, healthy life and a peaceful death in the midst of plenty, rather than a short life, ending in want or violence.

To secure this desire-based social order, competing foundations must be eliminated. Since all men share the same basic desires, the modern state is, in principle, global. Therefore, the existence of distinct nations and the patriotic sentiments that dispose us to prefer our homelands to strange lands must be eliminated. Thus Jensen dismisses nationalism as a regressive folly of old men. The world is also divided by ideologies, like Marxism. Jensen dismisses those as well. If mankind is not divided by ideologies or national identities, we will have peace, so we can get down to the business of abolishing want and satisfying desire— business like the CC&A deal with the Saudis.

However, when Howard goes back on the air to preach Mr. Jensen's vision of global capitalist utopia, he paints it in depressingly dystopian tones, for he sees that a world devoted solely to creature comforts and lacking identity, patriotism, and principles is a world without passion, nobility, and soul-expanding sentiments. It is also a world of self-indulgence, not self-edification. So it is a world without the tastes, standards, and strength of character necessary to resist the crowd. Thus it is also a world without individuality. Hence: "It's the individual that's finished. It's the single, solitary human being who's finished. It's every single one of you out there who's finished. Because this is no longer a nation of independent individuals. This is a nation of two hundred odd million transistorized, deodorized, whiter-than-white, steel-belted bodies, totally unnecessary as human beings and as replaceable as piston rods."

The End of History ushers in the age of the Last Man.

This perversely bleak utopia resembles Kojève's description of the universal homogeneous post-historical state as a realm of dehumanization, for desires don't set us apart from the animals, thus a society in which desire is sovereign and reason and sentiments are subordinate puts the distinctly human in service of the subhuman. It is a society of clever animals, not men. Such a depiction of utopia can only lead to its rejection, which was Kojève's intent, as I argue in my lecture "Alexandre Kojève and the End of History."[1]

Howard's depressive utopianism could only provoke revulsion. People started changing the channel, and *The Howard Beale Show* went into steep decline. Mr. Jensen, however, was adamant that Howard remain on the air and on message, regardless of the consequences. Thus Christensen, Hackett, and others at the network hatch a plot to have Beale assassinated, on air.

At this point, we get the payoff for the movie's funniest subplot: Christensen's plan to create a one-hour weekly dramatic series called *The Mao Tse-Tung Hour*, based on the real-life activities of a terrorist group called the Ecumenical Liberation Army (obviously patterned on the Symbionese Liberation Army). Christiansen gives the Communist Party complete control of the ideological content of the show. They can stick any Marxist propaganda they want on television as long as the show makes money, which pretty much sums up television today.

Christiansen's contact with the guerrillas is Laureen Hobbs

---

[1] In Greg Johnson, *From Plato to Postmodernism* (San Francisco: Counter-Currents, 2019).

(who is supposed to remind us of Angela Davis). Hobbs' transformation from pedantically rattling off Marxist duck-speak to hysterically ranting about contracts is absolutely priceless. Actress Marlene Warfield somehow manages to make dialogue like this hilarious:

> Don't fuck with my distribution costs! I'm getting a lousy two-fifteen per segment, and I'm already deficiting twenty-five grand a week with Metro. I'm paying William Morris ten percent off the top! . . . I'm paying Metro twenty percent of all foreign and Canadian distribution, and that's after recoupment! The Communist Party's not going to see a nickel out of this goddam show until we go into syndication!

The name Hobbs is supposed to call to mind Thomas Hobbes, the theorist of dog-eat-dog capitalism, though nobody, in truth, outdoes Marxists in cannibalism. Since Beale's show is in the slot before *The Mao Tse-Tung Hour* and dragging down its ratings, Hobbs agrees to have the Ecumenicals assassinate Howard Beale. It'll be a great two-hour opener for the new season!

The scene in which the network executives decide to murder Howard Beale is quite chilling. Every one of them is a sociopath. Moral considerations never creep in at all.

When the Ecumenicals kill Howard on live television, again the camera dollies forward and looms up over the kill, transmuting it into an image. Then we cut to four television screens, one tuned to each of the four networks. We simultaneously see and hear the coverage of the shooting as well as various commercials. Then the narrator proclaims over the cacophony: "This was the story of Howard Beale, the first known instance of a man who was killed because he had lousy ratings." As far as I know, television networks still do not resort to assassinations, but *Network* was dead right about the plunge of network television into gutter depravity and crude Left-wing agitprop.

Network offers a feast of truth on the media, popular culture, capitalism, feminism, Leftism, nationalism, populism, globalization, and decadence. *Network* is absolutely right that we need to worry about who controls the mass media, especially hostile aliens. But when *Network* raises the alarm about foreign influence on the American media, it names the wrong tribe of Semites.

Indeed, although the American television and movie industries are famously Jewish, *Network* portrays UBS as almost entirely non-Jewish. In the context of a TV network, a name like Max Schumacher sounds Jewish, but William Holden was not Jewish and neither is his portrayal of Schumacher. Of course, if Schumacher is supposed to be Jewish, we also have to note that he is the most decent character in the bunch. A minor character—little more than an extra—is named Barbara Schlesinger, a likely Jewish name, but she is played by Conchata Ferrell, who is not Jewish. Jews, however, are not confined to minor roles in the American media.

Everybody else at UBS is conspicuously white. Howard Beale is an English name, and Peter Finch, who played him, was of Anglo-Scottish ancestry. The main villains are named Christensen and Jensen, both Scandinavian names, and Hackett, an English name with Scandinavian roots. (Another corporate sociopath is named Amundsen in the script.) This is such a neat inversion of the truth that it cannot be accidental.

Indeed, the main reason there are so few Jews in front of the cameras in *Network* is that the main people behind the camera, writer Paddy Chayefsky and director Sidney Lumet, were both Jewish. One has to give them credit for all the truths that they did put on screen, but it was clearly dishonest of them to omit their own ethnic group's presiding role in the corruption and degeneracy of American television.

There's a lesson in that, too.

The Unz Review, May 13, 2020

ONCE UPON A TIME IN HOLLYWOOD

Some of my best reviews are about Quentin Tarantino, but this won't be one of them. Tarantino has gone from a director I loved (see my essay on *Pulp Fiction*), to a director I loved to hate (see my reviews of *Kill Bill I* and *Inglourious Basterds*), to a director I just hated (*Django Unchained*), to a director I just ignored.[1]

Tarantino's only great movie is *Pulp Fiction*, and at this point it is safe to declare that one a fluke. The rest of his works range from the distasteful (*Reservoir Dogs*), to amiable piffle (*Jackie Brown*), to nihilistic deconstruction (the *Kill Bill* movies), to genocidal—although self-deconstructing—anti-white Jewish wet dreams (*Basterds*), to genocidal anti-white black wet dreams (*Django*), to a movie I never bothered to see (*The Hateful Eight*).

And that brings us to Tarantino's ninth feature film, *Once Upon a Time in Hollywood*. I planned to skip this one too, but the reviews, both positive and negative, intrigued me, and quite to my surprise, I really liked this film.

Once Upon a Time in Hollywood does not touch on deep moral themes like *Pulp Fiction*, but it is better than the rest of Tarantino's films. It is not distasteful in the ways we have come to expect from him. It is not especially violent, gross, obscene, or anti-white. Basically, it is another *Jackie Brown*—well-crafted, likeable, and not particularly offensive. I am inclined to be grudging with superlatives in Tarantino's case, but *Once Upon a Time in Hollywood* is definitely his funniest film, and although he might cringe to hear it, it is also his most morally wholesome and satisfying story.

Once Upon a Time in Hollywood is set in Hollywood in 1969. It tells the story of two buddies, Rick Dalton (Leonardo Di Caprio), who stars in TV cowboy dramas, and his stunt double Cliff Booth (Brad Pitt). Rick's attempt to transition from TV into mov-

---

[1] See my reviews of *Pulp Fiction*, *Kill Bill: Vol. I*, *Inglourious Basterds*, and *Django Unchained* in *Trevor Lynch's White Nationalist Guide to the Movies*.

ies has failed, his series *Bounty Law* has been canceled, and he is now playing guest heavies in TV series, drinking a lot, and dreaming of restarting his career. Rick has lost his driver's license due to DUIs, so Cliff is now his driver and sidekick.

The main Dalton-Booth plotline, which meanders along at a rather leisurely pace, is intercut with two subplots, one about Cliff Booth meeting a member of the Manson "family" and visiting the Spahn Ranch, where they are squatting, to check in on its owner, George Spahn, whom Booth had met some years before while filming at his property. The other subplot is about Dalton's new neighbor, Sharon Tate (Margot Robbie), following her through her life in Hollywood.

Dalton, with the help of his loyal friend Booth, manages to pull out of his career slump by hard work, getting a grip on his drinking, and just general decency. He ends up in Italy, starring in three Westerns and a Eurospy romp, returning married to an Italian starlet, with fifteen pounds of pasta added to his frame.

He arrives home just in time to team up with Cliff and bring about a fairy-tale happy ending to one of Hollywood's most gruesome true stories, which makes sense of the *Once Upon a Time . . .* title, which I thought was an allusion to Sergio Leone, but that was just a clever diversion.

Once Upon a Time in Hollywood is a geeky, ultra-detailed nostalgia fest, filled with vintage cars and clothes, period songs and advertisements, and a fat volume's worth of TV, movie, and pop-culture trivia. The movie brims with actual historical characters, all of them well-cast and well-realized. The fictional characters are rich pastiches of still other historical characters. The clips and posters for fictional movies and TV shows are brilliantly realistic and often hilarious parodies. It's all very self-indulgent, but one has to admire Tarantino's immense energy, attention to detail, and devotion to historical authenticity.

But this poses a problem for today's SJW critics. Windbag Richard Brody at *The New Yorker* condemns the film as "obscenely regressive" and "ridiculously white." (I find *The New Yorker* obscenely progressive and ridiculously Jewish, but that's a topic for another day.) Brody is silent about the fact that some of these obscenely white characters and actors are Jewish, although in other contexts, of course, Jews are "diverse."

Once Upon a Time is Hollywood is all about historical exactness and verisimilitude. Hollywood in 1969 was an overwhelmingly white and Jewish town. It was swarming with liberals, hippies, and downright communists, but by today's PC-standards, such people seem like ultra-reactionaries.

But being true to the times is no defense in an industry that now peoples medieval and Elizabethan England with Negroes. It would have been a complete violation of Tarantino's commitment to historical accuracy to black up the cast, but artistic integrity means nothing compared to the imperative of The Great Replacement. I am sure Richard Brody would have no problem with Samuel L. Jackson playing Roman Polanski. Lord knows I wouldn't.

Tarantino has always made prigs squirm by putting racial epithets on the screen. Here, Rick Dalton sneers about "beaners," and Cliff Booth admonishes Dalton not to cry in front of Mexicans. They also refer constantly to dirty "hippies." In one of the funniest scenes in the film, Bruce Lee pretentiously holds forth on the set of *The Green Hornet* until Booth has enough, calls his bullshit, and then humiliates him in a fight.

Feminists actually pushed up their problem glasses, scrunched up their faces, and counted the lines spoken by women. They are not amused.

Dalton and Booth, moreover, are two-fisted "paleomasculine" heroes, brimming with strength, mastery, honor, and camaraderie. And at the end, the excessive TV and movie violence that moralists love to condemn is shown to be cathartic, redemptive, and downright hilarious.

Tarantino hasn't become a reactionary, of course. He's still a self-hating white shitlib. But he's also an artist with his own stubbornly-held vision, and he and the leading edge of the Left *Zeitgeist* have parted ways.

Once Upon a Time in Hollywood is full of Tarantino trademarks: a complex narrative structure, quirky characters and dialogue, a leisurely pace, banal foot fetishism, and a love of putting complex and intelligent dialogue in the mouths of Negroes. Although there are no Negroes in this film, so Tarantino accomplishes the same comic effect with an eight-year-old white girl. The performances by DiCaprio and Pitt are by turns affable and riveting. The scenes at the Spahn Ranch are utterly suspenseful and creepy, the closest Tarantino has come to creating a zombie flick.

I highly recommend this film, simply as well-crafted grown-up entertainment that does not go out of its way to insult the intelligence, race, or moral sensibilities of its overwhelmingly white audience.

The Unz Review, August 31, 2019

QUIZ SHOW

Robert Redford's 1994 film *Quiz Show* tells the story of the *Twenty-One* game show scandal of the late 1950s. Featuring a superbly literate and psychologically subtle script and outstanding performances by Ralph Fiennes, Paul Scofield, John Turturro, and Rob Morrow, *Quiz Show* dramatizes important moral issues and explores the corrupting influence of television in American life.

Quiz Show was a critical success but a box office bomb. To me, however, the most remarkable thing about *Quiz Show* is that it was ever made at all. For *Quiz Show* is not just a nostalgic portrayal of the self-confident, normatively white America of the 1950s, it is also a remarkably acute meditation on the role that television played in the fall of America's WASP elite and the rise of today's Jewish hegemony.

There are four principal Jewish characters in *Quiz Show*. Dick Goodwin (played by Rob Morrow) is an ambitious Harvard-educated lawyer whose memoir, *Remembering America: A Voice from the Sixties*, is the basis of the story. Herb Stempel (played by John Turturro) is a cringe-inducing, high-strung, quasi-autistic savant from Queens who became famous for his six-week winning streak on the game show *Twenty-One*, produced by Dan Enright (born Ehrenreich) and Albert Freedman. It turned out that the producers of *Twenty-One* rigged the show because champions with winning streaks attracted larger audiences and sold more Geritol.

When Stempel's ratings plateaued, Martin Rittenholm from Geritol (Martin Scorsese in a wonderful minor role) asked for a new champion.

Enter Charles Van Doren (played by Ralph Fiennes), the scion of America's white intellectual elite. Van Doren was the son of Pulitzer Prize-winning poet, critic, and Columbia professor Mark Van Doren and novelist Dorothy Van Doren. He was a nephew of Pulitzer Prize-winning biographer Carl Van Doren. Charles Van Doren earned a B.A. in Liberal Arts from St. John's College in Annapolis, an M.A. in astrophysics from Columbia

University, and a Ph.D. in English, also from Columbia. He also studied at Cambridge. At the time of the film, he was teaching English literature at Columbia.

The film offers an affectionate portrayal of Charles Van Doren's world. At a birthday party for his father Mark Van Doren (wonderfully played by Paul Scofield), the elder and younger Van Dorens carry on their conversation in quotes from Shakespeare and banter with Thomas Merton and Edmund "Bunny" Wilson. (The warm relationship between Charles Van Doren and his father is one of the best aspects of the movie.)

When Van Doren tries out for another Enright and Freedman quiz show, *Tic-Tac-Dough*, they steer him toward *Twenty-One*. When they propose giving him the answers, he rejects it as dishonest. But when Van Doren is on live TV, they give him a question that he had correctly answered in the tryouts. Stempel, meanwhile, takes a dive by giving the wrong answer to an easy question, and Van Doren is crowned the new champion. Van Doren objects to being, in effect, tricked into taking part in a rigged game, but Enright and Freedman salve his conscience by telling him that he is promoting higher educational standards to American schoolchildren. The money also helps.

Enright and Freedman are a pair of oily operators, but giving people answers was the least of their sins. After all, they had to give contestants the answers only because the questions were incredibly difficult. But seeing people answer difficult questions actually encouraged viewers to take education more seriously. Furthermore, as the suave gentleman from Geritol, Martin Scorsese, points out, if game shows can't manage the rise and fall of champions by feeding them answers or demanding they take falls, they can accomplish the same effect by simply making the questions easier, i.e., by lowering standards—with its predictable effect on the public mind—which is exactly what they did. Besides, nobody believes that in a magic act, the lady is actually sawed in two. The point is to entertain. And *Twenty-One* was not just entertaining, it was *edifying*.

Unfortunately, when Enright and Freedman made Herb Stempel take a dive, the unstoppable force of Jewish neuroticism crashed into the immovable object of Jewish unscrupulousness, and the result was a huge explosion. The highly neurotic Stempel was humiliated by being forced to fail on an easy question. He also lost his winnings in a bookie's "investment" scheme. Stempel threatened to expose Enright unless he got him back on TV. Enright tried to placate him and string him along with empty promises, carefully laying the foundation for discrediting him as insane by taping his rants and offering him free visits to a psychiatrist. Finally rejected, a vengeful Stempel went to a District Attorney, who convened a grand jury. But Enright managed to get the finding sealed.

The whole thing would have blown over rather than up were it not for the catalyzing agent of Jewish ambition, in the form of Dick Goodwin, trying to work his way out of a minor staff position in the House Committee for Legislative Oversight. Goodwin went to New York and eventually unraveled Enright and Freedman's whole scheme. A congressional hearing was called. Stempel finally returned to the spotlight he so craved and told his story. The president of NBC and the head of Geritol denied any knowledge of the fix and blamed Enright and Freedman. Enright and Freedman accepted full responsibility. Charles Van Doren, however, out of a typically white surfeit of conscience, gave an eloquent confession.

None of the people who lied faced any negative consequences. NBC and Geritol continued to rack up millions. Enright merely laid low for a few years then returned to the game show business where he too made millions. Freedman ended up working for *Penthouse* magazine.

Goodwin, who died in 2018, went on to be a speechwriter and an aide to presidents John Kennedy and Lyndon Johnson and also to senator Robert Kennedy. (His second wife, Doris Kearns Goodwin, is a presidential biographer plagued with charges of plagiarism.) Stempel went to college and ended up working for the New York Transportation Department. He still lives in Queens.

Charles Van Doren was the only person in the whole sordid affair to face negative consequences for his testimony, solely because he told the truth. After his run on *Twenty-One*, NBC had hired him for *The Today Show*. After his testimony, he was fired and forced to resign from his instructorship at Columbia. When caught in a perfect storm of Jewish unscrupulousness, neurosis, and ambition, his Aryan sense of honor was his undoing. Thus the story of Charles Van Doren can be seen as the epitome of the fall of the WASP ruling class and the rise of our hostile Jewish elite.

Quiz Show is surprisingly frank about Jewish ethnic hostility toward founding stock Americans. Dick Goodwin is portrayed as a vulgar *arriviste*. In the opening scene, he chomps a cigar while being shown an expensive convertible by an unctuous salesman. Later, when Charles Van Doren and his father treat him to lunch at the Athenaeum Club, his table manners are atrocious. He also remarks on the absence of Jews at the club. He bristles when people call him Mr. Goldwyn rather than Mr. Goodwin. Yet, for all that, he has a genuine admiration for the intellect, manners, and lifestyle of the Van Dorens—to the point that his shrewish Jewish first wife accuses him of being "the Uncle Tom of the Jews."

Stempel has unalloyed hostility to Van Doren, referring to him as an "uncircumcised prick." When Stempel realizes Goodwin is Jewish (as if there could have been any doubt), he asks how a guy like him could have gotten into Harvard. (Now we wonder how the descendants of the people who founded Harvard can get into Harvard.)

I don't know how closely the script hews to Goodwin's book, but I imagine such sentiments only made it into the film as part of a larger Jewish triumphalist narrative. If so, it strikes me as a miscalculation, because I can't imagine that such sentiments sit well with normal white moviegoers. This is why I include *Quiz Show* in my list of Goebbels Award winners, namely mainstream Hollywood films that Joseph Goebbels would have released without changing a frame.

I highly recommend *Quiz Show* to racially conscious whites. It is a beautifully realized portrait of the America that was ours, and it contains a surprising amount of truth about how we allowed it to be taken away from us, and by whom.

RICHARD JEWELL

2019 was the year of the "frustrated-white-loser-living-at-home-with-his-mom" movie. First there was Todd Phillips' *Joker*, an origin story of Batman's most memorable nemesis, starring Joaquin Phoenix as the clown himself. Then came Clint Eastwood's *Richard Jewell*, the true story of a Georgia security guard who discovered the Centennial Olympic Park bomb in 1996.

Jewell alerted the police, insisted they follow protocol when they were initially dismissive, and evacuated people from the area before the explosion, which killed two and injured more than 100. Jewell's vigilance and conscientiousness saved many lives. He was hailed as a hero. Then he was framed as a suspect by the FBI and the media and hounded mercilessly. Why? Because he fit "the profile" of a mad bomber: a "frustrated white male" who lived at home with his mother.

Both Leftists and the Alt Right tried to meme Phoenix's Joker into a symbol of white male rage and alienation. They did this long before the movie came out, based largely on hearsay, and many on the Right kept flogging this meme even after the movie belied it. For Phoenix's Joker is not a charismatic criminal mastermind. He's just a pathetic, vacant, mentally ill loser. Nobody would want to identify with him, not even pathetic, vacant, mentally ill losers.

Beyond that, there's nothing especially insightful about *Joker's* diagnosis of the modern malaise. Heartless rich people are cutting government programs, and Patrick Batemans are terrorizing people on the subway. It is true that during the Reagan years, thousands of mental patients ended up homeless, but most of *Joker's* vision of dystopia is just unimaginative Bolshevik boilerplate. Nor does *Joker* offer any positive lessons for white men to overcome their alienation and rage. *Joker* isn't the worst movie I saw in 2019 — that prize goes to *Star Wars: The Rise of Skywalker* — but it is certainly the most disappointing.

Richard Jewell is one of the best movies of 2019, with a brilliant script, excellent performances, and an important message. It is infinitely superior to *Joker* because it shows the true cause of white male rage and alienation. Richard Jewell is not a nutcase dumped into the gutter by Reaganism. He's simply an ordinary white man who fit "the profile." No, not the FBI profile, the *hostile elite* profile. Richard Jewell is the kind of white man that the American system increasingly blames for everything that is wrong with our society—while depending upon these men to keep the society going. It's a profile authored by people who regard white Americans as contemptible aliens. It is propagated through a thousand movies, TV shows, books, songs, and bits of journalism.

Richard Jewell is a fat, white, Christian, heterosexual, Georgia redneck with a heavy Southern accent. He likes guns and hunting, drives a pickup truck, believes in the American system, looks up to authority—especially men in uniforms—and wants a career in law enforcement, because he wants to protect people. He's kind-hearted, observant, attentive to the needs of others, and obviously desires to be liked. These are pro-social virtues, but he's also somewhat pathetic. Assholes and bullies regard him as an easy target. Yet he doesn't seem to be especially bitter, although he has good cause to be.

I vividly remember the Richard Jewell case. When he was being hailed as a hero in the media, they were obviously pained by the fact that he looked like a redneck from central casting. And when they turned on him, it was with an obvious relief and relish, because he looked like the kind of guy they spend all their time sniggering at and vilifying anyway.

You know very well that if even one or two of Jewell's traits had been altered—if he were thin, or female, or black, or gay, or a Yankee—the whole thing would have played out very differently. But Richard Jewell was *everything* the hostile elite loved to hate. And they almost lynched him for it.

In the opening scenes of the movie, Jewell (Paul Walter Hauser in his breakout role) is an office supply clerk in a law firm who strikes up an unlikely friendship with a young lawyer named Watson Bryant (Sam Rockwell). Bryant is presented as a cocky Chad. Jewell is presented as observant to the point of nosiness and obsequious to the point that we feel embarrassed for him.

Viewers with modern Leftist prejudices immediately dislike both men. Bryant is "toxically masculine," and Jewell has "low self-esteem." But the film then brilliantly shows that Jewell's sharp eyes and punctilious desire to please others are what allows him to save lives, and Bryant's cockiness is what allows him to save Jewell.

Richard Jewell offers a scathing portrait of two of the hostile elite's enforcement arms: the mainstream media and the FBI, personified by *Atlanta Journal-Constitution* reporter Kathy Scruggs (played by Olivia Wilde) and FBI agent Tom Shaw (a fictional character played by Jon Hamm). Both are arrogant, ambitious, manipulative, and dishonest—and the system rewards them for this behavior. They team up to frame Richard Jewell as a terrorist and ruin his life because they are utterly indifferent to truth and see him as a perfect patsy, for he "fits the profile" of the system's number one enemy. He personifies the America they want to destroy. They really are "enemies of the people," and it really is them or us.

It was perfectly reasonable for the FBI to look into Jewell. The bomber, Eric Rudolph, really was a frustrated white male. People really do plant bombs for attention. They also fake hate crimes for attention and even make their own children sick. And Jewell's record could be taken to show signs of this sort of malignant narcissism. He was fired as a sheriff's deputy and a campus security officer for overstepping his authority, which could be taken for self-importance although it is probably just the same over-zealousness that made him a hero in the Olympic Park bombing, and once Jewell was in the media spotlight, he was humble and gracious, not self-aggrandizing.

But the FBI did not just look into Jewell. They tried to frame him. What's more, they tried to use his patriotism, respect for authority, and desire to do good to destroy him. Eastwood is brilliant to hone in on this point again and again. It is a lesson that all white people need to learn.

This is not our country anymore. It is not our government. It is not our FBI. It is not our media. All of these are in the hands of our enemies. All the authoritative institutions of our society have been hollowed out, taken over, and repurposed to our dispossession and destruction. And one of the chief tools this system uses to destroy us is our own patriotism and naïve trust in the people who despise us. *Richard Jewell* repeatedly hammers home this moral obscenity.

This is one of the most important lessons we can teach, for when people cease to trust the media and the government—when they see them as a hostile elite, as enemies of the people—that is the beginning of populism. We have come a long way since 1996.

Many decent white people cringe when they look at Richard Jewell. Part of that reaction is healthy, because fat people are gross and unhealthy. Poor Richard Jewell died at the age of 44 from diabetes and heart disease. The stress of being framed as Public Enemy Number One surely did not help. I wish that Jewell had a longer, healthier life, and I hope that Paul Walter Hauser pulls a Chris Pratt body transformation.

But most of these negative reactions simply spring from anti-white hate internalized from the media, as well as the shameful American mania for exalting oneself by denigrating other whites. The truth is, we are all Richard Jewell. We are all targeted for destruction, and a smaller waistline and a better haircut won't save you in the end.

What saved Richard Jewell? He knew his rights and asserted them. When he suspected that he was being framed, he called a lawyer with genuine character, Watson Bryant. Jewell slipped up a few times because of his trust in the government, his unassertiveness, and his desire to help. Bryant was there for support, but in the end, Richard Jewell was sufficiently smart, suspicious, and self-assertive to walk away a free man. He is an example to us all.

It would also be helpful if our people learn to see every reporter as a Kathy Scruggs and every cop as a Tom Shaw. There would be a lot fewer hit pieces and frameups.

Richard Jewell is a populist classic, which is why the enemies of the people have tried to bury it with silence or screeching. Every white person needs to see this superb film.

The Unz Review, January 29, 2020

A STAR IS BORN

I could have happily lived the rest of my life without seeing any of the now four versions of A Star Is Born (1937, 1954, 1976, 2018). But on a long flight, I decided on a whim to watch the latest version, starring Bradley Cooper and Lady Gaga. I like Bradley Cooper as an actor, and this is also his directorial debut. I was also curious about Lady Gaga, whom I had never actually heard. (Can I refer to her as "Gaga" for short?)

Much to my surprise, I loved A Star Is Born, and although I am sure this pun has been used a million times, I was absolutely gaga about the lead actress's performance. It is not a perfect movie, but it is so captivating and emotionally powerful that quibbling seems like heartlessness and ingratitude.

Bradley Cooper is an amazingly versatile and charismatic actor, and now we can add director and musician to his talents. Cooper plays Jackson Maine, a forty-something rock star whose music seems like country or folk in some scenes, hard rock and grunge in others (in short, wipipo music). I think he is supposed to make us think of Chris Cornell or Curt Cobain.

Maine is a brooding artist type with a drink and drug problem. He is losing his hearing, which adds to his isolation. Cooper voices him with a sort of gruff cowboy/stoner monotone, which is annoying but realistic. He is constantly leaning in to conversations to hear better, or mishearing and misunderstanding people. But with Cooper, it somehow adds to the character's charm and autistic ingenuousness.

One night, after a concert, Maine is looking for a place to continue drinking and ends up at a drag bar where he sees Ally (Lady Gaga) perform "La vie en rose." It was a dangerous choice that invites all sorts of invidious comparisons. Aside from a tantalizing bit of "Over the Rainbow" earlier in the film, this was the first time I had heard and seen Lady Gaga. Her French is wobbly, and I feared she would butcher the song with the vulgar mannerisms of Broadway or soul, but the few lines she belts out are actually thrilling.

The most masterful stroke of her performance, however, is

what she *doesn't* sing. When she notices Cooper, she freezes for a moment and forgets to sing "Et, dès que je l'apercois alors je sens en moi mon coeur qui bat" (And when I notice him, I feel inside me my heart beating)—a gesture which pretty much stopped my heart dead. From that moment on, I was in love with this film.

"La vie en rose" is about the rapture and blindness of love, which of course foreshadows what is to come. But Gaga's performance did not prepare me for what was in store musically. There was a bit of unpleasant belting in a parking lot which made me cringe, but Gaga's next song, a duet with Cooper called "Shallow," was truly astonishing. Cooper is really good, but Gaga's voice is electrifying, combining power with emotional subtlety.

A few comparisons come to mind: Judy Garland, Cher, K. D. Lang, Adele, Dulce Pontes. But really, Lady Gaga is in a class by herself. I am one of those people who literally get chills from powerful music, but Lady Gaga is the only pop singer who has ever had this effect on me. (Needless to say, Lady Gaga could deliver the best James Bond song ever.)

Musically, I thought everything would go downhill after "Shallow," but only a few scenes later, Gaga topped it with "Always Remember Us This Way," an utterly heartbreaking distillation of the relationship that forms between Cooper and Gaga's characters. If this song does not bring a tear to your eye, check your pulse. You're probably dead.

I was also impressed with Gaga's performance as an actress. There is not a flat or a false note. Just freshness and authenticity. I suspect that the character of Ally is not too far from Lady Gaga herself. Both Cooper and Gaga brilliantly portray artists because, well, they *are* artists.

And for all the egotism, insecurity, and drama that surrounds it, the core of all art is still a kind of self-transcendence, the creation of meaning and beauty. The more you share physical goods, the less you have for yourself. But meaning and beauty can be shared with the whole world without reducing one's own store. Both artists beautifully capture the magic of creation and performance, as well as all the little things that can get in the way.

Maine is fascinated with Ally and wants to get to know her. Naturally, she suspects it is just a pick-up, but sexually Maine is jaded and probably impotent. He is actually more interested in her as an artist and a person. A few scenes later, when their relationship has deepened, they practically race each other to a hotel room (a beautiful touch). But as soon as Maine gets inside, he passes out drunk.

Maine is at the peak of his career, but his hearing loss and addictions already map out his decline. He has everything he wants and feels like sharing. Ally has talent but lacks self-confidence. Maine gives her the encouragement she needs to share her songs with the world, and a star is born. They also fall in love and marry, and the dramatic conflict in the rest of the film springs from the opposite trajectories of their careers.

It is impossible not to like Jackson Maine, and this brings me to my only serious criticism of the script. It is easy for Cooper to play Maine as a really nice guy because he's written that way. But performers with drug and alcohol problems are generally not nice normal people, with just a little addiction issue off to the side. They often have serious personality disorders. They can be narcissistic, manipulative, borderline, bipolar, etc. They put the people around them through hell. Frankly, though, Cooper could have still made such a character into an irresistibly charismatic hot mess.

But there's only the slightest hint of that kind of ugliness and jealousy in the film, and frankly it seems at least partially justified, for Maine is rightly disgusted with the music Ally makes when she goes commercial. She sounds like those soulless wind-up autotune divas that I hear everywhere on the radio dial for a few tense seconds as I frantically search for something better. (A horrible thought crosses my mind: Maybe Gaga really is one those autotune divas.)

But what am I complaining about? If Cooper played Maine as a charismatic monster, it might have added realism to the character and challenges to the actor — but it would also have made *A Star Is Born* into a far less tragic and emotionally powerful film. Let somebody else make *that* film.

I highly recommend *A Star Is Born*. I won't say anything more about the plot. Through some miracle, I didn't know the end, despite the immense commentary surrounding all four versions, so I approached the movie naïvely and enjoyed it all the more. I don't want to deny you the same pleasure.

The Unz Review, June 16, 2019

STAR WARS:
THE RISE OF SKYWALKER

In memory of Raven.

Even I didn't expect *Star Wars: The Rise of Skywalker* to be this bad. It is simply a terrible movie: derivative, incoherent, arbitrary, superficial, and deeply boring and uninvolving—despite, or maybe because of, the frenetic action sequences, dazzling duels, and effects so special they'll leave carbon scoring on your eyeballs.

The Rise of Skywalker is 2 hours, 22 minutes long, which is long enough, but it feels even longer. I saw it in a half-empty theatre, and when Harrison Ford showed up on the screen, a whole row of people began streaming toward the exits. It would have been the last straw for me too, but I had my duty to you, dear reader, to sustain me.

There's no way to "spoil" a movie this bad, thus I am going to give a running summary of the plot. So if you don't want to hear it, now is the time to angle your deflector screens and warp on out of here, or whatever.

The Rise of Skywalker is the third installment of Disney's *Star Wars* sequel trilogy. The die was cast in the first installment, *The Force Awakens*, directed by Jar Jar Abrams. Instead of coming up with original stories and a new cast of characters, Abrams and Disney decided to do something calculated, cynical, and easy: milk nostalgia for the original trilogy by bringing back the main cast (Mark Hamill, Carrie Fisher, Harrison Ford, the droids, the walking carpet) and shooting a derivative remake of the original *Star Wars* and parts of *The Empire Strikes Back*, but this time as an inept farce.[1]

Somehow the Republic has been defeated and a new Empire has risen, turning the victory of the first trilogy into defeat and all their striving into naught. Instead of a male hero, this time

---

[1] See my review of *The Force Awakens* in *Return of the Son of Trevor Lynch's CENSORED Guide to the Movies.*

we have a Mary Sue, Daisey Ridley's Rey, who takes to the lead like a fish to a bicycle. And instead of an imposing male villain, we have an Emo man-child try-hard, Adam Driver's Kylo Ren, who basically comes off as a parody of Darth Vader.

Since *Star Wars* fans are not exactly the most mature and discerning cinephiles, they squealed, grunted, and buried their noses in this slop while Disney rubbed their hands together in glee and raked in untold millions of shekels.

The second installment, *The Last Jedi*, directed by Rian Johnson, continued in the same vein, with point by point, sometimes shot-by-shot retreads of *The Empire Strikes Back* and *Return of the Jedi*.[2] But this time the director's cynicism and contempt for the story and the fans were so transparent that he provoked a rebellion.

There were many objections: Luke throws away his lightsaber, Luke dies, Leia can suddenly do Force magic, Supreme Leader Snoke is killed off, Rey's parents are nobodies, etc. Some of these objections may be silly. (Imagine actually caring about non-entities like Snoke and Rey.) But *Star Wars* fans were awakening to the fact that Disney was exploiting them and holding them in contempt while taking their money.

This gave the impetus—and Gamergate provided the template—for the great *Star Wars* boycott of 2018 that tanked the movie *Solo*.[3] As we shall see, *The Rise of Skywalker* does attempt to placate at least some of the more superficial critics of *The Last Jedi*.

Since Abrams and Johnson managed to remake and mock the whole original trilogy in only two films, Abrams was in an uncomfortable position in *The Rise of Skywalker:* he might have to actually *come up with something original*. Of course he tries to minimize the shock of doing something really new by bringing back the original cast some more. Luke and Han Solo are both dead, but Luke comes back as a ghost and Han as a figment of his son's imagination. Carrie Fisher really is dead, but Abrams

---

[2] See my review of *The Last Jedi* in *Return of the Son of Trevor Lynch's CENSORED Guide to the Movies.*

[3] See my review of *Solo* in *Return of the Son of Trevor Lynch's CENSORED Guide to the Movies.*

cleverly incorporates unused footage from the first movie. He also finds Billy Dee Williams in carbonite to reprise the role of Lando Calrissian. But the greatest surprise is that he resurrects Emperor Palpatine.

Yes, I know, the last time we saw Emperor Palpatine he was thrown down a shaft in the second Death Star, followed by a big explosion that we interpreted as the release of malign energies when he went splat at the bottom, followed by the destruction of the whole damn Death Star, to add an even greater air of finality.

But, as in the Road Runner cartoons, when Wile E. Coyote falls to his death through a portable hole, or blows himself up with a bomb, or gets an anvil dropped on his head, only to be magically resurrected moments later for further adventures with the bird, Palpatine is back to spare Jar Jar Abrams the necessity of coming up with a new villain after Rian Johnson casually dispensed with Snoke.

The trouble is that, for all his Gungans and Ewoks and juvenile dialogue, George Lucas' *Star Wars* still had a bit more realism and existential heft and credibility than Road Runner cartoons.

The Rise of Skywalker begins *in medias res* as Kylo Ren, the new Supreme Leader, battles to find a Sith McGuffin that allows him to fly to a hidden planet, where he finds Palpatine alive. (Yes, he appears to be on life support. But more than forty years have passed.)

Still, we have questions. If Palpatine was merely injured, how exactly did the Empire fall? Why didn't he just dust off his skirts and continue the war? Why in the galaxy did he retreat to this remote, hidden planet (Mordor, or something)? Why did he set up Snoke as his cat's paw rather than rule directly? Why did he not step forward when Snoke was killed? Why did he allow Ren to take over? How, given his exile, did he build a vast fleet of new star destroyers armed with planet killing lasers? Why was Ren searching for him? Etc. Of course none of it makes sense, which means that resurrecting Palpatine is arbitrary, dumb, and unintelligible.

Oh, and you'll love this: The First Order was just the beginning. When Palpatine launches his new fleet, then we will have *the Final Order.*

Palpatine orders Ren to kill Rey because he fears her. But why is Ren now taking orders from Palpatine?

Meanwhile, Poe Dameron, Findu Nuffin, and Chewbacca meet a contact who tells them of a mole in the First Order. They escape by performing as many as six impossible stunts before breakfast, jumping wildly in and out of hyperspace while the enemy fighters manage to still follow them. (So they can do that now?) Then we see Rey doing dangerous and impossible feats, training under her new Jedi master, Leia.

This too has the credibility of a Road Runner cartoon, and it seems very silly in the universe of *Star Wars*, where even though there are all sorts of magic and advanced technology, there is still a sense of rules and limits, which helps the viewer suspend disbelief.

Jar Jar Abrams explicitly mocks his suspension of Lucas' rules (and our disbelief) when Stormtroopers start flying. "They fly now?" asks Findu incredulously. Throughout this film, lot of us were thinking "They *x* now?" incredulously. But *incredulity is a barrier to actually getting into the story.* Which is one reason this film is so goddamn boring.

When Poe, Findu, and Chewie return to base, they bicker like children with Rey. Rey and company are as surprised as we are by Palpatine's return, so they go to the exotic planet of Pasadena to search for a McGuffin that Rey just happens to find in one of Luke's books. This second McGuffin will lead to the first McGuffin, which will lead to Mordor or something.

There's no hemming and hawing and hesitation in Abrams' script. No problems to stump the characters. No sense that military campaigns need more than just a locker-room huddle to plan. Just a series of arbitrary McGuffins to move them from one chase, space battle, monster, or sword duel to another. But somehow the movie is still 142 minutes long, and somehow it seems even longer.

On Pasadena, our heroes conveniently just bump into Lando Calrissian, who conveniently knows just where to look for the second McGuffin in the desert: the abandoned ship of a Sith assassin, which has just been sitting there for twenty-odd years, untouched by the Sith, unstripped by Jawas. Hell, by all appearances, the local teens have not even "partied" in it. Conveniently, even the battery has not run down, so our heroes can escape on it later. Our heroes also find the assassin's bones and a dagger which is inscribed with Sith "runes" — naturally the most evil people in the universe write in runes — giving the location of the McGuffin that gives the location of the Sith planet.

But, since C-3PO is programmed not to translate Sith (hate speech is barred in his terms of service), this new bit of arbitrariness requires a visit to yet another planet, Kimchee, where a tiny puppet extracts the info from 3PO's head. This whole digression, as well as the stupid idea of inscribing what is in effect a memo on an ancient-looking dagger could have simply been avoided by putting a post-it note on the ship's dashboard giving the McGuffin's location, or better yet, a direct route to the Sith planet. It wouldn't have been any dumber, and it would have streamlined the movie considerably.

Kylo Ren uses his Force bond with Rey to find her on Pasadena. He reaches out through space and time and somehow snatches her necklace off, which she just so happened to acquire on Pasadena, so Ren goes there to meet her. But if Ren can snatch a necklace off her across untold light-years, why can't he just magically intuit her location? In fact, he *does* magically intuit where she is. So why not give her coordinates to his lackeys? Why does he have to use "analysis" to determine where the necklace came from? And why assume she is on the planet where the necklace is from? (Imagine if she had bought the necklace on a different planet. Girls who like to travel do that, you know.)

Ren and the First Order show up on Pasadena. Rey goes to confront him, taking down Ren's TIE fighter with a lightsaber. But, this being a Road Runner cartoon, he walks away from the fiery crash. The First Order capture Chewbacca and the *Newmanium Falcon*. Rey uses her magic powers to try to prevent the First Order transport from leaving the planet. (She can do that now.) But the transport explodes, killing Chewbacca. But don't worry, this being a Road Runner cartoon, we soon learn that

Chewie was on a *different* transport.

The ancient-looking dagger contains coordinates to the Sith McGuffin on the second Death Star which was built, what, forty years before? And wasn't the Death Star blown to atoms anyway? Conveniently not. It crashed on "the nearby forest moon of Endor" (rinse, repeat), and although it landed in an ocean "on the nearby forest moon of Endor," the location of the McGuffin conveniently is above the water line. Conveniently, the ominous metal doors still have electrical power as well, and they are not even locked. Rey grabs the McGuffin and has a vision of herself turned evil.

Then Ren shows up, grabs the McGuffin, and breaks it. The only way she is going to get to Mordor is with him. Then they fight. Leia uses the Force from clear across the galaxy to distract Ren (she can do that now), and Rey stabs him. Leia dies, and Rey feels so bad that she uses magic to heal Ren's wound. (She can do that now.) Ren, who tried to kill his mother in the last movie, now feels remorse. Rey steals Ren's ride while he is distracted by a vision of his father, Harrison Ford. Ren has blown up entire planets, *but there's still good inside him*. This stupidity, at least, is Lucas'. Ren throws away his weapon. He's going to be a good boy now.

There's also a sequence where Findu and Poe infiltrate the First Order command ship to rescue Chewbacca, which turns out to be absurdly easy. But I don't remember how it quite fits with the rest of the story because by this time it had become so overcomplicated that even my big brain was getting fatigued.

Also, Ren magically communicates to Rey that her parents weren't exactly nobodies. You see, *her father was Emperor Palpatine's son*, so that makes her Palpatine's granddaughter. Yes, Palpatine now has a son. Yet that didn't prevent Palpatine from having Rey's parents killed for hiding her from him, because even when she was a toddler, he feared her powers and wanted her dead. (This, presumably, all took place decades after Palpatine's presumed death.)

It was great drama when Darth Vader told Luke Skywalker that he was his father. But this new revelation barely attains the level of farce. (I wasn't the only one in the theater who scoffed.)

Perhaps Disney's next *Star Wars* trilogy can focus on the adventures of Palpatine's nephew's girlfriend's roommate.

Discovering that her grandfather is the Emperor messes with Rey's head, so she decides to have a good cry on the planet of Achoo, where Luke hid out. When she arrives, she burns Kylo's starship. She tries to throw her lightsaber into the fire, but the ghost of Luke Skywalker catches it and tells her that a Jedi's weapon deserves more respect. Then he convinces her to go back to the fight.

But how? She just burned her ride. Fortunately, Luke uses magic to raise his x-wing fighter from the bottom of the ocean, where it has been for how many years? Conveniently, it is in perfect working order. Luke also gives her Leia's lightsaber, because she's now been retconned as a Jedi too, and in a flashback, we see that she was even better than Luke. Also, somehow the McGuffin on Ren's ship was not consumed by flames, so Rey uses it to find Mordor where she will confront the Emperor.

When Rey arrives on Mordor, she transmits its location to the Resistance, who mobilize to attack Palpatine's fleet. When Rey meets Palpatine, he demands that she kill him and take his place on the Iron Throne. When he dies, his spirit and the spirits of the other Sith will live on in her. (They can do that now.) Then Kylo Ren, now reverted to good boy Ben Solo, somehow shows up to help Rey. But somehow his henchmen the Knights of Ren also show up. For some reason they are now on Palpatine's side, so he has to fight them. Too bad he threw away his weapon in a fit of pique. Rey loans him a lightsaber.

When Ben shows up, Palpatine has a change of plan. You see, Ben and Rey have so many midichlorians or something that they constitute a "Force Dyad." (They have those now.) It turns out that a Force Dyad is just the thing that Palpatine needs to get off life support. So he drains them to rejuvenate himself. Then he's back to wanting to kill Rey.

No, Palpatine is not crazy. If he were crazy, how could he negotiate such extreme mood swings?

Palpatine throws Ben down a hole, but this being a Road Runner cartoon, he climbs back out. Palpatine attacks the Resistance fleet with Force lightning. (He can do that now.) Rey manages to drag herself back into the fight, and, using both Luke and Leia's lightsabers, she manages to kill Palpatine. Then she dies from the strain. Ben Solo then brings her back to life, whereupon she kisses him, then he dies.

Meanwhile, a diverse array of Resistance fighters destroys Palpatine's fleet. My favorite moment is when Findu and a frizzy-haired mulatto chick lead a cavalry charge across the top of a Star Destroyer. (This stupidity is simply a continuation of Lucas' Viet Cong inspired idea of primitives—Ewoks, Gungans—defeating high-tech Imperial armies.)

Then we have long drawn-out scenes of celebration, including a couple of cat ladies kissing. The movie ends with Rey on Tattooine, burying Luke and Leia's lightsabers near the house where he grew up. A passerby asks Rey's name, and she says "Rey Skywalker." And, in a bit of *symbolism*, we see the ghosts of Luke and Leia as Tattooine's twin suns set.

Clearly when Luke prevents Rey from throwing away her lightsaber, and when we are told that Rey's father was Palpatine's son, Jar Jar was trying to placate some of the fan objections to *The Last Jedi*. Aside from the apparent lesbian cat-lady kiss—and who are we to assume their genders anyway?—Abrams actually seems to go out of his way to make this movie as inoffensive as possible.

For instance, the long-feared love match between Rey and Findu never happened. Nor does the Asian chick Rose end up with Findu. Instead, the introduction of the frizzy-haired mulatto chick on Endor seems to be setting him up with a woman of his own race. Even the bad guys are racially and sexually diverse, with strong womyn and magic Negroes genociding whole planets along with the white guys with British accents.

Indeed, the only demographic that gets slighted in *The Rise of Skywalker* are the Gungans. This movie contains all manner of humanoid and alien diversity, pretty much every species we have seen in the other films, *except for the Gungans*. The Gungans are conspicuous by their absence, which to my mind makes them the key to the whole damn movie. Where are the Gungans? They *must* be involved. And if they are not in front of the camera, they must be *behind the camera*. Director Jar Jar Abrams, for one. When you think about it, crypto-Gungan influence seems to be the only possible explanation for a movie this dumb.

The Rise of Skywalker has really only one redeeming feature: John Williams' lovely music, but in this case, the score does not add depth to the movie but simply highlights how shallow it is. *The Rise of Skywalker* isn't Ed Wood bad or Coleman Francis bad, such that you might just succumb to the temptation to see it anyway. It is just plain bad, a painful waste of time and a cruel mockery of Lucas' original mythos and the millions of fans who found meaning and pleasure in it. Jar Jar Abrams and Disney have killed *Star Wars*. Let's hope the fans stay away in droves and kill the careers of the people responsible for this cynical and disgusting desecration.

The Unz Review, December 20, 2019

STARSHIP TROOPERS

Robert A. Heinlein's *Starship Troopers* (1959) marked his transition from writing juvenile pulp science fiction to serious novels of ideas, in this case setting forth a highly reactionary and militarist political philosophy. Paul Verhoeven's 1997 film of *Starship Troopers* takes quite a few liberties with Heinlein's plot but manages to capture its spirit and communicate its key ideas. Although Verhoeven's film was enormously expensive and received mostly negative reviews, it was a box office success and since then has established itself as a classic military, science fiction, and coming-of-age film.

Of course Verhoeven could not film a straightforward adaptation of a novel that glorifies war and denigrates democracy in favor of something that sounds like fascism. So he claimed his movie was satire. But that's not how the fans see it. Like Stanley Kubrick's *Full Metal Jacket*, *Starship Troopers* contains over-the-top depictions of brutal military training and combat that actually function as recruiting propaganda. Moreover, many viewers find Verhoeven's depiction of a fascistic military meritocracy highly appealing on both aesthetic and philosophical grounds.

Starship Troopers is the story of how Johnny Rico (played by Casper Van Dien) becomes a man and a citizen of the global state known as the Federation. *Starship Troopers* is set around 300 years in the future. Some time right about now, civilization broke down due to democracy and the social sciences (read: Leftism). However, as in the aftermath of the First World War, military veterans put an end to the chaos and established a new order, in which the vote is restricted to citizens.

Citizenship is awarded to those who volunteer to do federal service, placing their lives at risk for the body politic. Those who do not volunteer are called "civilians," which implies that national service simply is military service. Civilians enjoy the protection of their basic human rights, but they do not have "civil rights" to participate in government.

Heinlein's system is appealing, because it recognizes that there are two basic types of human beings: collectivists, who are willing to sacrifice their lives for the common good, and individualists who prize their own lives over the common good. One can also draw the same distinction in terms of the importance of honor. When forced to choose, the warrior prefers death to dishonor, honor being understood in terms of his role as protector. Those who prefer dishonor to death can be called bourgeois. In the novel, Heinlein also distinguishes between "men" — who choose lives of honor — and mere "producing-consuming economic animal[s]," who choose lives of ease.

Which is likely to be better governed: a society that reserves political power to an honorable minority proven to have the courage and responsibility to risk their lives for the common good — or a society that gives equal power to everyone, allowing the selfish, cowardly, and irresponsible majority to outvote their betters? The answer is obvious.

Heinlein's proposal is appealing because it combines the best features of aristocracy and democracy. Aristocracies were, of course, based on risking one's life for the common good. But heredity is a bad way to perpetuate such a system, because people don't always breed true. Noble ancestors beget unworthy heirs, and every noble line has common ancestors when one goes back far enough. Democracy recognizes that leadership virtues can be found in all social classes, but it fails by politically empowering everyone indiscriminately, simply by virtue of being born.

Whether one is born a son of a prince or a son of the people, both aristocracy and democracy inevitably assign political power to inferior people through the principle of heredity. The best system, however, assigns political power only to the most responsible. The best way to recruit such people is to discard hereditary status and allow each individual, in each new generation, to determine his own status — by choosing to be a citizen or a civilian — and then giving those who choose citizenship the appropriate training.

The extreme brutality of the military training depicted in *Starship Troopers* seems excessive from the point of view of simple military necessity. But making citizenship dangerous discourages fundamentally bourgeois types from volunteering. When Johnny Rico ("rico" is Spanish for "rich") tells his very rich, very bourgeois parents that he wants to volunteer for federal service, his mother's immediate objection is that "People get killed in federal service." (Of course, she later learns that people get killed by opting out as well, when she and her husband are obliterated by the hostile alien species known as arachnids or bugs.) Then Johnny's parents try to wheedle him out of his choice by offering him an expensive vacation. (In truth, though, Johnny does not reject his parents' offer out of a desire for a harder and more heroic life. He's just infatuated with a girl. But this is a coming-of-age story, which means that at the start, Johnny has to be immature.)

Although the world of *Starship Troopers* is militaristic and meritocratic, it is quite pointedly not racist or sexist. All races are represented, and women can aspire to any position, including combat roles. Men and women even bunk and shower together in the military. This is absurd, of course, given the importance the regime places on both military efficiency and simple biology. There are, for instance, federal studies to find psychics, who might be the next step of human evolution. Also, one needs a license to have children, which implies some sort of eugenic measures. Such a society would not put women in combat, especially in a genocidal war of survival. Women can produce far fewer children than men, which makes women precious and men expendable in warfare. Therefore, they cannot have equal rights to choose combat. Moreover, such a society would not conclude that the races are basically the same, so that a stable and functional multiracial society is possible.

Despite the explicit multiracialism of Heinlein's novel, Verhoeven massively Aryanizes his cast and setting. Heinlein's Johnny Rico is a Filipino. Verhoeven's Rico is a squared-jawed Nordic archetype, and his Buenos Aires looks like a rich, heavily Nordic North-American suburb where everyone speaks English. All the main characters have blue eyes: Carmen Ibanez is played by Denise Richards; Dina Meyer plays Isabelle "Dizzy" Flores; Michael Ironside plays the teacher/lieutenant Jean

Rasczak; Neil Patrick Harris plays Carl Jenkins; Patrick Muldoon plays Zander Barcalow; Jake Busey plays Ace Levy; Clancy Brown plays Zim; Brenda Strong plays Captain Deladier; and so forth.

It seems odd that Verhoeven reduced the diversity of Heinlein's cast. No filmmaker would ever do that today. I would like to think that he was simply guided by strong aesthetic considerations. I'd also like to think that he wanted heroes with whom his majority North-American white audience could better identify. But perhaps he simply thought a more Nordic cast made for a better "parody" of fascism. If so, we have to thank him for making the right choice for the wrong reasons.

The basic story of *Starship Troopers* is rather simple. High-school senior Johnny Rico is in love with Carmen Ibanez, who has much shallower feelings for him. Carmen is planning to sign up for federal service. Johnny decides to join as well, hoping to impress Carmen. His parents oppose his decision, Johnny rebels, and his father cuts him off. Johnny goes off to boot camp. Dizzy Flores, who is in unrequited love with Johnny, follows him. Johnny begins to excel at training. Carmen dumps him. When one of Johnny's comrades dies due to his negligence, Johnny decides to quit and go home. But then Buenos Aires is destroyed by the arachnids, and Johnny rushes back to join the fight.

The war with the arachnids is utterly brutal. Due to his competence and the high casualty rates on his missions, Johnny is promoted from private to corporal to sergeant to lieutenant. He sees many friends and comrades die. He becomes detached from his pain over the breakup with Carmen. He comes to feel compassion for Dizzy.

At the beginning of the film, Mr. Rasczak chides Johnny for repeating the words of the textbook on citizenship without really knowing their meaning. When Dizzy dies, Johnny fully understands what it means to give one's life for the common good.

But Johnny also repeats other lines from Rasczak, who is later his lieutenant: "I only have one rule. Everyone fights. No one quits. If you don't do your job, I'll shoot you." You have a rank, "Until you're dead or I find someone better." "Come on you apes! Do you want to live forever?"

Perhaps we are supposed to sneer at Johnny for being unoriginal, inauthentic, or high on the f-scale. But Johnny Rico has transcended all such concerns because he has transcended his ego by doing his duty. He has followed the path of the Karma Yogi. He has also become a bit like the arachnids: lacking ego, he is a perfect member of society. But they are born that way, whereas he had to attain detachment through suffering and effort.

Many critics have sneered at Verhoeven's central cast—Van Dien, Roberts, Meyer, and Muldoon—because they are perfect looking but "wooden." One of the extras on my disc is a screen test with Van Dien and Roberts in which they generate real heat. Verhoeven dampened that for the final film, again, perhaps to suggest that the characters are shallow fascist Barbie and Ken dolls. Or maybe Verhoeven wanted the characters to deepen emotionally as they experience suffering and compassion, which is exactly what happens with all of them as the story unfolds. In any case, *Starship Troopers* can be deeply moving, especially the deaths of Dizzy and Rasczak.

From a technical point of view, *Starship Troopers* is a brilliant achievement. I recently rewatched it on Blu-ray on a large-screen OLED TV, and I found the special effects to be stunningly realistic. The arachnids are genuinely terrifying. Basil Poledouris' score is also highly effective.

Two scenes, though, are particularly powerful to me. When Johnny Rico has dropped out of federal service and is leaving base, we see hundreds of soldiers going about their business. Then, suddenly, some of them break ranks and start running. Others follow. And Johnny, not knowing what is happening, joins in. News of the destruction of Buenos Aires has hit. "War! We're going to war!" one of his friends shouts. This scene wonderfully communicates the sense of being swept up in historical events that are larger than oneself.

At the end of the film, as Johnny emerges from the darkness of the bug city, he again sees large crowds of soldiers running.

But this time, the meaning is reversed. Johnny has flushed the brain bug into the arms of his comrades, who have captured it, and this is not the beginning of the war, but the beginning of its end. Johnny Rico is no longer just a passive speck buffeted around by history. He has become an agent of history.

How was it even possible that such an appealing anti-liberal movie was ever made?

We are all supposed to have cold shudders when Johnny Rico screams, "Kill them! Kill them all!" as he and his fellow soldiers are swarmed by terrifying arachnid warriors—or when Zander Barcalow spits out the words, "One day, someone like me is going to kill you and your whole fucking race" to an arachnid brain bug—or when Carl Jenkins psychically probes the brain bug then exultantly proclaims, "It's afraid, it's afraid!" After all, surely not all arachnids are like that. Surely things can't be that black and white. But while shitlibs soil themselves, healthy people cheer such sentiments and work them into countless edgy Right-wing memes.

I have two hypotheses that might explain this film.

The first is that Paul Verhoeven did a good job because he fundamentally liked the story. Then, when the predictable *oy veying* about fascism started up, he claimed that he was parodying the whole thing. There are some definitely parodistic elements in the film clips of the republic's propaganda. But the main story is quite "real" and played pretty much straight.

The second hypothesis is that Verhoeven delivered a good film essentially by accident. The smugness and psychological shallowness of Leftists often causes them to defeat themselves. They assume that simply restating Rightist ideas is enough to refute them, so they sometimes accurately communicate them to receptive audiences.

Whatever the explanation, *Starship Troopers* is an anti-liberal classic which has done far more to promote than to undermine Heinlein's vision of military meritocracy.

The Unz Review, April 25, 2019

STORYTELLING

Storytelling (2001) is the most politically incorrect movie I have ever seen. Indeed, it is so un-PC that it could never have been made today.

Director Todd Solondz is a really sick guy. His films *Welcome to the Dollhouse, Happiness, Palindromes,* and *Life During Wartime* can justly be accused of fixating on bullying, rape, pedophilia, abortion, suicide, and murder. I find them utterly distasteful, and I cannot recommend them to anyone. But of course, these films have been hailed as courageous by critics, who delight in breaking down barriers to everything sordid and terrible in man.

But even our transgressive cultural elites have lines that cannot be crossed, which explains their comparative silence about *Storytelling*. For example, while Solondz's other films are extensively summarized on *Wikipedia*, as of this writing, this is the *full* summary of *Storytelling*:

The film consists of two stories that are unrelated and have different actors, titled "Fiction" and "Non-Fiction." College and high school serve as the backdrop for these two stories about dysfunction and personal turmoil.

Fiction
"Fiction," starring Selma Blair, "Vi," is about a group of college students in a creative writing class taught by a black professor (Robert Wisdom).

Non-Fiction
"Non-Fiction," starring Paul Giamatti and John Goodman, is about the filming of a dysfunctional suburban New Jersey family as their teenage son (Mark Webber) goes through the college application process, and faces the trials and tribulations of late teenage years.

Autobiography
The original version of the film featured a third story

entitled "Autobiography," concerning, among other things, a closeted football player (James van der Beek). The main character has an explicit sex scene with a male partner (Steven Rosen); the entire story was cut from the final version.

Note that the paragraph about the part of the film that was cut is actually longer than the descriptions of the stories that made it into the final cut. Why the reticence? You'll see.

I will comment on the entire plot of "Fiction," the shorter of the two stories, and let you explore "Non-Fiction" on your own.

"Fiction" begins with two college kids, Vi (Selma Blair) and Marcus (Leo Fitzpatrick) *in flagrante*. Vi climaxes as she rides Marcus, then sinks to the bed. Marcus then clumsily tries to interest Vi in hearing his short story for tomorrow's class.

There's really something off about this guy. It turns out that Marcus has cerebral palsy. Sensing that Vi is tiring of their relationship, he observes that she no longer sweats during sex. "The kinkiness is gone. You've become . . . kind," he says ruefully. Vi is turned on by sexual degradation, like fucking a "cripple," a "freak." But when she starts to feel for Marcus, she is less turned on. One wonders if he has seen this before.

The next day, Marcus reads his story in class. This is the ending:

> But when he saw her, it was as if he could walk like a normal person. His legs didn't swing, his arms didn't spaz away. He wasn't a freak any more, for she made him forget his affliction. No more cerebral palsy! From now on "CP" stood for "cerebral person." He was a cerebral person.

It is truly excruciating, but since Marcus is a cripple, the students are kind. My favorite comment is: "It kind of reminded me a little of Faulkner, but East Coast and disabled." To which other students chime in: "Or Flannery O'Connor. She had multiple sclerosis [sic; actually, she had lupus]." "And

Borges. He was blind." Then, with perfect comic timing, another adds, hopefully: "Updike had psoriasis."

At this point Catherine (Aleksa Palladino)—the brunette, bespectacled, hook-nosed teacher's pet—takes over: "I found the whole thing to be a little trite. Its earnestness is, well . . . it's a little embarrassing." There's a lot wrong with Marcus' story, but calling it out for earnestness is simply a cliché of decadent postmodern ironism.[1] The worst thing about Marcus' story is not that he is earnest, but rather that he isn't earnest at all. He isn't trying hard, because he prefers to coast on the politically correct deference he receives as a cripple.

Finally, the teacher speaks. Mr. Scott is a tall, imposing black man. He is a Pulitzer Prize-winning author of books like *A Sunday Lynching*. He is known for being "aggressively confrontational," and he does not disappoint:

Catherine is right. The story's a piece of shit. You express nothing but banalities and, formally speaking, are unable to construct a single compelling sentence. You ride on a wave of clichés so worn, in fact, it actually approaches a level of grotesquerie. And your subtitle, "the rawness of truth," is that supposed to be a joke of some sort? Or are you just being pretentious?

On the one hand, Mr. Scott's un-PC frankness is refreshing. But in another way, his speech is actually quite PC. He goes well beyond frankness into sadism. A white professor would never behave in such a way. White people have to be sensitive, especially to cripples. But Mr. Scott is a black man in academia. Thus he enjoys a bubble of PC deference that allows him . . . certain liberties.

After class, Marcus attacks Vi for not coming to his defense. His parting words are "You just want to fuck him, like Catherine and every other white cunt on campus." That evening, Marcus calls Vi to break up. After she hangs up, she refers to him as a "fucking cripple" and goes out to a bar, looking to "get laid."

---

[1] See Greg Johnson, "Postmodernism vs. Identity" in *From Plato to Postmodernism*.

At the bar, Vi runs into Mr. Scott. She is hilariously awkward. He's a total asshole. Naturally, she finds him irresistible. "You have beautiful skin," he says, then grabs her hand. They go to his apartment.

Vi goes to the bathroom to freshen up. There she finds an envelope of photographs. The first ones she sees are of Catherine, nude and tied up. Other women follow, perhaps some of the other girls in her class. Vi is shaken. To recover her composure, she repeats "Don't be a racist. Don't be a racist." Her gut is telling her to flee, but her PC programming overrides it.

This is how countless white women fall victim to black predators.

When Vi emerges from the bathroom, Mr. Scott tells her to strip, turn to the wall, and bend over. He's not one for foreplay. He just wants to rut, doggie-style. As he enters Vi, he commands her: "Say 'Nigger fuck me.'" Vi is flustered. "Oh, bu . . . uh . . . I can't say that." Technically she can; she's just not supposed to. He insists, and she complies, repeating "Nigger, fuck me hard! Nigger, fuck me hard!" Clearly, they are both getting into it. Cut to Marcus' dorm room. Vi knocks on the door. She has been weeping. They hug, and Marcus notes that she's all sweaty.

At the next session of the class, Vi reads her latest story. This is how it ends:

> So John flipped her around and slammed her against the wall. Jane braced herself: she thought about her mother. She thought about Peter. She thought about God . . . and rape. "Say, 'Fuck me, nigger. Fuck me hard.'" John's flesh abraded her soft skin. There would be marks. She acquiesced and said what he asked her to say, and did what he asked her to do. She had entered college with hope, with dignity, but she would graduate as a whore.

The reactions of the class are exactly what one would predict given the PC victim hierarchy. When faced with a white woman accusing a black man of sexual impropriety, there is no hesitation. Feminist sisterhood goes out the window. Her classmates, most of them white and female, condemn the story as "ugly," "perverted," "mean-spirited," "a little bit racist," "completely racist," "totally phallocentric," and "weirdly misogynistic."

Note the strange alchemy by which a woman writing about a traumatic sexual experience with a black man becomes "misogynistic." Merely complaining about female objectification and victimization is not "misogyny." In fact, it is practically the definition of feminism. But something changes when the predator is a black man. Like all politically correct terms, "racist" and "misogynist" have basically one meaning: a bad white person. These words are deployed solely to denigrate whites and celebrate non-whites. Thus a white woman is a misogynist if she complains about being sexually objectified or raped by a non-white man. This is the mentality that has led the feminist Left to remain silent about the mass rape and sexual harassment of white women by black and brown men in Europe and North America.

Once again, Catherine is the master of PC-speak. She must be a graduate student, maybe Mr. Scott's graduate student assistant.

It was confessional, yet dishonest. Jane pretends to be horrified by the sexuality that she in fact fetishizes. She subsumes herself to the myth of black male potency, but then doesn't follow through. She thinks she "respects Afro-Americans," she thinks they're "cool," "exotic," what a notch he'd make in her belt, but, of course, it all comes down to mandingo cliché, and he calls her on it. In classic racist tradition she demonizes, then runs for cover. But then, how could she behave otherwise? She's just a spoiled suburban white girl with a Benneton rainbow complex. It's just my opinion, and what do I know? But I think it's a callow piece of writing.

To some extent, Catherine is right. The story is dishonest. Mr. Scott (the "John" to Vi's "whore") is not a rapist. Vi simply had a hot, consensual sexual encounter that made her feel dirty. But rather than own up to her ambivalent feelings, she wants to disown them by claiming to have been raped. False accusations of rape are common on college campuses because feminists encourage women to think they can withdraw consent after the fact. But Vi has discovered that white women are lower than black men in the PC victim hierarchy.

Catherine is, however, wrong to claim that Vi is the "real racist." Mr. Scott gets off on being called a "nigger." It isn't something we can talk about these days, but I am sure a lot of black people do. Vi is offended by that and feels guilty for going along with it.

Mr. Scott seconds Catherine's charge of callowness:

> Callow and coy. Jane wants more, but isn't honest enough to admit it. In the end, she returns to the safety of her crippled (translation: sexually impotent) boyfriend.

Marcus bursts out, "This is bullshit! Her story was the truth!" The class responds: "It's unbelievable!" "It's clichéd!" "It's disgusting!"

"But it happened!" Vi protests.

Ever unflappable, Mr. Scott continues:

> I don't know about "what happened," Vi, because once you start writing, it all becomes fiction. Still, it certainly is an improvement over your last story: There is now at least a beginning, a middle, and an end.

And that is the end.

Mr. Scott's position is post-modern Leftism in a nutshell. Truth doesn't matter. Everything is fiction. Facts don't matter. Only narratives matter.

What structures the narratives? The rules of political correctness. Basically, everyone in the story behaves badly because of political correctness. The students don't care about truth. They simply lie to flatter whoever holds the highest victim card.

Those who hold the cards exploit them to abuse people with impunity. Marcus wrote a lousy story because he thought he could skate by on pity for being a cripple, even though such pity ruined his relationship with Vi. Mr. Scott is a sadist with students both in and out of the classroom because his blackness lets him get away with it. Vi uses her emancipated woman card as a pass to pursue degrading, kinky sex. And when she feels a little too degraded, she retcons the experience into a "rape" and tries to use it as a club against Mr. Scott. But perhaps Vi does not know the rule that black men can rape white women with impunity.

This is one of the most systematic, subtle, penetrating, and brutal satires of political correctness ever made, and it takes only about twenty minutes.

The last hour or so of *Storytelling* is called "Non-Fiction." It is equally brutal and brilliant, but I will let you discover it for yourself. I will, however, leave you with my proposed edit to the *Wikipedia* summary:

"Non-Fiction," starring Paul Giamatti and John Good-man, is about a resentful Left-wing Jewish filmmaker whose documentary mocking an obnoxious upper-middle-class suburban Jewish family is cut short when the family is gassed to death by their Salvadoran maid.

This is Solondz's idea of comedy, and, believe me, you'll laugh until you feel dirty and want to accuse him of mind rape.

How does Solondz get away with it? Apparently, like the Coen brothers and Larry David, he isn't worried about being accused of racism or anti-Semitism because he's Jewish. Solondz, in short, uses political correctness against itself. But with satire this good, I'll take it wherever I can find it.

The Unz Review, July 25, 2020

THE STRAIGHT STORY

When I saw *Blue Velvet* and *Twin Peaks*, I was convinced that David Lynch is an essentially conservative and religious filmmaker, with a populist and mystical bent. Arguing that thesis was an uphill battle as his work got increasingly dark in the nineties. Many people interpreted Lynch's portrayals of quirky, salt-of-the-Earth white Americans as parody, his mysticism as arbitrary weirdness, and his depictions of evil and violence as inconsistent with having a conservative and religious moral center. (They'd probably argue the same thing about Flannery O'Connor as well — and just as wrongly.)

Then came 1999's *The Straight Story*, which reprises all the wholesome, life-affirming, and sentimental elements of Lynch's earlier works without the darkness, terror, and demonic evil. *The Straight Story* is so wholesome, in fact, that it was rated G and released by Disney.

The Straight Story is the story of Alvin Straight (1920–1996), a small-town Iowan who at the age of 73 decided to visit his stroke-stricken brother 240 miles away in Wisconsin. What makes Straight's journey interesting is *how* he did it. Alvin didn't have a driver's license because his eyes were bad. So he put a hitch on his riding lawnmower, hooked up a small trailer full of fuel, food, and camping equipment, and set out for Wisconsin, driving five miles an hour along the side of roads and camping in the fields at night. All told, the journey took six weeks, including breakdowns and repairs. (Then a nephew drove Alvin and his lawnmower back home.)

The basic characters and outline of *The Straight Story* are based on fact, but many of the details strike me as pure Lynch. Lynch did not, however, write the screenplay, although it was co-authored by his longtime collaborator (and third wife) Mary Sweeney. Perhaps Lynch was attracted to the project because it was already sufficiently "Lynchian."

The entire cast of *The Straight Story* is white, and they are Lynch's trademark quirky, good-hearted, small-town Americans.

Alvin Straight is beautifully portrayed by Richard Farnsworth, who was nominated for the Best Actor Oscar. Alvin is a soft-spoken, gentle man who stubbornly tries to cling to his independence and dignity as old age and illness strip them from him. Farnsworth lived his role. He was suffering from metastatic prostate cancer while filming and took his life the next year at the age of eighty. He brings Alvin to life with warmth and gentle humor. He is particularly powerful when relating sad memories, such as his daughter Rose's loss of her four children, and his terrible guilt about accidentally killing a member of his own unit during World War II. But to me the most touching scene is simply watching Alvin's face as he silently overhears the bad news that his brother Lyle has had a stroke.

Sissy Spacek is wonderful as Alvin's slightly "special" (perhaps autistic) daughter Rose. Everett McGill, of *Dune* and *Twin Peaks* fame, plays Tom, a John Deere salesman. Harry Dean Stanton (*Wild at Heart, Twin Peaks: Fire Walk with Me, Inland Empire, Twin Peaks: The Return*), has an almost wordless role as Alvin's brother Lyle.[1] The rest of the cast are local Midwesterners, and they are uniformly excellent.

As Alvin makes his journey, he dispenses bits of wisdom to the people he meets.

In one scene, he camps with a surly teenage runaway girl who slowly warms to him. Alvin intuits that she is running away because she is pregnant and urges her to return home. She can only think of the enmity of her family, but Alvin suggests there is strength in family as well, using a very concrete and primal metaphor: the fasces. An individual twig can be broken, but tie them together in a bundle, and they become strong. The next morning, the girl is gone. But she communicated her decision by leaving a bundle of sticks.

In another scene, Alvin and a fellow WWII veteran share painful memories of friends they lost. But the Germans are not dehumanized. In fact, Alvin mentions that at the end of the war, "We were shooting moon-faced boys." The war is simply presented as a senseless waste of life, which it was.

---

[1] See my reviews of *Dune* and *Wild at Heart* in *Return of the Son of Trevor Lynch's CENSORED Guide to the Movies.*

The Straight Story is a warm and sentimental portrait of the American Midwest and its people. Lynch filmed it on location, on the actual route Alvin took. He also filmed every scene in the order in which it appears. In short, Lynch took Alvin's journey. *The Straight Story* contains Lynch's most beautiful nature photography. It is set during harvest time, with rippling fields of ripe grain, vivid sunsets, and autumn leaves, all suffused with gold.

Yet, despite its seeming straightforwardness, Lynch characterized *The Straight Story* as his "most experimental movie" thus far. To my eyes, it is an experiment in being naïve and spontaneous. One scene plays gently with movie conventions. We see Alvin driving his tractor down the road away from us, then the camera slowly pans up to the beautiful blue sky—then slowly back down to Alvin, who, of course, has only gone a few more feet. Whenever I saw this scene in a theater, it always provoked gales of good-natured laughter, because if this were any other movie, and Alvin were riding anything other than a lawnmower, he would be just a dot in the distance.

There are many Lynchian touches beyond the affectionate portrayals of quirky and sometimes grotesque Midwesterners. Lynch's trademark depiction of technology as an ominous and dehumanizing force—using loud mechanical thrumming and screeches—is used to good effect with a grain elevator at night and also huge semi trucks looming over Alvin and his vulnerable, hobbit-scale technology.

When Alvin's brakes give out and he comes hurtling down a hill, the sequence is viscerally real. Like Alvin, we feel out of control and jarred to our bones. Yet the backdrop of a burning building gives the scene an apocalyptic and surreal quality.

When Alvin sees a deer killed by a hysterical female motorist, he of course uses it to replenish his supplies, cooking it over a fire—while surrounded, somehow, by lawn statues of deer out in the middle of nowhere.

Lynch is a director who believes in the reality of the supernatural. (See, especially, my review of *Lost Highway*.) There is only one scene that suggests such powers in *The Straight Story*, and it is masterfully handled. The real Alvin Straight's tractor conked out just short of his brother's house, and he was towed the rest of the way by a local farmer. In Lynch's film, when Alvin's tractor dies, a man on a much bigger tractor pulls up. We see the whole thing from a distance, too far to clearly hear the dialogue. Lynch has used the same technique in two earlier scenes of the movie. We also get no closeup of the farmer's face. He seems to simply suggest that Alvin try starting his tractor again, and lo, it works. The big tractor then pulls in front and leads Alvin to the driveway of his brother, pointing to the turn, then continues on with a wave goodbye. The big tractor/little tractor contrast, the uncanniness of the distance, and the lack of any explanation for why Alvin's tractor started again all suggest a bit of well-deserved divine intervention, after a wonderful demonstration of American ingenuity, independence, and self-help.

Another outstanding feature of *The Straight Story* is longtime Lynch collaborator Angelo Badalamenti's beautiful score, which is the best thing he has composed since his iconic music for *Twin Peaks*.

The Straight Story received universal acclaim from critics and Lynch fans, but it did not break out of those circles to become a box office success, nor is it well represented on home video. The DVD has no extras, and the only Blu-ray I could find is Japanese. The CD of the soundtrack and the book of the script are also long out of print. *The Straight Story* is long overdue for a critical reappraisal—and a Criterion Collection Blu-ray with all the trimmings—for it is truly one of Lynch's finest works.

The Straight Story is a film about American pluck and ingenuity, the importance of family, the necessity of forgiveness, and growing old with independence and dignity. If you have conservative and populist tastes, love Americana, and are looking for a wholesome, artful, and deeply touching story you can enjoy with your whole family, see *The Straight Story*. It is the last film most people would expect from David Lynch, but it comes straight from his heart.

The Unz Review, June 15, 2020

THE TALENTED MR. RIPLEY
& PURPLE NOON

Anthony Minghella's *The Talented Mr. Ripley* (1999) has been one of my favorite films since I saw it on the big screen while living in darkest Atlanta. A few years later, post-red pill, I bought the DVD and was struck anew at the brilliance of the script, performances, and direction. But I was also struck by the sheer *whiteness* of this film, which is set in 1958 and 1959 in New York City and Italy (Rome, Venice, the Bay of Naples). There's nothing new about the idea of "escapist" entertainment. But when I first watched this film, I was not aware that one of the things I was escaping from was diversity.

Minghella's movie is based on Patricia Highsmith's 1955 novel of the same name. Most film adaptations of novels are inferior to the original, but not Minghella's. Spoilers ahead: To talk about the novel and its adaptations, I am going to have to summarize the story. But the film has not been in the theaters in twenty years. And don't worry: You'll still want to see it.

Highsmith's Thomas Ripley is not a likeable character. He's simply a sociopath who makes money through forgery and other scams. In his early twenties, Ripley meets shipping magnate Herbert Greenleaf at a party. Ripley was passingly acquainted with his son, Dickie, at Princeton. The elder Greenleaf pays Ripley to go to Italy and persuade his wastrel son to come back and work for the family business.

In Italy, Ripley ingratiates himself with Dickie and becomes increasingly attracted to his lifestyle. Dickie's girlfriend Marge Sherwood is skeptical of Ripley, accusing him of being homosexual, and eventually Dickey tires of Ripley as well, especially after he catches Ripley wearing his clothes and imitating his mannerisms.

On a trip to San Remo, Ripley murders Dickey, assumes his identity, breaks off his relationship with Marge, and moves to Rome. Dickey's friend Freddie Miles locates the Rome apartment where Ripley is living as Dickey. Ripley kills Miles and dumps his body.

Since Dickey is now a murder suspect, Ripley can no longer lead his life. Thus Ripley leads Dickey's family to think he has committed suicide and begins to live in Venice under his own name. Mr. Greenleaf transfers Dickey's trust fund to Ripley, in accordance with a will that Ripley has forged. Ripley ends up wealthy and free, but fears that he may eventually pay for his crimes.

It is a cleverly written book, and even though Ripley is not a sympathetic character, Highsmith manages to slowly seduce the readers into becoming accomplices in his crimes.

Minghella's adaptation is far more three-dimensional and ultimately tragic. But Minghella understands that to make Tom Ripley tragic, he must also evoke some sympathy and admiration. Thus Minghella's Ripley (one of Matt Damon's finest roles) is not introduced as a calculating sociopath. Instead, he is an American middle-class everyman, an insecure, upwardly-mobile phony, an impoverished aesthete whose good looks and good taste offer him an entrée into high society. (Ripley slides into a slow-burning murderous rage when a Princeton silver-spoon describes his apartment as "bourgeois.")

Ripley plays classical piano. (Bach's Italian Concerto is one of his favorites.) One day, Ripley substitutes for a pianist at a classical recital, borrowing the fellow's Princeton jacket. When Herbert Greenleaf spies the jacket and asks Ripley if he knew his son Dickie at Princeton, one gets the feeling that Ripley lies with no specific aim, just a general desire to ingratiate and keep the conversation going.

Mr. Greenleaf's offer allows Ripley to enter a world of beauty and high culture he cannot otherwise afford, transported from his noisy basement apartment in the meatpacking district in a chauffeured limousine—the driver telling him that the Greenleaf name opens a lot of doors, foreshadowing what Ripley will do with that name—to a Cunard luxury liner for a first class voyage to Italy.

When Ripley arrives in Mongibello, the fictional town on the Bay of Naples where Dickie and his girlfriend Marge Sherwood are living, the chemistry is far more complex than in Highsmith's novel. Marge, beautifully played by Gwyneth Paltrow, is charmed rather than repelled by Ripley. And Ripley's relationship with Dickie—brilliantly played by Jude Law—is far more intense.

According to Highsmith, the character of Ripley is not homosexual. That was just Marge's jealousy speaking. (A lesbian herself, Highsmith certainly had no hang-ups about homosexuality. She just didn't see Ripley that way.) In Minghella's film, however, Dickie Greenleaf is fearsomely handsome and charismatic, and Tom Ripley doesn't just fall in love with his money and lifestyle, he falls in love with the man himself, and he is tormented by Dickie's own seeming ambiguity on the subject. These changes to the story send the dramatic tension and conflict off the charts and make Ripley's eventual murder of Dickie a tragic crime of passion, not merely a sociopath's cold-blooded kill.

Minghella's treatment of the murder of Freddie Miles (loathsomely played by Philip Seymour Hoffman) and the aftermath is very close to the book. When Ripley reverts to his own character, leaving behind the beautiful wardrobe and apartment he has purchased with Dickie's money, he makes a fateful choice, taking Dickie's rings, which were gifts from Marge. As he closes the lid of his piano, a single blurred reflection divides like an amoeba into two separate faces. Ripley is Ripley again.

Later in Venice, Ripley meets with Mr. Greenleaf and Marge. When Marge finds Dickie's rings in Ripley's flat, there is a tense scene, in which Ripley panics and contemplates killing Marge to silence her. The whole thing is absurd. Marge is certain that Dickie never took off his rings. All Tom had to do was say that Dickie took off his rings whenever he contemplated being unfaithful to Marge, which is plausible and probably even true. In short, Minghella's movie has the audience making up better lies than Ripley. Thus the film is far more adept at making the audience Ripley's accomplices than Highsmith's novel.

Mr. Greenleaf has hired a private investigator, Alvin Mac-Carron, to investigate Freddie's death and Dickie's disappearance. It turns out that Dickie once violently assaulted a Princeton classmate. They have concluded that Dickie probably murdered Freddie in a similar rage and then committed suicide. To thank Ripley for his loyalty—and to buy his silence—Greenleaf has decided to give Ripley a portion of his son's trust, making him a wealthy man. As in the novel, it looks like Ripley is going to get off Scott free.

But no. Minghella's movie also introduces new characters, who add dramatic tension and tragic pathos. When Ripley arrives in Italy, he meets Meredith Logue, bewitchingly played by Cate Blanchett. Again on an apparent whim, he lies and introduces himself as Dickie Greenleaf, a lie that will have consequences when he runs into her again in Rome after having killed Dickie and assumed his identity. Meredith has excellent taste, so she and "Dickie" become friends, shopping and attending the opera—Tchaikovsky's *Eugene Onegin*, in which the title character kills a friend in a duel. Then they seem to slip into a romance, although one has to wonder if she is really Ripley's type, being a girl and all.

Peter Smith-Kingsley, played by Jack Davenport, is a musician and musicologist living in Venice. He is dangerous to Ripley's ruse because he is friends with Meredith, who knows Ripley as Dickie, and with Marge, who knows him as Ripley. This makes for some tense cat-and-mouse drama. Smith-Kingsley is also homosexual, and given their mutual interest in music, he is a good match for Ripley, so when Ripley leaves Rome for Venice, he and Peter become lovers.

At the end of the movie, Ripley and Peter leave on a boat for Athens. Once out to sea, Ripley bumps into Meredith. This is a problem. She knows Ripley as Dickie, and she knows Peter, who knows him as Ripley. She's traveling with family, so he can't just toss her overboard. And they can't just stay in the cabin, because Peter has seen them together. (Kissing, no less.)

At this point, Ripley could have just come clean with Meredith about how his impulsive imposture, when he thought he would never see her again, snowballed because he could never summon up the courage to come clean. She probably would have accepted it. He could have even come clean with Smith-Kingsley about *everything*, and he probably would have accepted it. But instead, Ripley strangles Peter, probably the only person who ever loved him. Ripley may never be arrested, but he's never going to "get away with" this kind of crime.

It is a wrenchingly tragic conclusion to an incredibly rich and powerful drama, and far more satisfying than Highsmith's tiny, *pro forma* nod to the fact that Ripley, though untroubled by a conscience, will always fear the police.

The Talented Mister Ripley is one of the few films I find simply flawless. The script is brilliant both literarily and psychologically. The performances are uniformly excellent. These are Matt Damon's and Jude Law's best roles. It is Minghella's best-directed film: an unapologetically Eurocentric, absolutely voluptuous vision of Italy at its most beautiful and America at its civilizational peak. Try it if you want to escape into the world of 1950s and early-1960s glamorous romantic thrillers like *To Catch a Thief* or *Charade*. *Ripley* turns darker than those films, but it is also more emotionally powerful and rewarding.

If you can't get enough of *Ripley*, I've got good news: There's another big screen adaptation, René Clément's 1960 film, *Plein soleil (Purple Noon)*, starring Alain Delon in his first major role. *Purple Noon* is highly absorbing, but as a work of art, it falls far short of Minghella's film.

Delon's Ripley is simply a cold sociopath, although one wants him to be more, because Delon is stunningly handsome. None of the other characters are particularly likable either. Dickie Greenleaf (called Philippe here) is simply a bully, and Marge is a shrew. Freddie Miles is exactly the same. Minghella clearly cast his Dickie and Miles to look like their counterparts in *Purple Noon*.

Minghella's treatment of the death of Freddie Miles also owes a lot to *Purple Noon*. In *Purple Noon*, however, Ripley calmly cooks and eats a meal while Miles lies dead in the next room, a nice way to indicate sociopathy.

Whereas Minghella's departures from Highsmith add depth and drama, Clément's diminish the story, particularly the end, when Ripley gets caught. Let that be a lesson to you.

This ending was probably necessary in 1960, for *The Talented Mr. Ripley* in all of its incarnations drives moralists to distraction. Highsmith's Ripley is a sociopathic murderer as anti-hero, the kind of thing that was hot during Generation Existential. Clément brings him to the screen as a pinup. If he didn't get caught, French men would have pretended to be sociopaths too, French girls would have thrown themselves at them, and 1968 would have come early. When Minghella's film came out, I heard it denounced as diabolical because it makes a sympathetic anti-hero out of a "gay serial killer." But I'm not buying it. Save it for Hannibal Lecter, Sweeney Todd, and Dexter. Minghella's Ripley is just good Will Hunting gone bad.

The Unz Review, March 4, 2020

TWELVE MONKEYS

Twelve Monkeys (1995) is Terry Gilliam's last great movie. It is a masterful work of dystopian science fiction, with a highly imaginative plot, a tight and literate script, fantastic steampunkish sets and props, and compelling performances from Bruce Willis, Brad Pitt, and Madeline Stowe. Gilliam is usually far too ironic and self-conscious to deliver emotionally satisfying work. But in *Twelve Monkeys*, we see stylistic elements and themes from earlier Gilliam films—*Time Bandits, Brazil, The Adventures of Baron Munchausen, The Fisher King*—applied to much darker material with such virtuosity that it no longer seems labored and calculated. Nor does it smother real feeling.

I'd like you to watch this film, so no major spoilers. Most of what I will say can be inferred from the trailer. In the back story of *Twelve Monkeys*, practically the whole human race was wiped out by a virus in 1997. The survivors live underground, in totalitarian lockdown, under a Permanent Emergency Code, ruled by a politburo of scientists, a whole committee of Dr. Strangeloves.

In 2035, the scientists somehow invent a way to travel back in time. They wish to send someone to the past, just before the outbreak of the plague, in order to . . . No, they don't want to *prevent* it. If the plague never happened, none of them would be ruling over the pitiful remnants of the human race. Instead, they simply want a pure sample of the virus, before it mutated. Their motives are never made clear. Is it for pure research? Would an earlier strain of the virus allow them to create a cure?

Bruce Willis plays James Cole, a prisoner, who has been pressured into "volunteering" to be sent back in time. But the equipment is a little tricky, so he first ends up in Philadelphia in 1990—six years too early—where he is arrested and confined to a mental institution, because that's what one does with people who claim to have come from the future to prevent the human race from dying in a pandemic.

Cole meets a sympathetic psychiatrist, Dr. Kathryn Railly (Madeline Stowe), and a mental patient Jeffrey Goines (Brad Pitt), who is a radical environmentalist and animal rights advocate. Cole tries to escape to complete his mission, but he is captured and locked in a cell, from which he mysteriously disappears. Apparently, the scientists have put implants in his molars that allow them to pull him back into the future, where he is debriefed and then returned to the past, first ending up in the trenches of WWI, where he is shot in the leg, then finally arriving in 1996.

Six years after her encounter with Cole, Dr. Railly has published a book on the "Cassandra complex": people like Cole who warn society of impending disasters but are not heeded. After Railly gives a lecture on her book and signs copies, Cole kidnaps her. He needs her help. He now believes that the virus will be released by Jeffrey Goines and a radical environmentalist group called the Army of the Twelve Monkeys. Cole is afraid that during their time in the mental hospital, he actually gave Goines the idea of wiping out the human race with a plague. (If you are going to construct a story around time travel, you might as well milk it for every paradox.)

Railly, of course, is terrified. But she does not go to pieces. She's a doctor. She tries to understand Cole and convince him to let her go as he drags her through his quest for the origin of the virus. Philadelphia in 1996 turns out to be almost as dystopian as Philadelphia in 2035. After some harrowing misadventures with Railly, Cole is pulled back into the future.

When the two are apart, a delightful role reversal takes place. Railly comes to believe Cole is not a madman. He really is from the future. Cole, however, comes to think that he's actually mad. He does hear a mysterious voice that is never explained. The scientists also, frankly, act a bit crazy. And really, doesn't the whole story sound a bit insane?

When Cole is returned to the past, he seeks out Railly because he wants her to cure him, only to discover that she has taken up his mission with the manic intensity of a true believer. You laugh when you see it, but the real delight comes in retrospect, when you see that it was completely inevitable.

After Cole and Railly get back on the same page, they go after the Army of the Twelve Monkeys, only to find . . . Well, I'm not going to say any more about the plot, save that there are many more twists and turns for you to enjoy.

Twelve Monkeys isn't a "deep" film. It doesn't invite us to ponder philosophical or theological issues. It doesn't seem to be an allegory for anything else. It doesn't need to be. The world it creates and the story it tells are highly satisfying in themselves: by turns surreal, terrifying, funny, and moving.

The lead performances are remarkable. Bruce Willis is compelling as a man who is heroic despite all his doubts, fears, and failings. Brad Pitt is charismatic and hilarious as Jeffrey Goines. But Madeline Stowe steals the film. She is not only beautiful, she is highly intelligent, so she is completely convincing as a psychiatrist.

Twelve Monkeys is not just intellectually stimulating and emotionally compelling, it is also visually striking from start to finish, with imaginative sets, beautifully constructed shots, and a gauzy glamor that bring to mind Hitchcock. (One of the settings is a Hitchcock film festival.)

Twelve Monkeys is set within a materialistic, scifi universe, but what you see is almost never what you get, because madness and false memories can systematically estrange us from reality. Gilliam methodically mirrors events in the "real world" with movies, television shows, and commercials so that the boundaries between fantasy and reality are sometimes hard to trace.

Twelve Monkeys is also mercifully free of political correctness. (Particularly when Cole calls a wrong number in 1990.)

In fact, I can't think of a single false note in the entire film, not even the music. Given this film's cinematic forebearers and touchstones, I was not expecting Paul Buckmaster's score, which riffs off Astor Piazzolia's Argentine tango music. But it works.

Even though *Twelve Monkeys* was released in 1995, it seems quite topical in the age of Corona-chan. So if you are looking for some more lockdown viewing, I highly recommend it. It is a depressing vision of the future, but it will make you feel lucky. James Cole had a lot more to complain about than we do, and he bore it far more admirably.

WISE BLOOD

John Huston's *Wise Blood* (1979) is one of his lesser-known films, but it deserves a wider audience. Based on Flannery O'Connor's 1952 novel of the same name, *Wise Blood* is the most faithful screen adaptation I have ever seen, largely because the screenwriter truly loved and understood the source material. The script was written by Benedict Fitzgerald, who knew Flannery O'Connor from childhood. In fact, she was his babysitter. Benedict Fitzgerald is the son of classicist Robert Fitzgerald and his wife Sally, who were close friends of O'Connor. Benedict Fitzgerald also shares O'Connor's Catholic faith. Later he went on co-author the script of *The Passion of the Christ* with Mel Gibson.

Fitzgerald may have had an influence on the cast as well, since they pretty much perfectly accord with O'Connor's descriptions. The cast includes two of my favorite movie weirdos, Brad Dourif and Harry Dean Stanton, as well as Ned Beatty.

When I first saw *Wise Blood*, I found it baffling. People said things that just didn't make sense: "Jesus is a trick on niggers," "Nobody with a good car needs justification," etc. People wreck cars and even blind themselves for no apparent reason. I found myself wondering "What *is* this shit?"

Beyond that, *Wise Blood* is an ugly movie to look at. Everything looks cheap, tacky, and run down. The colors are washed out. But the film's grimy materiality conceals the lofty religious and metaphysical issues that animate this story.

Wise Blood is a dark comedy about serious matters, a Catholic satire on modern materialism and the Protestant South. (*Wise Blood* touches on many of the same themes as Evelyn Waugh's *The Loved One*, which is my all-time favorite comedy.[1])

The hero of *Wise Blood* is 22-year-old Hazel Motes, played by Brad Dourif. "Motes," of course, are specks of dust, and Hazel

---

[1] See my review of *The Loved One* in *Return of the Son of Trevor Lynch's CENSORED Guide to the Movies*.

is often shortened to "Haze," which suggests imperfect vision, just as "Hazel" suggests vision because it is an eye color. Haze, however, believes that his eyes are wide open, and they see only the material world. Atoms, of course, are tiny motes as well. And a haze of motes suggests that atoms get in the way of true vision. Haze's grandfather was some sort of Protestant preacher, but Haze rejects all religion. We learn nothing else about his family.

At the opening of the movie, Haze returns home from a war. In O'Connor's novel, it would be the Second World War, but Huston sets the movie in the 1970s. Haze has been wounded, but he won't say where, and apparently has some sort of pension. He finds the family home deserted and in ruins. His grandfather's grave in the back states that he has "Gone to be an angle" (sic).

Haze was deeply marked by his grandfather's preaching but is in full rebellion. He wants to free himself of Christianity and fully immerse himself in nature. He wants to be loyal to the Earth. O'Connor hints that Haze might be a kind of Nietzschean. When he asserts that "Jesus is a trick on niggers" and "Sin is a trick on niggers," it sounds like Nietzsche's claim that Christianity is a slave revolt in morals.

The comedy of *Wise Blood* is that, despite his best efforts, Haze can't escape the pull of Christianity. To put the military behind him, Haze buys a suit and hat, then dumps his uniform in the trash. But as soon as people set eyes on Haze, everyone thinks he is a preacher. It is the hat, as well as his grim intensity.

Haze then takes a train to the city of Taulkinham to do some things he has never done before. As one of my students told me years ago, she could hardly wait to leave her small Southern town for Atlanta, so she could "sin." Haze evidently has the same idea, since his first order of business is to seek out a fat whore named Leora Watts. It seems degrading to pay a fat woman for sex, but perhaps that's the whole point.

In Taulkingham, Haze runs into a blind preacher, Asa Hawks (Harry Dean Stanton) and his illegitimate daughter Sabbath Lily (Amy Wright). Hawks interrupts a salesman demonstrating a potato peeling machine, the "Miracle Peeler," by passing out tracts and begging for money. Haze and Sabbath Lily flirt as Haze tears up one of the preacher's tracts.

In the crowd is eighteen-year-old Enoch Emery (Dan Shor), who works at the zoo. People don't like Enoch, basically because he's an idiot. Enoch complains that people aren't friendly. Enoch pathetically latches on to Haze, who isn't friendly to him either, even though Enoch in some ways represents what Haze wants to be: a wholly natural man. Enoch doesn't think much about Christianity or anything at all. He follows his "wise blood" — instincts, intuitions, compulsions. O'Connor being a Catholic, she depicts the man who follows the wisdom of the blood as a fool.

Haze and Enoch follow Hawks and his daughter. Hawks can tell that "some preacher's left his mark" on Haze, asking "Did you follow me for me to take it off or to give you another one?" When Hawks begins begging and passing out leaflets again, Haze is so incensed that he delivers his own sermon.

> Don't I know what exists and what don't? Ain't I got eyes in my head? Am I a blind man? Let me tell you somethin'. Maybe you think that you ain't clean because you don't believe. Every one of you are clean, and I'll tell you why. If you think it's because of Jesus Christ crucified, you're wrong. I ain't saying he wasn't crucified, but I say it wasn't for you. I'm gonna start a new church . . . the Church of Truth Without Jesus Christ Crucified. And it won't cost you nothin' to join my church.

In a parting shot to Hawks, Haze spits, "What do I need Jesus for? I've got Leora Watts."

The next day, Haze buys a car. In the novel is it described as a "high, rat-colored car," but in the movie it is red and white. ("High rat" suggest *heirat*, the Greek word for priest, and Haze later uses the car as a pulpit.)

Haze doesn't just want to use the car to leave Taulkinham, he also wants to live in it. But the car is a piece of junk and stalls out on the first hill outside of town. Haze looks over, sees graffiti on the side of the road about Jesus, and has a flashback to his childhood, peeing his pants as his grandfather preaches fire and brimstone, pointing to him: "Jesus will never leave him, ever. Jesus will have you in the end."

Haze then turns back toward Taulkinham. Interestingly, the car works again when he turns back. Taulkinham is associated with Jesus. Haze's car is his means of escape. But, as we shall see, he never manages to escape. Jesus has him in the end.

Haze wants to find Asa Hawks. Enoch said he knew where Hawks lived, so Haze heads for the zoo where he finds Enoch making faces and hurling insults at the monkeys. Enoch promises to show Haze where Hawks lives, but he tries Haze's patience by insisting that he first show him something at the MVSEVM: a dried up, shrunken man. Enoch has a strong fascination with the subhuman.

Haze locates the boarding house where Hawks and his daughter live. He goes to the door and knocks. The door is opened by the landlady, Mrs. Flood, played by Mary Nell Santacroce. Haze asks to rent a room. The dialogue is quite droll.

MRS. FLOOD: What do you do?
HAZE: I'm a preacher.
MRS. FLOOD: What church?
HAZE: Church of Truth without Christ.
MRS. FLOOD: Protestant . . . or, or somethin' foreign?
HAZE: Oh, no, ma'am. It's Protestant.

Once ensconced in the rooming house, Haze sets out to preach on the streets of Taulkinham. He unmasks Asa Hawks as a fraud who had promised to blind himself for Jesus but whose nerve failed. Hawks flees town. Sabbath Lily, who is utterly cynical, seduces Hazel. She says that they are both alike: pure filth. But Sabbath Lily likes it, whereas Haze doesn't. Sabbath promises to teach Haze to like it too.

One day, Enoch Emery hears Haze preaching:

What you need is somethin' to take the place of Jesus . . . somethin' that would speak plain. Now, the Church

Without Christ don't have a Jesus. But it needs one. It needs a new Jesus . . . one that's all man, without blood to waste . . . that don't look like any other man, so you'll look at him. Give me such a Jesus.

Haze, of course, is speaking metaphorically. He knows there is a God-shaped hole in human nature, and if Jesus is ejected, something else will have to take his place.

But another trait of human nature is that some people inevitably take metaphors literally. Enoch Emery is such a person. He knows exactly what Haze is talking about: all man, without blood, who looks unique. So Enoch puts on a disguise, sneaks into the MVSEVM, smashes a glass, and scampers off with the shrunken man. In the novel, once back in his room, Enoch creates a shrine for him. In the movie we see a brief shot of the shrunken man standing at the head of Enoch's bed while he looks on in awe. O'Connor is suggesting that even Enoch has a God-shaped hole, but when the superhuman is closed off, the subhuman takes its place.

Enoch is soon spooked by the New Jesus, so he brings it to Hazel. Sabbath receives it and thinks it is cute. When she enters the room with her head draped, carrying the shrunken man like a baby in her arms—a grotesque parody of the Madonna and Child—Hazel is enraged, smashes the "baby" against a wall, and tosses it out the fire escape. Sabbath is hysterical.

After Enoch drops off the package, he hears a van announcing that Gonga will be making an appearance outside the local theaters to promote his new film. Gonga is a man in a gorilla suit. There will be free passes for anyone brave enough to shake Gonga's hand. Enoch gets in line, and when Gonga shakes his hand, it is the first kind gesture he has experienced, perhaps in his entire life. He is so delighted that he goes through the line again and again, until Gonga finally tells him to go to hell.

Stung, Enoch waits until Gonga returns to the van, then assaults him and steals his gorilla costume. Enoch puts on the gorilla suit. In the novel, he ceremoniously buries his clothes, implying that this is more than a change of costume. Then

Enoch/Gonga wanders through the town, asking people to shake hands with him, as they scream and flee.

The Gonga episode is a parody of the Christian doctrine of the incarnation. Just as God puts on a man suit to redeem humanity, Enoch puts on a gorilla suit to spread kindness. But when man goes down a level in the great chain of being, he loses his humanity. Enoch is the New Jesus made flesh, as opposed to the dried-up simulacrum he gave to Sabbath.

One night when Haze is preaching on the hood of his car, he is noticed by a radio preacher named Hoover Shoats (Ned Beatty). Beatty thinks that Haze has talent, but needs to promote himself better, so he steps in, introduces himself as Onnie Jay Holy (pig Latin for Johnny Holy), and shows Haze how it is done. Within moments, the Church of Truth Without Christ mutates into the Church of Christ Without Christ, then the Holy Church of Christ Without Christ, suggesting that there's no escaping Jesus in the end.

But Haze's doctrine that man is innocent of original sin is not changed by Holy, just sweetened. In Holy's telling, it is pure Rousseau. Man is naturally good. We are born full of sweetness and love. But society drives our sweetness deep inside us. The purpose of religion is to return us to our innate innocence and goodness.

Aside from these truths, Holy declares that their new church has other advantages: there's nothing foreign about it, and it's up to date, at the cutting edge of progress. Join this church, and nobody will get the truth before you.

Haze angrily denounces Holy, who then threatens to run Haze out of business. Haze needs some competition, and Holy can get "prophets for peanuts." The next night Holy makes good on his threat. He dresses a drunkard up as Haze, and the first schism of the Church of Truth Without Christ is launched. Haze waits until they finish, then follows the fake prophet, runs his car off the road, demands that he strip off his suit and hat, then runs him over and kills him. To Haze's disgust, the dying man begins to confess his sins.

The next day, Haze decides it is best to leave town. He stops to get some gas. His radiator is leaking, his gas tank is leaking, and his tires are about to give out. But Haze insists that his car will get him anywhere he wants to go, and that "This car is just beginning its life. A lightning bolt couldn't stop it." A lightning bolt, of course, is often seen as a tool of divine punishment. But Haze does not think he is tempting fate.

Turns out he's wrong. When Haze gets outside of town, he is pulled over by a policeman. When Haze asks why, the policeman, who speaks very gently, says "I just don't like your face." Then the policeman asks Haze to follow him down the road to the "prettiest view you ever did see." When they arrive, he asks Haze to get out of the car, whereupon the policeman sends it over an embankment and into a pond. Haze then returns home with a package of quicklime and blinds himself.

The whole sequence is utterly shocking and bizarre. But there is a deeper meaning and logic. Haze's car is not just a car. Haze buys the car as a home, not just a means of transport. He also claims that "Nobody with a good car needs to worry about nothin'." More strikingly, he declares that "Nobody with a good car . . . needs to be justified." Here justification specifically means justification before God.

So in Haze's mind, there is an equation between his car, his home, and a world without sin and redemption. Haze's car is the material world without God, which he thinks is an adequate home, a view that O'Connor the Catholic presents as a delusion. Haze's car is falling apart around him. He has three encounters with mechanics but is in complete denial about the wreck he is driving.

What is the connection between Haze's car and vision, such that when deprived of his car, he deprives himself of his sight? Haze declares that his car "Wasn't built by a bunch of foreigners or niggers, nor one-armed men. It was built by people with their eyes open . . . who knew where they was at." Haze's this-worldly metaphysics is correlated with an empiricist epistemology. Seeing is believing. In one of his sermons, Haze counsels forgetting the past and not worrying about the future. In short, live in the present, which can be seen with one's eyes. (He also recommends hunting one's conscience down and killing it. One only regrets the past.) Thus the loss of his car is a loss of faith in the faculty of vision. Thus Haze blinds himself to see deeper.

But why in the world did the policeman wreck Haze's car? Just as the car is not a car, the policeman is not a policeman. To crack the Flannery O'Connor code, one needs to be on the lookout for unobtrusive acts of divine intervention in an utterly fallen and bleak world. The first such act is when a one-armed mechanic gets Haze's car running again and asks nothing for his trouble. It doesn't make sense in terms of the earthly economy. In the novel, the policeman who destroys Haze's car has uncannily blue eyes. In the movie, he speaks with a strange gentleness and detachment. He's more than a policeman; he's an angel.

Why does the first angel (the mechanic) get Haze's car started and the second (the policeman) destroy it? It has everything to do with Haze's destination. In the first case, Haze wanted to get back to Taulkinham. In the second, he wanted to get away from it. Haze's primary motive for buying the car is to flee Taulkinham. But the car also represents his flight from anything divine and non-material. God wants Haze in Taulkinham, because that is where Jesus will get him in the end.

The last act of *Wise Blood* is both moving and bizarre. Sabbath Lily wants nothing to do with a real blind man, so she runs off, leaving Haze in the care of Mrs. Flood.

Mrs. Flood is horrified to discover that Haze spends most of his time walking with rocks in his shoes, a form a penance he adopted as a child. He also wraps his torso in barbed wire. He does it because he "ain't clean." Haze feels the need to pay for his sins. Mrs. Flood declares "There's only one kind of clean," and Mr. Motes has blood on his shirt, blood on his sheets. Mrs. Flood will have none of it:

> It's like one of them gory stories that some people have quit doin'. Like boiling in oil or being a saint or walling up cats. I wouldn't be surprised if you wasn't some kind of a agent of the pope or g-got some connection with somethin' funny. . . . You-you might as well be one of them monks. You might as well live in a in a monkery.

Mrs. Flood is right in her common-sense Protestant way. Haze is mortifying himself to get right with God *on his own*. But if that were possible, then Jesus and the church would be unnecessary. In short, Haze is still a member of the Church of Truth Without Christ. But if Jesus saves us through his suffering, then there's no point in our "works" of self-mortification, which is why Protestants have quit doing such morbid things.

Mrs. Flood thinks Haze is crazy, and she's probably right. She wants to be rid of him, but she needs his money. In the book, she hatches a plot: she'll marry him, secure his pension, and then clap him in an insane asylum. But then something uncanny happens: Mrs. Flood actually comes to love him. She really does wish to marry Haze and take care of him. By omitting her initial plans, the movie obscures just how dramatic Mrs. Flood's change of heart is, shearing away any sense of the miraculous.

When Mrs. Flood proposes marriage to Haze, he quietly gets up and walks off into a downpour as Mrs. Flood pours out her heart to him. This heartbreaking scene is beautifully acted by Mary Nell Santacroce. Mrs. Flood tells him not to return, but soon she is so worried that she calls the police, who eventually find Haze, suffering of exposure, and bring him back to Mrs. Flood. They prop him up on a daybed in her living room. Mrs. Flood tells Haze he can stay on his own terms, but there's no answer. Hazel Motes is dead. The End.

Wise Blood's best features are its script and performances. Dourif is riveting, with a seething, rattlesnake intensity. Stanton is loathsome. Beatty looks just like a hog. The hardest roles are probably Mrs. Flood and Enoch Emery, but they are brilliantly brought to life by Mary Nell Santacroce and Dan Shor.

The movie's only real weakness is the director. John Huston delivered many classic films—*The Maltese Falcon* (1941), *The Treasure of the Sierra Madre* (1948), *The Asphalt Jungle* (1950), *The African Queen* (1951), *The Misfits* (1961), *The Man Who Would Be King* (1975), and *Prizzi's Honor* (1985)—in a transparent, prosaic, workmanlike style. He was no *auteur*.

Beyond that, Huston was not a religious man. He saw *Wise Blood* as merely a parody of superstitious hicks. Benedict Fitzgerald convinced him that it is a religious movie and that, in the end, "Jesus wins." But in the crucial scenes where God intervenes, Huston was dead to what was going on. He gives us no clue that anything uncanny is happening at all.

The same is true of the score is by Huston's frequent collaborator, Alex North (born Isidore Soifer), which leans heavily on "The Tennessee Waltz" and "Simple Gifts," as well as a couple of cues that can only be described as "hick caper music." But North gives us no sense of the uncanny when it would have added meaning, for instance in the scenes with the one-armed mechanic, the dying false prophet, or the policeman who wrecks Haze's car.

Imagine how David Lynch would have directed *Wise Blood*. Lynch is a perfect director for O'Connor, since he shares her love of the grotesque, her affection for ordinary people, her humor and compassion, and her feel for the numinous. Lynch is a master of suggesting the presence of the uncanny. He has even worked with Brad Dourif and Harry Dean Stanton.

But even in the age of endless remakes and reboots, Huston's *Wise Blood* is likely the only version we will ever get. I had not seen *Wise Blood* since the '90s when I popped in the Criterion Collection DVD to write this review. I was surprised at how reactionary *Wise Blood* seems in the current year. I doubt that it could have been made today. So we should be grateful for this film, despite its flaws.

I recommend John Huston's *Wise Blood* to serious-minded lovers of dark comedy and Southern Gothic. But, better yet, if you are a reader, skip the image and go straight to the original: Flannery O'Connor's *Wise Blood*. As the world slides deeper into decadence, O'Connor will increasingly be seen as a one of America's greatest artists of the Right.

The Unz Review, March 25, 2020

INDEX

Numbers in bold refer to a whole chapter or section devoted to a particular topic.

Busey, Jake, 180

C
Cabaret, 41, **42–46**
Caine, Michael, 99, 100
Cannavale, Bobby, 137
Cannavale, Jack, 137
Cardinale, Claudia, 109
Catholicism, 55, 73, 112, 203, 205, 209
Centennial Olympic Park bombing; Atlanta Olympics bombing, 162
Charade, 198
Charlottesville; Unite the Right, 5, 6
Chastain, Jessica, 100
Chayevsky, Paddy, 116, 139, 143, 151
Christianity & Christians, 2, 12, 27, 45, 51, 55, 161, 204–205, 208
Christie, Julie, 62, 65
class, 68, 72, 78, 92, 103, 107–13, 159, 178, 189, 195
Clément, René, 198–99
The Clone Wars, 135, 137
college, 18, 19, 32–33, 183–84, 186, 188
coming of age, 18, 177, 179
Cooper, Bradley, 164–66
Costello, Jef, 68
Counter-Currents, 6
crime (genre), 18, 19, 89, 90, 92, 94
Cruise, Tom, 51–52, 55, 58, 61
Cullen, Brett, 102

D
Damon, Matt, 98, 100, 195,

198
The Dark Knight Trilogy, 100, 101; Batman, 160; Bruce Wayne, 103
Dark Triad, 12–13, 64
Davenport, Jack, 197
Dead Presidents, 11
death, 17, 34, 46, 50, 68, 70–71, 87, 112, 127, 128, 133, 134, 148, 170, 178, 181, 189, 196, 198
Delon, Alain, 107, 198
De Niro, Robert, 103–104
detective fiction, 96
Devlin, F. Roger, 30
Di Caprio, Leonardo, 14–15, 152
Disney, 89, 135, 137, 168–69, 173, 176, 190
dispossession, 9
diversity, 1, 7, 9, 94, 154, 175, 180, 194
Django Unchained, 152
Dockery, Michelle, 47, 89
Dourif, Brad, 203, 211, 212
Downton Abbey, **47–49**, 89
dreams, 25, 28, 31, 46, 57, 60, 87, 121, 122, 124–27, 133, 134
Driver, Adam, 169
drugs, 12, 23, 24, 30, 59, 89, 102, 164, 166
Drunken Angel, 92, 96
Duke, David, 6
Dunaway, Faye, 139, 140
Duvall, Robert, 139, 140
dystopia, 83, 86, 148, 160, 200, 201

ABOUT THE AUTHOR

Trevor Lynch is a pen name of Greg Johnson, Ph.D., Editor-in-Chief of Counter-Currents Publishing Ltd. and the *Counter-Currents* webzine (http://www.counter-currents.com/).

He is the author of *Confessions of a Reluctant Hater* (San Francisco: Counter-Currents, 2010; expanded edition, 2016), *Trevor Lynch's White Nationalist Guide to the Movies* (Counter-Currents, 2012), *New Right vs. Old Right* (Counter-Currents, 2013), *Son of Trevor Lynch's White Nationalist Guide to the Movies* (Counter-Currents, 2015), *Truth, Justice, & a Nice White Country* (Counter-Currents, 2015), *In Defense of Prejudice* (Counter-Current, 2017), *You Asked for It: Selected Interviews*, vol. 1 (Counter-Currents, 2017), *The White Nationalist Manifesto* (Counter-Currents, 2018), *Toward a New Nationalism* (Counter-Currents, 2019), *Return of the Son of Trevor Lynch's CENSORED Guide to the Movies* (Counter-Currents, 2019), *From Plato to Postmodernism* (Counter-Currents, 2019), *It's Okay to Be White: The Best of Greg Johnson* (Hollywood: Ministry of Truth, 2020), *Graduate School with Heidegger* (Counter-Currents, 2020), and *Here's the Thing: Selected Interviews*, vol. 2 (Counter-Currents, 2020).

He is editor of *North American New Right*, vol. 1 (Counter-Currents, 2012); *North American New Right*, vol. 2 (Counter-Currents, 2017); *The Alternative Right* (Counter-Currents, 2018); *Dark Right: Batman Viewed from the Right* (with Gregory Hood, Counter-Currents, 2018); Julius Evola, *East & West: Comparative Studies in Pursuit of Tradition* (with Collin Cleary, Counter-Currents, 2018); Collin Cleary, *Summoning the Gods: Essays on Paganism in a God-Forsaken World* (Counter-Currents, 2011); Collin Cleary, *What is a Rune? & Other Essays* (Counter-Currents, 2015); Jonathan Bowden, *Western Civilization Bites Back* (Counter-Currents, 2014); Jonathan Bowden, *Extremists: Studies in Metapolitics* (Counter-Currents, 2017), and many other books.

His writings have been translated into Czech, Danish, Dutch, Estonian, Finnish, French, German, Greek, Hungarian, Norwegian, Polish, Portuguese, Russian, Slovak, Spanish, Swedish, and Ukrainian.

www.ingramcontent.com/pod-product-compliance
Lightning Source LLC
Chambersburg PA
CBHW030940150426
42812CB00064B/3080/J